IMAGES
of America
CAMP MAQUA

On the Cover: This group of campers, pictured in the early 1930s on the shores of Loon Lake, shows a fairly undeveloped shoreline. This spring-fed, 400-acre lake, which reaches depths of over 100 feet, was clean and clear for the camp's waterfront activities. Summer homes were sparse until a few decades later, when the area with 60 lakes within 60 miles became a vacation destination for families from the southern part of Michigan. (Courtesy of Great Lakes Bay Region.)

IMAGES
of America

CAMP MAQUA

Kathryn A. Baker

ARCADIA PUBLISHING

ISBN 978-1-4671-1491-2

Published by Arcadia Publishing
Charleston, South Carolina

Printed in the United States of America

Library of Congress Control Number: 2015940477

For all general information, please contact Arcadia Publishing:
Telephone 843-853-2070
Fax 843-853-0044
E-mail sales@arcadiapublishing.com
For customer service and orders:
Toll-Free 1-888-313-2665

Visit us on the Internet at www.arcadiapublishing.com

This book is dedicated to the girls whose lives were enriched by Camp Maqua, and to the families who now own the property and cherish its history.

Contents

ACKNOWLEDGMENTS

This book would never have been possible without the loan of archival documents and photographs from the YWCA Great Lakes Bay Region, under the directorship of Lisa Perrault Grills. The thorough records of this branch, where the humble beginnings of Camp Maqua first took root, were so valuable to my research. Many articles found in the YWCA archives that are cited in this book in general terms come from local Bay City newspapers but were impossible to identify specifically.

I wish to express loving thanks to my husband, Bill, who allowed me to retire from our business for this project of my heart, and for allowing my soul to rest at Maqua every summer.

Many thanks to Sascha (Marsha) Immerman—truly one of the most passionate Maqua campers ever—who helped me for many summers through her investigative camper searches and organization. Olivia Baker and Kate Cooley were wonderful transcriptionists, with keen young tech minds when I needed them. But, most of all, thanks to the women who shared their stories and photographs to help document a camp that was important to many.

INTRODUCTION

Between 1924 and 1978, thousands of young girls came through the doors of Camp Maqua, which means "The Birches." Built on the Loon Lake property in Hale, Michigan, the camp was originally conceived in a small beach town near Bay City. There, 65 girls camped on wooden-floored tents in the summer of 1916 after the board of directors of the YWCA agreed to rent a cottage on the Bay shore, near Killarney Beach.

In its second year, the camp operated from the McCormack cottage on Ricomah Beach, where the large porch became a dormitory and each girl set up her cot. The Tierney cottage at Aplin Beach was purchased two years later for $1,000, under the directorship of Vera Merriman.

The camp program at Aplin Beach was originally planned for use by "business and industrial girls" and was used on weekends and vacation periods under the guidance of Dr. Mary Williams. It proved to be so successful that younger girls asked for a camp program. The short- term solution was the loan of YMCA Camp Iroquois, at Sand Lake, for a two-week period in 1922. The Aplin Beach cottage was sold in 1925, and $1,650 was used to purchase Maqua.

That summer, a committee—consisting of Mr. and Mrs. E.B. Perry, Mr. and Mrs. C.T. Clark, Mr. Clift, Mr. and Mrs. F.W. Urch, and Dr. William Karr—searched for an appropriate property for a permanent camp. A campsite fund was established, and pledges and donations came in from individuals, merchants, and companies (mostly from Bay City) who believed in the vision of the camp.

The 64-acre parcel on Loon Lake was purchased on October 17, 1924, and construction began—under the chairmanship of Mr. C.T. Clark—on November 17, 1924. By December 24, the lodge was ready for the interior work, and an icehouse had been built and filled for the winter. On April 6, construction resumed, and on May 11, 1925, the camp was formally dedicated and completed. The total cost for the lodge, huts, toilets, road, fence, swamp draining, water system, deck, storehouse, tree planting, and icehouse amounted to $9,645.89.

Equipment for the camp was purchased, and an initial payment of $500 was made for the Dutton farmhouse on the shores of Loon Lake. During the first two years of operation, the farmhouse was used for sleeping quarters, cooking, and indoor activities, and in the 1940s an upper screen porch was added.

A permanent camp on Loon Lake opened on July 15, 1924, with Helen Graves as the first director. She was also the secretary of the Bay City Girl Reserves Department at the time. The lodge was furnished with tables, benches, cupboards, and a beautiful fieldstone fireplace—dedicated to Dr. Mary Williams, whose efforts resulted in the camp's founding. A hostess room with a small porch was added to the lodge in 1929, as well as two guest rooms that were furnished by Mrs. E.B. Perry in memory of her husband, who was also devoted to camp life.

In 1927, the boathouse was built, which stored waterfront supplies. In 1937, an elaborate, timber-covered pavilion was built, with a second-level sundeck off the upper story, and used for "recreational activities." In 1938, the upper room was remodeled to house more campers.

The craft hut, with its small stone fireplace, was also built behind the boathouse in 1927. It was designated for arts and crafts activities. A screened porch was added in 1938, which provided extra work space.

The original cabins were 14 feet by 18 feet and held four metal bunk beds for eight campers and one cot for the counselor. Later, the cabins in Senior Village, built in 1959, were increased to 16 feet by 20 feet. There were 12 free-standing cabins on the property, but staff and campers were also housed in the lodge, on top of the boathouse, and in Dutton.

It is unclear how many cabins were constructed in those first years, but all were built by the Alladin Company, owned by Mr. Otto Sovereign of Bay City. He also donated the cook's cabin and garage, which later housed the caretaker. The Business and Industrial Girl's Club also donated two cabins through the YWCA.

The grass tennis courts, which were sponsored by a club of business girls at the YWCA, were built in the early 1920s. A second renovation with re-rolling took place in 1930. In 1940, two new cement courts were constructed with a donation from Mr. Calvin, who had given the same amount for tennis courts at Camp Iroquois. There was also a mortgage-burning ceremony at the Saginaw Bay Yacht Club in 1937 after an anonymous donor had paid off the $3,000 debt.

In 1933, an outdoor chapel was built for worship services. It was located on the top of the hill at the north end of camp, overlooking the lake, and featured log benches, a wooden cross, and a podium. The area came to be known as Chapel Hill.

The archery range, with a protective hilly mound behind the targets, was located on the east side of the lodge beside the road that led to the horse corral and tack house. Farther into the woods lay the riflery lean-to and range, and horse trails ran throughout the property.

Around 1936, additional property was purchased from the D&M Railroad, on the southwest section of the camp, for back taxes. In 1963, an additional 23 acres were purchased from Ira Schofield for $10,000, and in 1969 more than 60 acres were purchased from John Webb for $300 an acre. In 1958, property adjacent to the camp, complete with an unfinished cabin, were put up for sale, and there were concerns that if it were rented it would be "disastrous" to the camp. As a result, fencing was erected from the waterfront and extended beyond the counselor's retreat, which was situated beside the fence.

The old farmhouse, Dutton, had been used as a health unit, a nature center, and sleeping facilities over the years. Later, the cook's cabin was also utilized as a nature center. In 1961, a new prefabricated infirmary was built, located on the road adjacent to the lodge that led to the tennis courts. It housed the nurse, who had her own room and bathroom, plus a sick bay. In 1966, the building was enlarged, and plasterboard was added to the interior.

Camp bathroom facilities, affectionately called "brownies," were originally primitive wooden structures without flush toilets, but later two cinder-block bath houses were constructed. In the early years, bathing often took place in the lake. The facility closest to the waterfront, built in 1952, had two showers, toilets, and a Bradley hand-washing basin. The senior girls' brownie was built in 1966 below Chapel Hill.

The YWCA Camp Committee was responsible for hiring staff, raising funds for improvements and repairs, publicity, fee structures, and program ideas. They met several times a year and fostered creativity in many girls through "Live Y'er" programs, Stay at Home Camps, rallies, reunions, and speakers within the local school systems. They solicited volunteers for work weekends at the camp, enlisting many of their own board members, junior chamber of commerce groups, Kiwanis, Omicron Clubs, and more.

The American Camping Association administered yearly inspections at the camp. Following a 1957 report, which granted Camp Maqua 938 points out of 1,000, the board members proudly added "Accredited by the American Camping Association" to registration brochures. Random inspections were also performed by the health department for kitchen procedures, which maintained a high standard of cleanliness, and the Department of Social Welfare from the State of Michigan, which inspected the grounds, facilities, camper-to-counselor ratio, and safety procedures. Camp

Maqua always maintained high scores and a stellar reputation and continually made improvements to its facilities.

The camp directors hired by the YWCA were often teachers who had their summers off, who then hired counselors from local colleges and universities. Many of the women who had camped as young girls returned as counselors-in-training when they aged out of the camp, becoming role models for the next generation as they earned their full counselor status.

There is no complete list of names for the camp's directors, due to missing records, but the following list has been made as complete as possible: 1924, Helen Graves; 1926, Margaret Whyte; 1927, Laura Epple; 1928, Ann Albright; 1929, Marie Lemberger; 1933–1934, Wilma Lewis; 1936, Ruth Buckwalter; 1943–1944, Margaret Fletcher; 1945, Mrs. Andrew Lowery (Maqua chairwoman); 1946, Margaret Fletcher; 1947, Mrs. Harrison Plum (Maqua chairwoman); 1948, Mrs. Livingston Thomas (Maqua chairwoman); 1950–1952, Dorothy Jane Dickey; 1953, Kathleen Geerlings; 1954, Janet Adams; 1955–1958, Kathleen Dillinger; 1959, Shirley Rausch; 1960–1962, Alice Bishop; 1963–1969, Dorthe Balaskas; 1970–1971, Barbara Haggart; 1972–1974, Sue Patenge; 1975, Carol Niemann; 1976, Delphine Evans; 1977, Ken Dike; and 1978, Margaret Meakin.

In 1928, registration fees started at $7.50 per week for local girls, while out-of-town girls paid an extra dollar. By 1935, rates had increased to $11 per week, and by 1952 it was $35 for the two-week sessions. By 1975, registration was $70 a week for local girls and $125 for two weeks.

Over the years, parents and their daughters established family traditions on the way to camp, stopping their cars loaded with trunks and suitcases to eat at certain restaurants on the road. Other campers boarded buses from the YWCA and rode together. By the time they arrived at camp and checked in for their many activities, they had taught the new girls the words to many of the camp songs, which was the thread that wove the camp experience together.

In 1926, campers packed their bags with sheets, pillowcases, toilet articles, a bathing suit and cap, dark bloomers or knickers, middy blouses and ties, heavy hose, and a Bible or prayer book. Suggested items included a camera, a tennis racquet, nature study books, a flashlight, and a musical instrument. In later years, items that could be used for costumes were packed, as well as shorts, T-shirts, and jeans, while sleeping bags replaced bedrolls.

Campers aged 8 to 16, many who had relatives that previously attended or were cheerful returnees, dashed to their assigned cabins to select their favorite bunks. As they unpacked—under the sometimes familiar names written on walls in lipstick and toothpaste—they acquainted themselves with their bunkmates and counselor, who soothed homesick girls and first-timers or hugged familiar faces. Many of the girls requested certain cabins with friends, sisters, or girls they had met at camp in years past.

Reveille was from 7:30 a.m. to 8:00 a.m., and by 8:45 a.m., the "hoppers" were getting tables ready for breakfast as the flag ceremony completed. The first activity began at 9:30 a.m., and free time was mid-morning. A free swim at 4:30 p.m. followed more afternoon activities, and by 6:00 p.m. the flag had been lowered and dinner was complete. Evening programs consisted of skits, songs, and laughter, which preceded traditional campfires. Taps were blown at 9:00 p.m., and it was lights out for the day. Sunday's programs were filled with different activities, such as Mass at the local Catholic church or an interdenominational service held high on Chapel Hill.

The program for the camp, according to a *Bay City Times* article from 1958, was built on "modern educational principles and directed by a staff of skilled leaders and counselors." The staff organized activities consisting of games, drama, arts and crafts, horseback riding, tennis, riflery, archery, swimming, boating, nature and camp craft, and sports. Approximately 100 girls gained new skills, confidence, relationship skills, and leadership during each session under the watchful eye of budding staff leaders.

Money was deposited into accounts by parents for girls to purchase candy, ice cream, stationery, stamps, and souvenirs at the camp store, or "trading post." Mail call was always the highlight of the day since phone calls and visits from home were rare. During the early years, Sundays were for visitors, who were often entertained by water festivals or skillful sporting demonstrations.

Over the years, attendance began to drop, and by 1971 the finance committee felt the burden of two large property payments. The YWCA camp committee made the decision to merge with YMCA Camp Iroquois on Sand Lake, which had been in operation since 1915 and was also struggling. They felt that by combining their resources on the larger Loon Lake property, one camp could survive.

The camp was renamed Camp Maquois and became coed in 1976 under new leadership. The sessions were restructured to consist of four, one-week coed sessions, two one-week girls-only sessions, and one week for boys only. While the camp still hosted 100 campers per week, the experiment was not a success, and Camp Maqua closed its doors in 1978. The property was sold to the Sukenik family in 1979, and they developed the property into 10 separate parcels and remodeled the lodge into two dwellings under one roof before selling all of the property.

One

Off to Camp Maqua We Go!

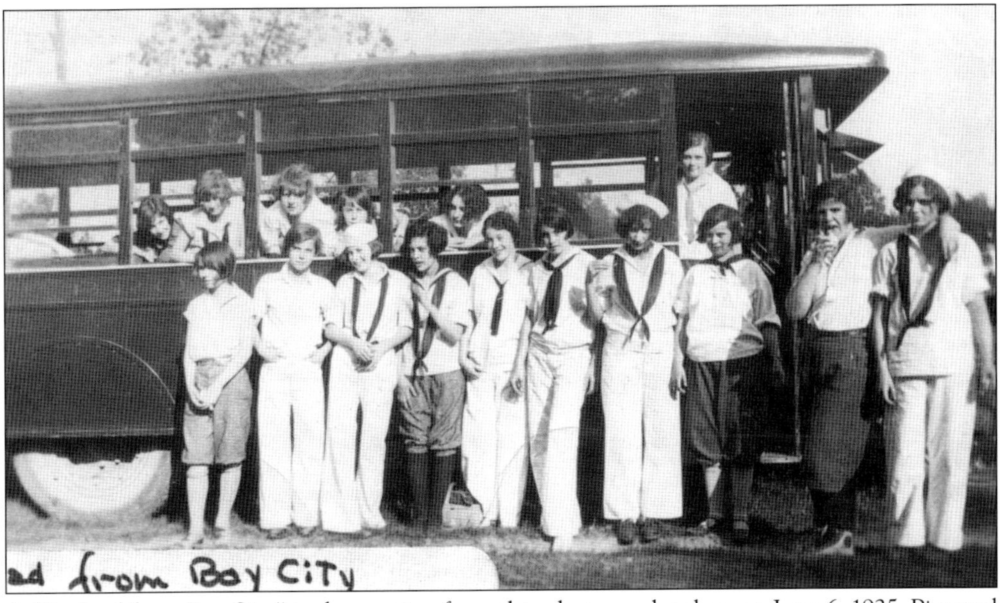

A "Busload from Bay City" is the caption from this photograph taken on June 6, 1925. Pictured from left to right are (first row) Char McKinnon, Marguerite Vollander, Lib Nelson, Beulah Beason, Marion Williston, Kay Woodbury, Sibby Miller, Dodie White, Kippy Plum, and Beth Miller; (second row) Edith Wright, Betty Smith, Petie Baumgarten, Marion Young, Ernestine Perry, and Catherine Belworthy. (Courtesy of YWCA Great Lakes Bay Region.)

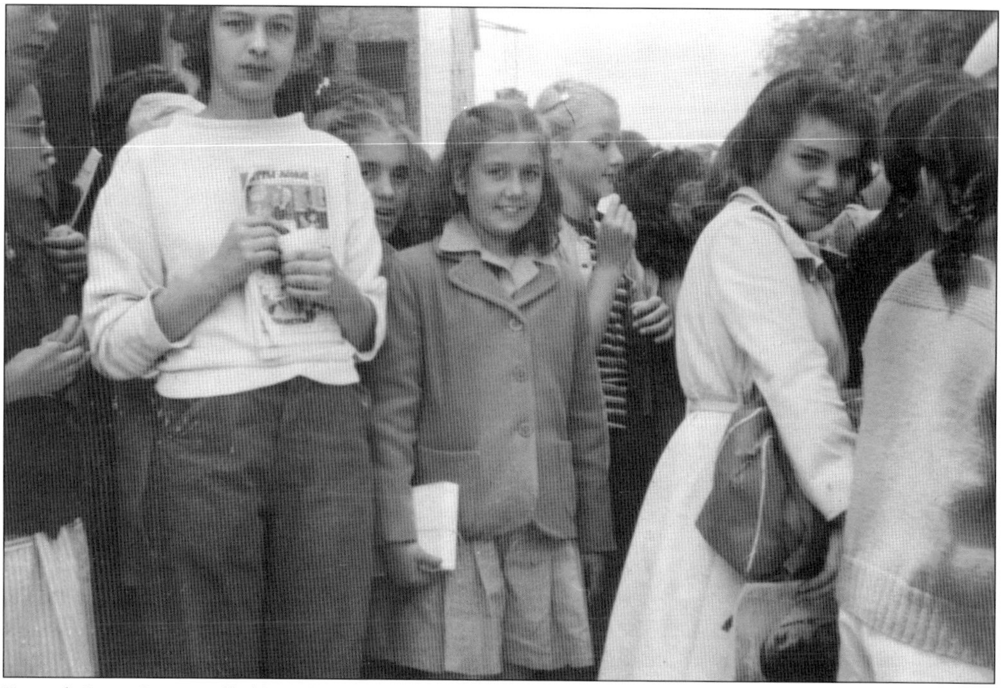

Friends Joan Cooper (left) and JoAnn Grotenraff (right) pose with Judy Rowden (center) in 1949 as they board the bus outside the YWCA. Judy recalled that one of the board members from the "Y" came aboard the bus and announced she and all her friends were in the coveted Hut Nine on the water. The girls knew it was their favorite since they were all returning campers. (Courtesy of Judy Rowden Sauve.)

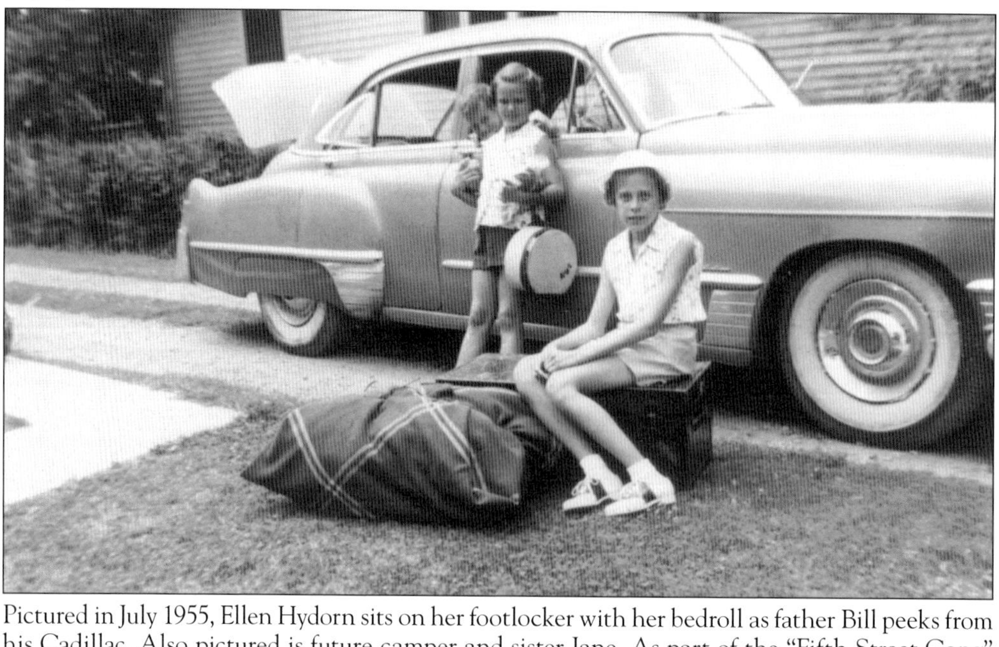

Pictured in July 1955, Ellen Hydorn sits on her footlocker with her bedroll as father Bill peeks from his Cadillac. Also pictured is future camper and sister Jane. As part of the "Fifth Street Gang" from Bay City, which included Jan Moore, Kay Mary Young, and Penny Mitchell, Ellen could not wait for her second camp experience. (Courtesy of Ellen Hydorn Campbell.)

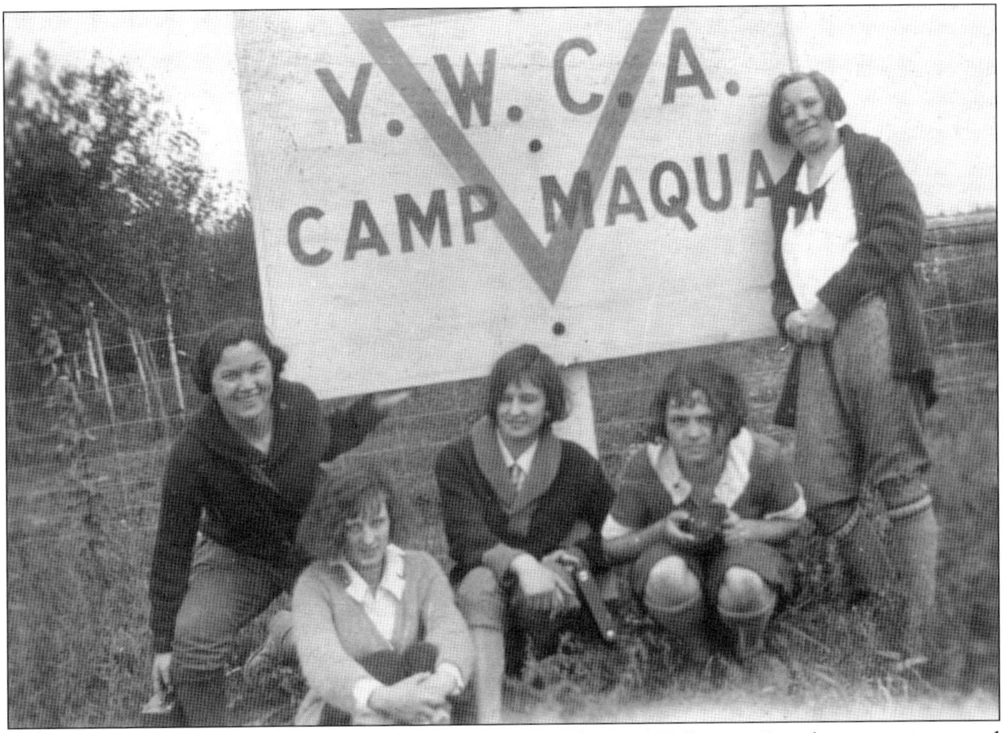

Prior to the purchase of the Camp Maqua property, Aplin and Killarney Beaches were sites used for the Employed Girl's Department of the YWCA. This undated, but presumably mid-1920s, photograph features five young girls at the crude entrance to one of the sites. (Courtesy of YWCA Great Lakes Bay Region.)

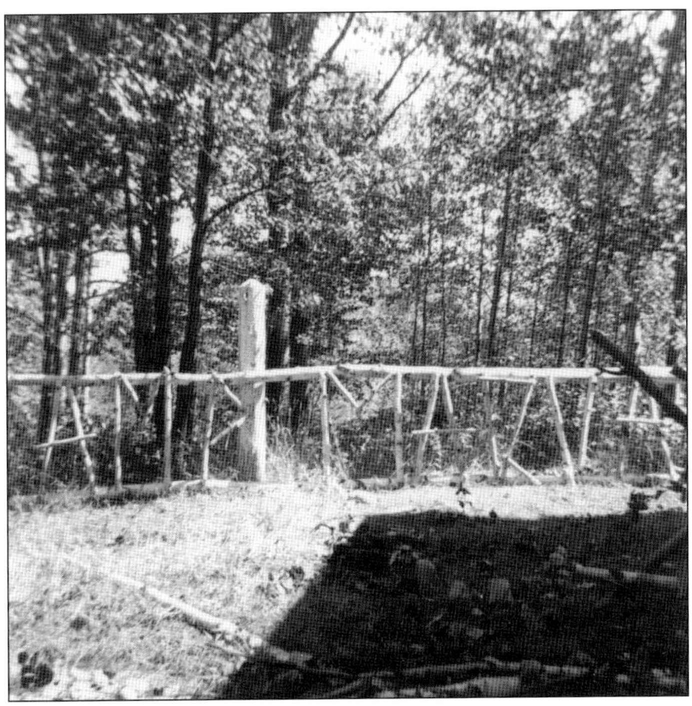

This birch log–entrance sign was built in 1951 by sisters Pat and Nancy O'Tool, Ann Gunn, and a few other girls, who braved mosquitoes and sweltering heat in bathing suits and plastic raincoats. Maqua is Native American for "The Birches," which are abundant on the property. (Courtesy of Pat O'Tool Smith.)

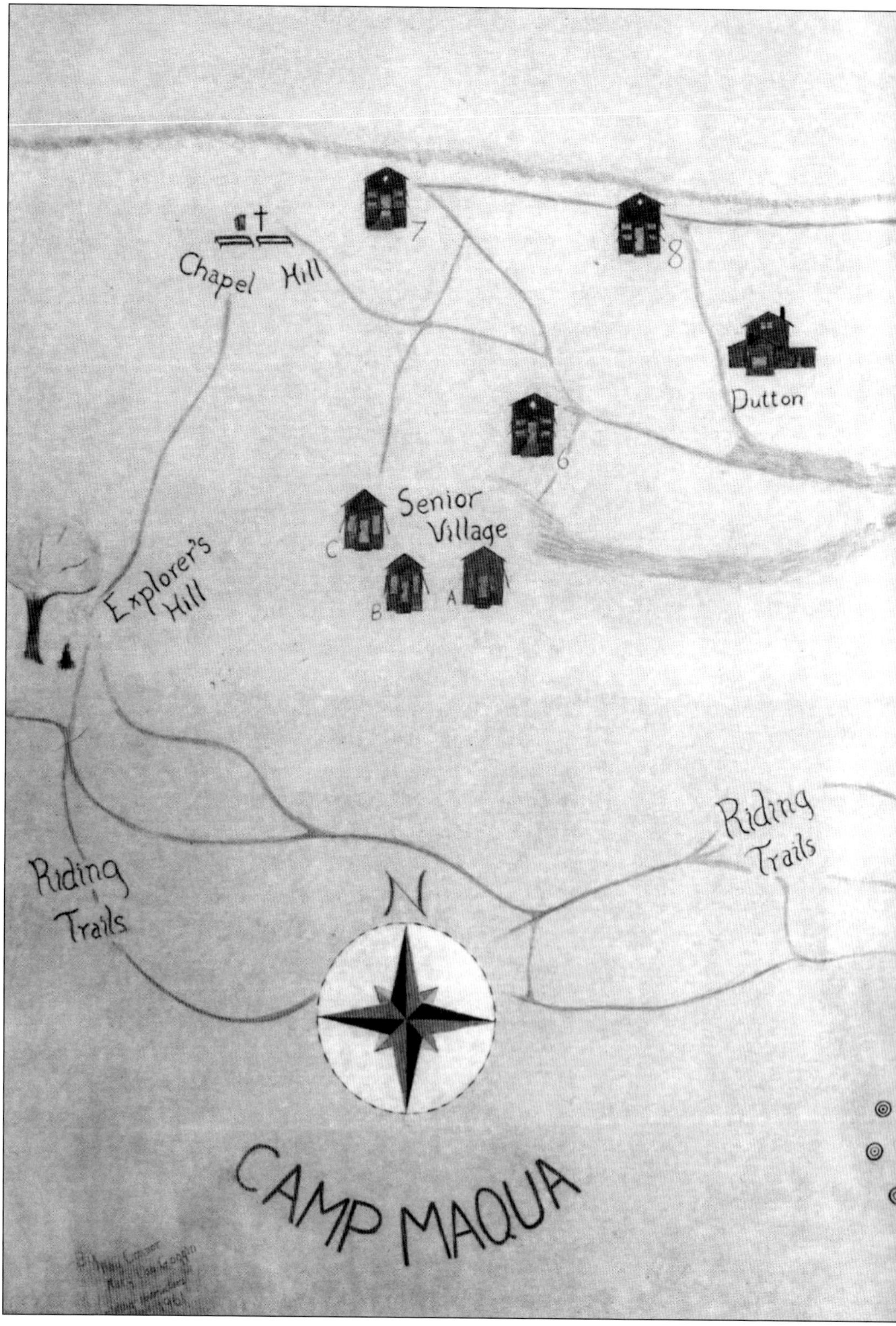
Chapel Hill
7
8
Dutton
6
Senior Village
C
B
A
Explorer's Hill
Riding Trails
N
Riding Trails
CAMP MAQUA

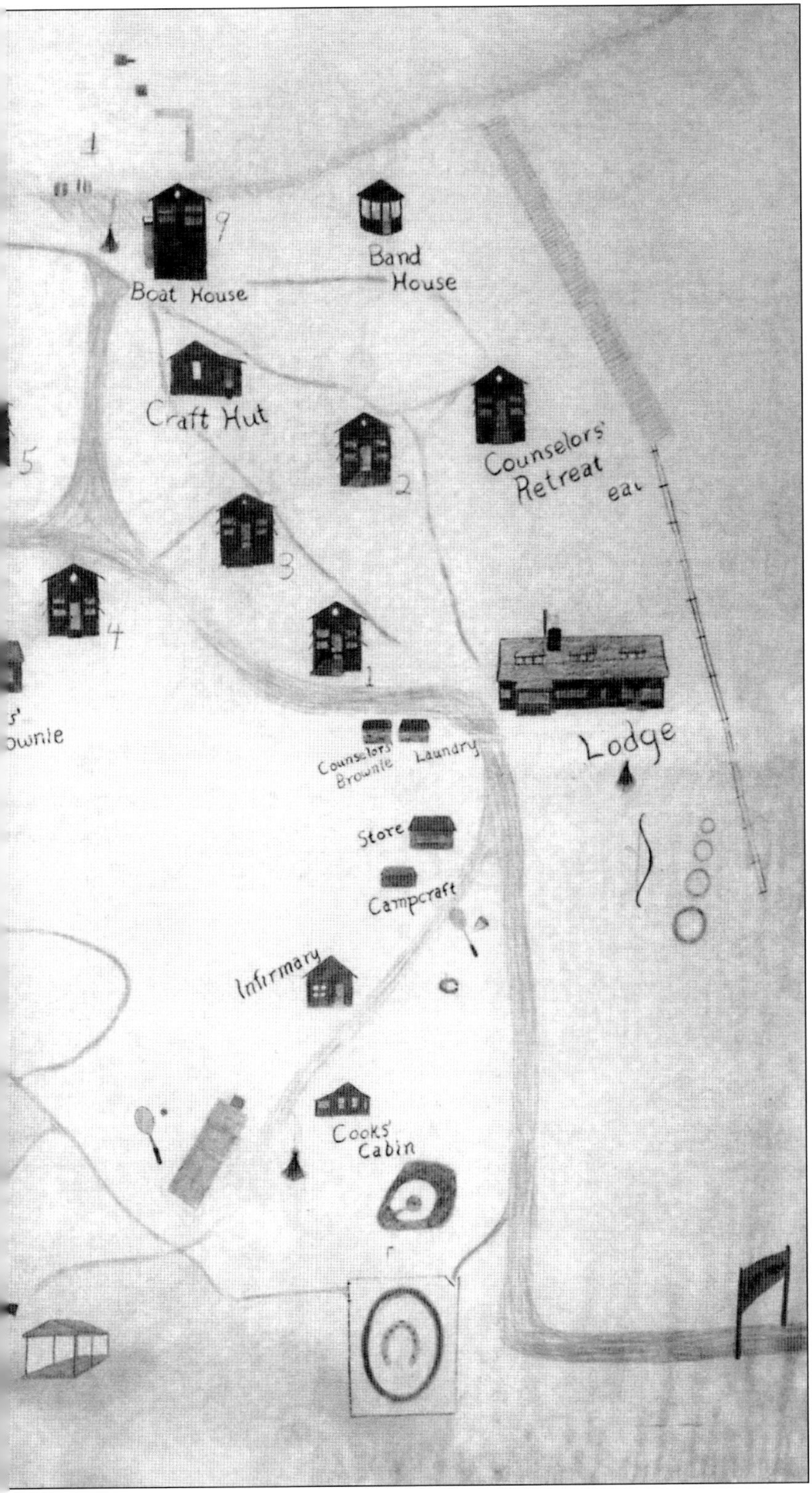

In 1961, riding instructors Mary Lou Goggin and Kay Connor fashioned a 10-foot-by-14-foot map using muslin and crayons. The map illustrates the placement of each cabin and activity area as they were placed that year. Many of the buildings remain intact, including the lodge, boathouse, craft hut, camp brownies, and six huts. Today, the trails are still mowed, and the corral and tennis courts remain. (Courtesy of Anne Trahan.)

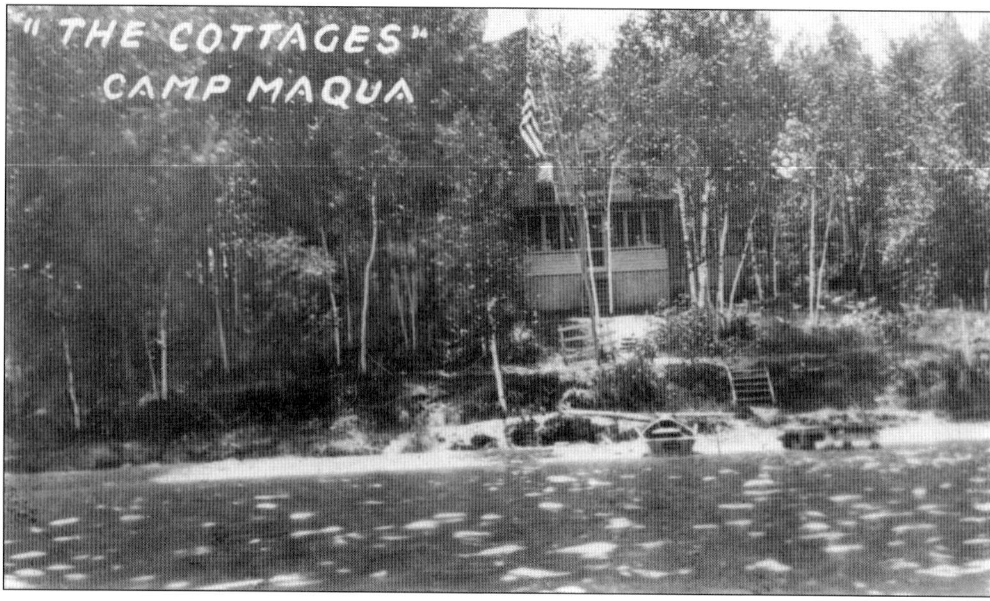

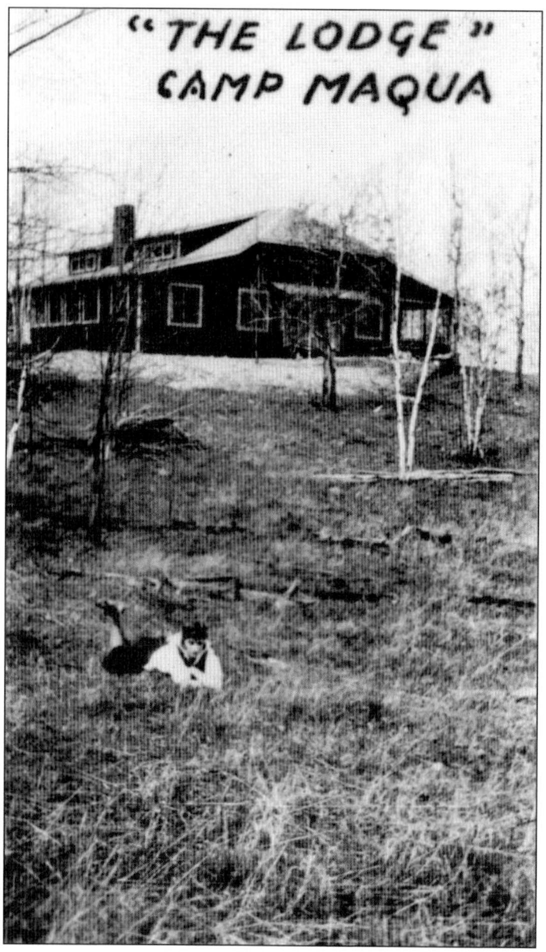

In the early 1920s, a series of miniature postcards of the property and buildings were tucked inside tiny envelopes and mailed from camp. This postcard, titled "The Cottages," shows the Dutton farmhouse—the only building on the camp property at the time of purchase in 1924. It was considered a story-and-a-half house. (Courtesy of YWCA Great Lakes Bay Region.)

One of the earliest photographs of the lodge is dated to 1925, taken lakeside. This view shows a path toward the lodge, which leads up a very barren hill. The 64-foot-long screened porch was comfortable for indoor activities, shuffleboard, ping-pong and relaxing on swings, hammocks, and rolled paper wicker furniture. (Courtesy of YWCA Great Lakes Bay Region.)

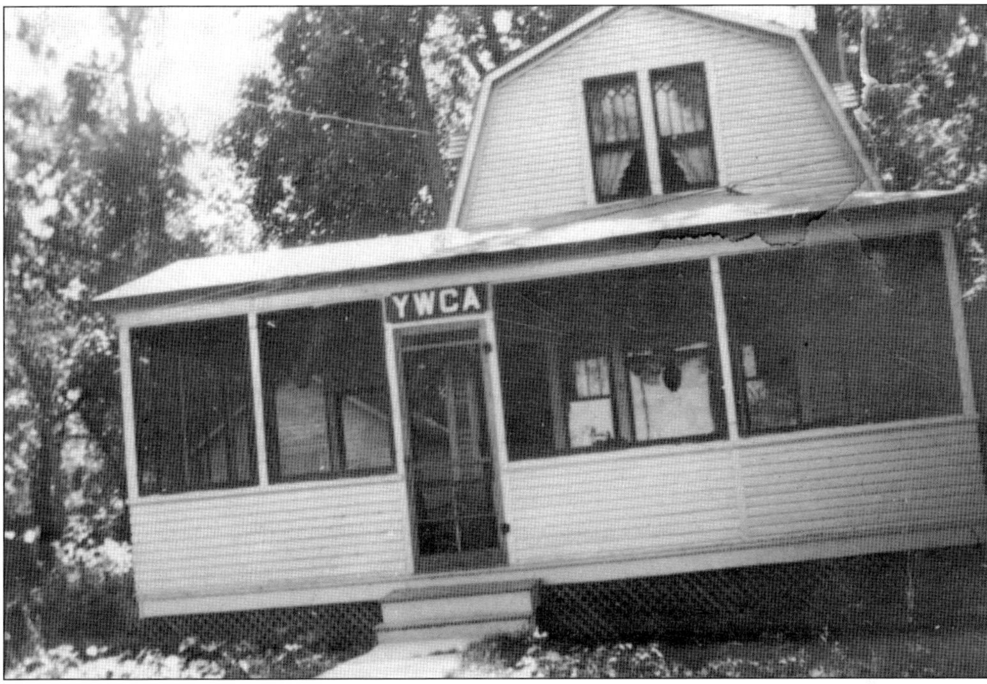

A handmade birch-bark album, entitled "Camp Maqua Employed Girl's Department 1925–1928," holds beautifully preserved photographs from the beginning years of camp, including the front and back elevation of Dutton. Above, the entrance door with the YWCA sign is clearly seen from the roadside leading to a screened porch that was the center of camp life for all indoor activities during the early years. Below, the back door faced Loon Lake, where another porch housed campers on cots. (Courtesy of YWCA Great Lakes Bay Region.)

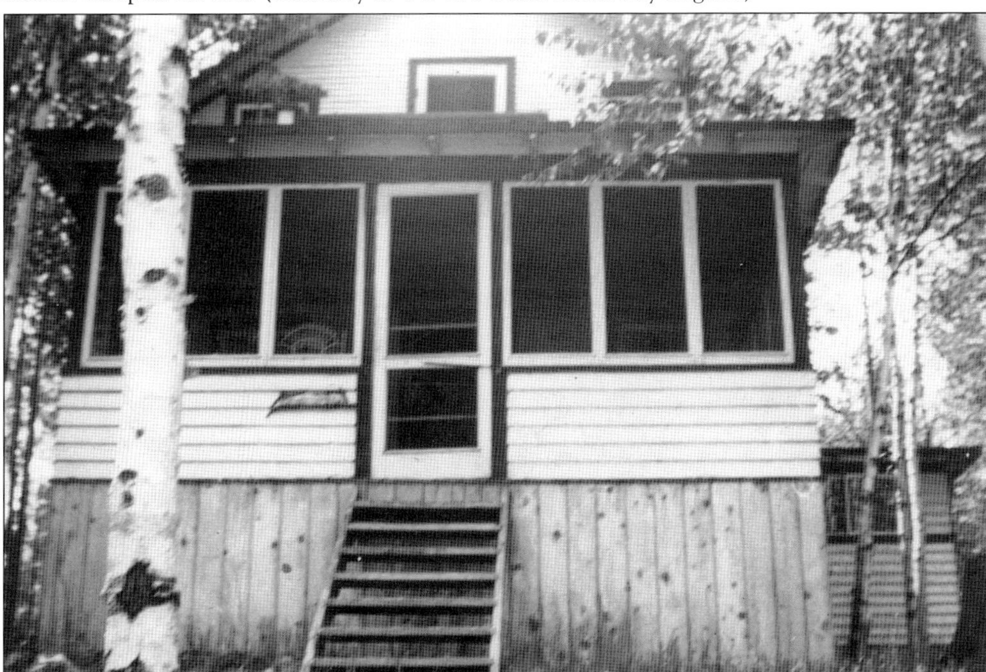

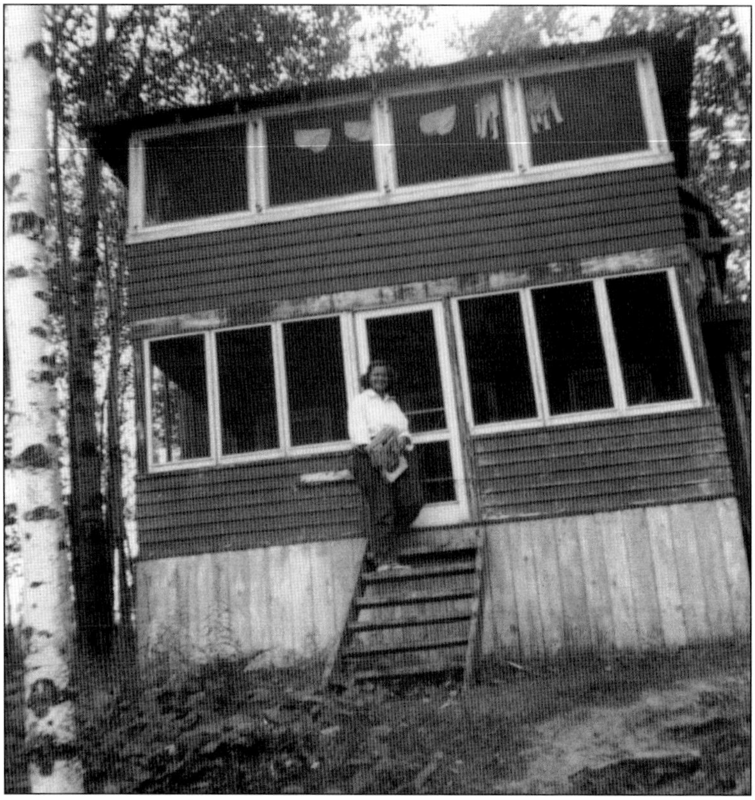

Over the years, Dutton served as inaugural camping quarters, a staff residence, the Health Unit or Infirmary, and the Nature Center. In 1940, an additional screened porch was added to the upper story, which allowed room for extra sleeping quarters when needed. Seemingly always in a state of disrepair, Dutton remained standing for years after the camp closed. (Courtesy of Sascha Immerman.)

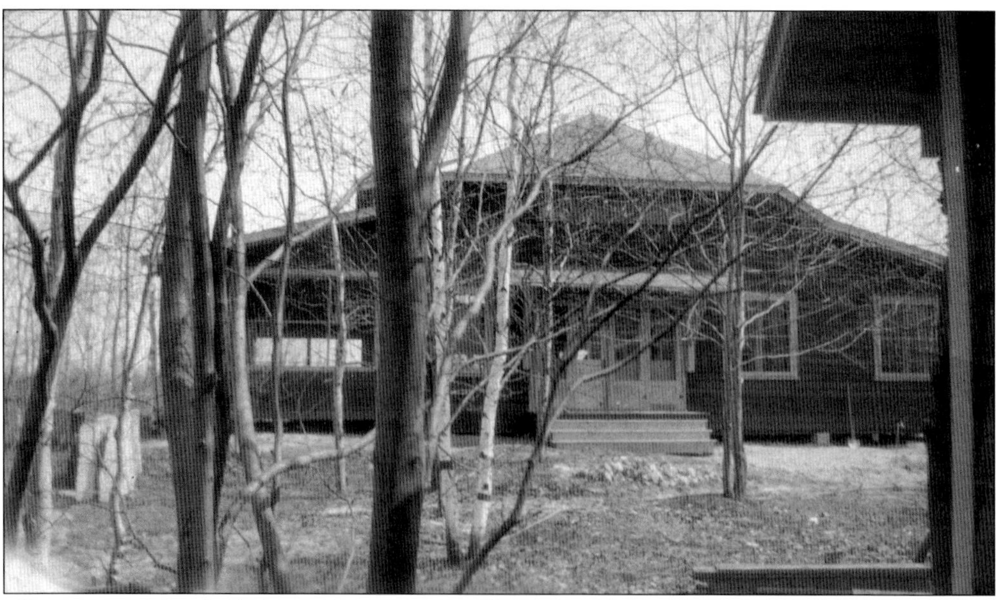

The main site for the lodge, selected on October 17, 1924, by a general committee, was under the direction of Mr. E.B. Perry. This early view, taken from the steps of Hut One, overlooks the entrance from the west side of the lodge. The annex, which was to the right, housed the kitchen, storeroom office, and a hostess bedroom, which led into the main dining hall with a fireplace. (Courtesy of YWCA Great Lakes Bay Region.)

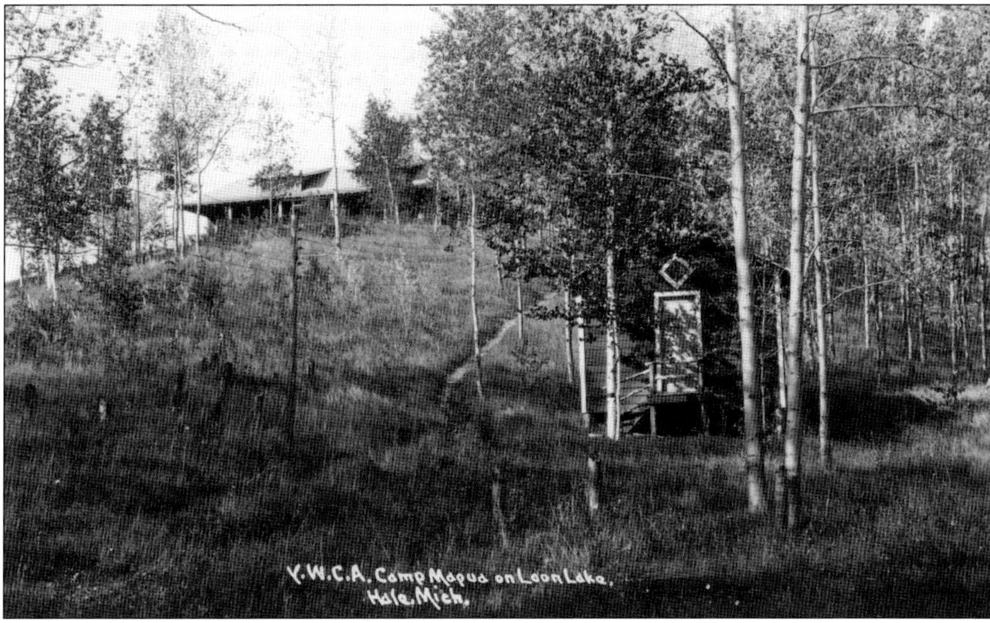

This early postcard, presumed to be from the late 1920s or early 1930s based on tree growth, was found on eBay by the present owner. The hut in the foreground was situated by the lakeshore to the right of the boathouse. The path leading to the lodge became a road later on, which led to the top of the hill. (Courtesy of Kathryn A. Baker.)

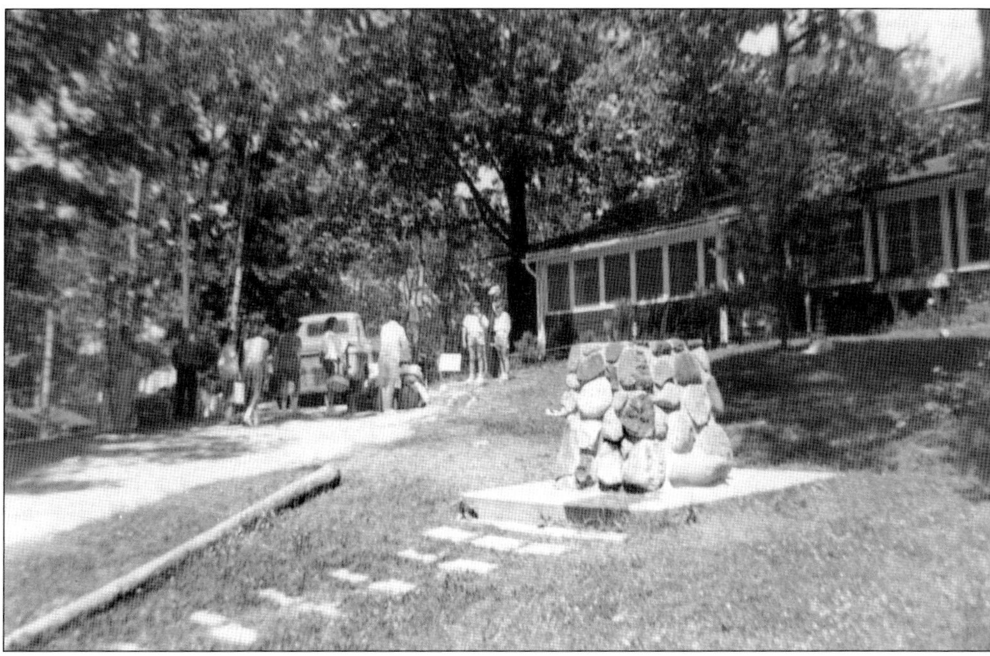

In 1924, the road leading into camp began at the south end of the property, but it would later be relocated to the north. Staff would assist campers with their belongings and assign a hut at registration. Taken in 1957, this photograph shows the drinking fountain and entrance to the lodge, which would have been the first look at the camp for newly arrived girls. (Courtesy of Pamela Watson Roberts.)

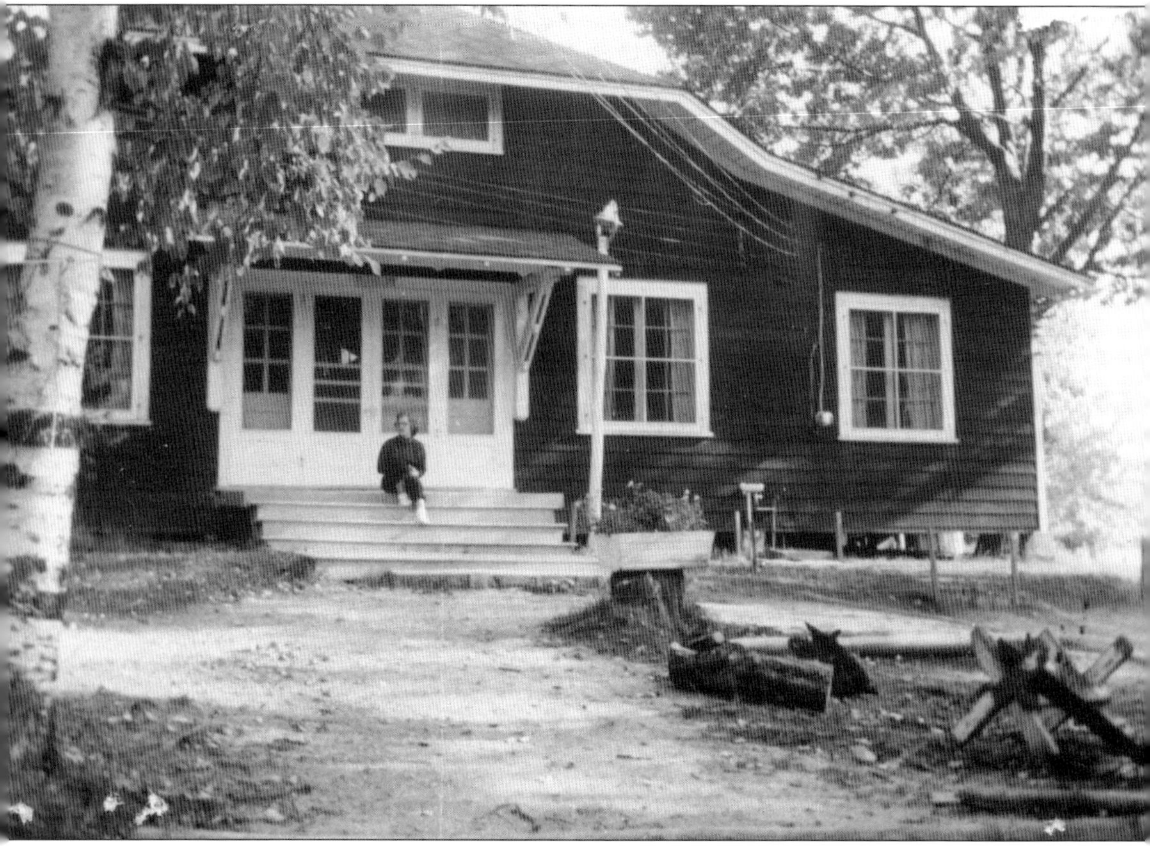

The west side of the lodge was the main entrance to the building's living area. A young woman sits on the steps leading up to the doors, and the camp bell can be seen to the right of the door. Taken in the 1930s, this photograph was probably snapped from Hut One, which sat a few yards from the lodge and housed younger campers. (Courtesy of YWCA Great Lakes Bay Region.)

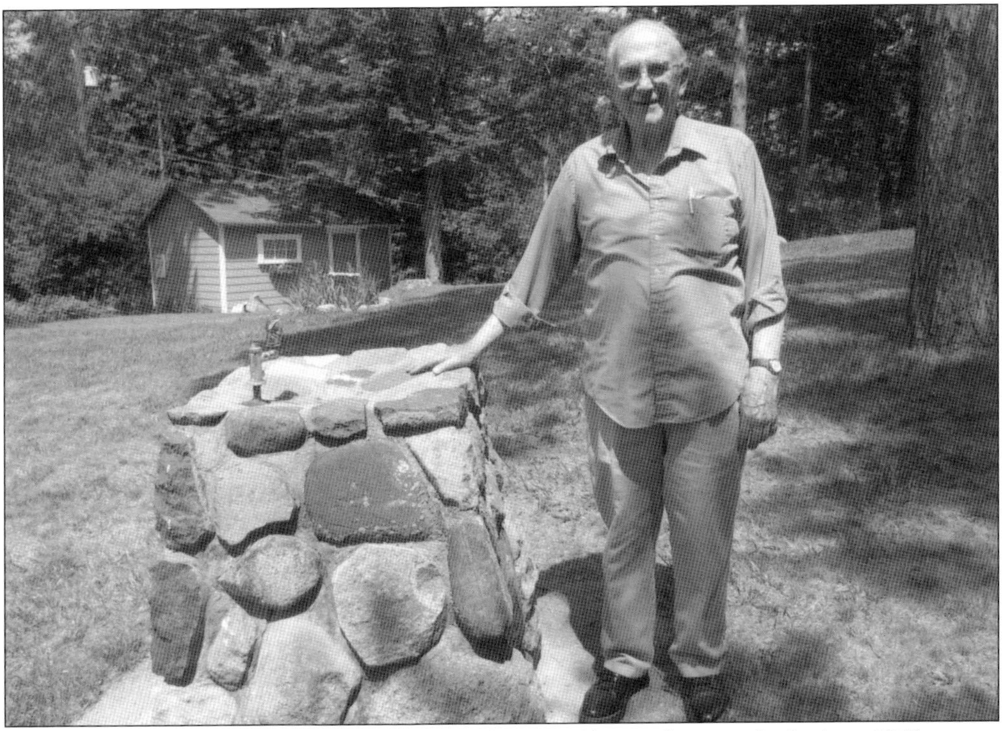

Above, Stewart Watson stands beside the Michigan fieldstone fountain he built in 1955, posing for the present property owner. For years, he helped his parents, "Ma and Pa Watson," with general maintenance around the camp. Three copper pennies are embedded in the top of the fountain to represent the film *Three Coins in a Fountain*, which was popular that year. Pamela Watson and her niece Cheri Sierocki were 10 years old in the photograph below and shared a cabin in the summer of 1956, when Pam's mother Lynn was the cook for camp. Holding her dog Squeaker, Pam shares a drink with her niece. (Courtesy of Pamela Watson Roberts.)

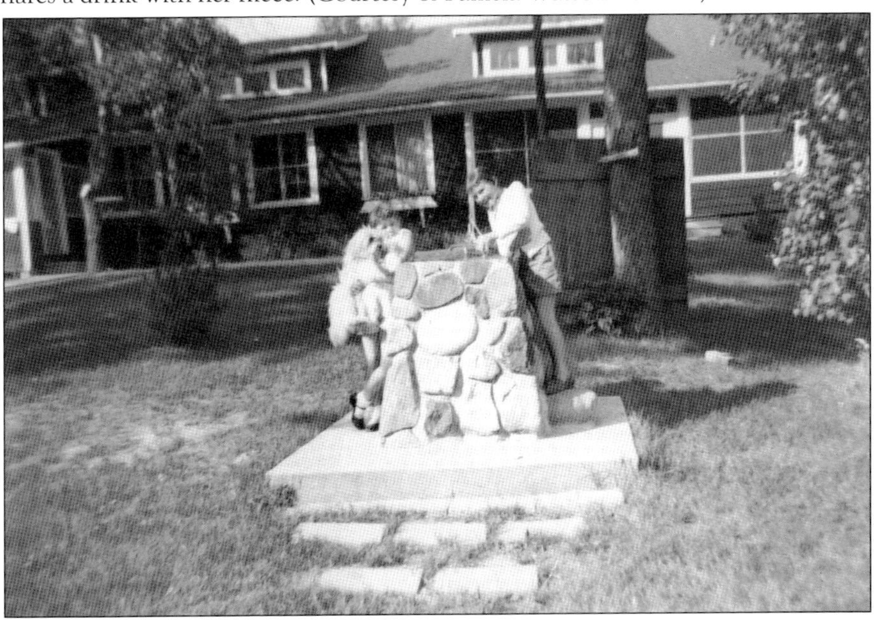

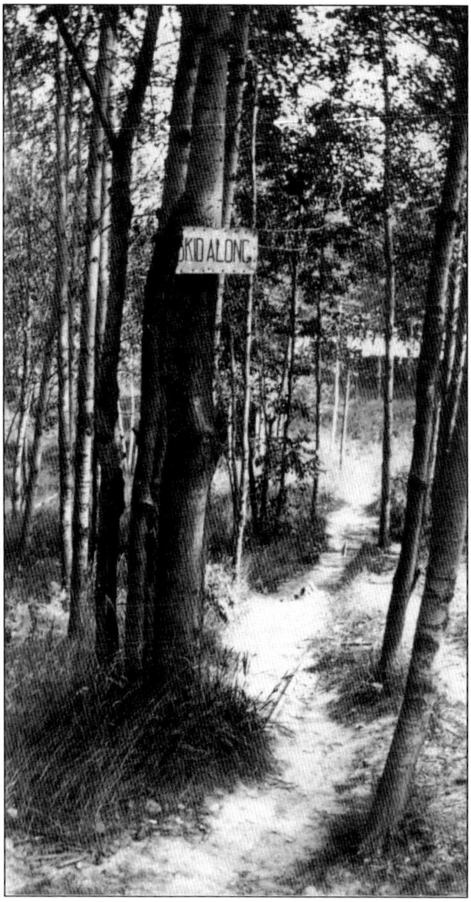

A mid-1920s image features a winding trail used by campers. Tree lined, and with a sign posted on one of the larger trees, the Skid Along Trail lacked steps to break a fall and may have been truly steep enough to slide down. Many trails were blazed throughout the property. (Courtesy of YWCA Great Lakes Bay Region.)

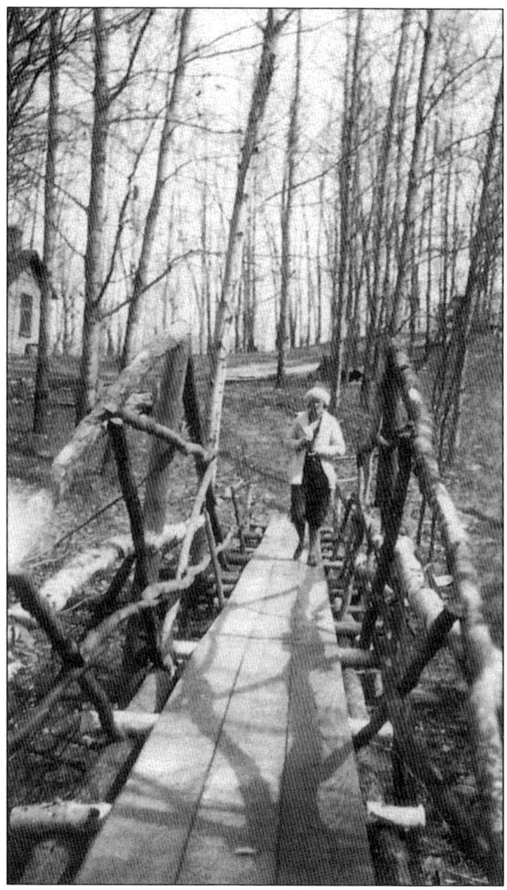

A young woman is seen crossing the rustic bridge, which spanned a ravine on the camp property in the early 1920s. The variation in elevation necessitated this practical solution. The property's low swampland and high trails appealed to both hikers and riders on horseback. (Courtesy of YWCA Great Lakes Bay Region.)

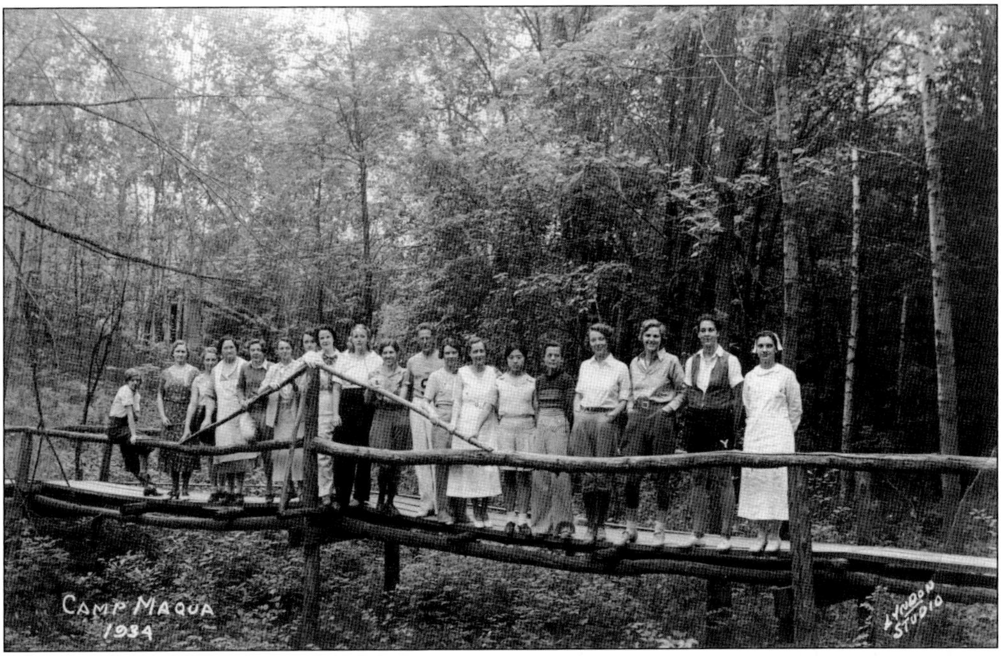

Campers and counselors enjoyed the 50-foot-long rustic bridge, which was a picturesque spot for photographs. Above, swimming and lifesaving director Mary Madore, third from right, poses with other staff members in 1934. Although their names are not available, it is easy to identify some of their duties by the nurse's cap, jodhpurs, and cook's apron. A solitary male stands among the women. The photograph below was taken in the late 1930s as the girls pose with a counselor in their swim attire. (Above, courtesy of Candy Camerden; below, YWCA Great Lakes Bay Region.)

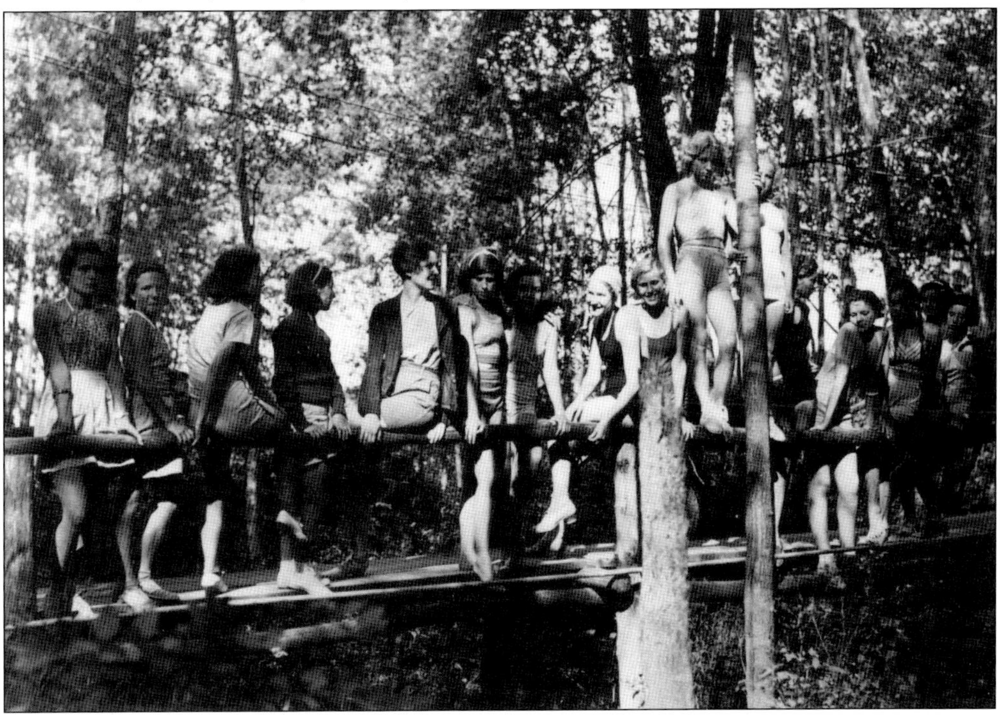

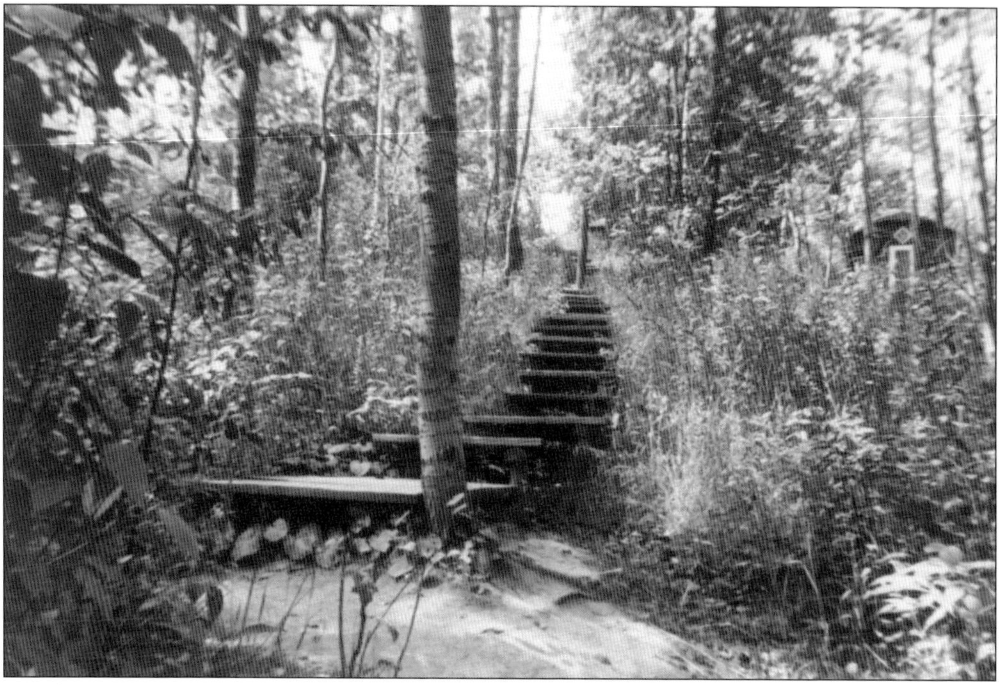

In July 1955, these stairs led up to Hut Two. The stairs always seemed such a long climb when young campers had to run up and down them all day. Amy Johns recalls vivid memories of her days in the 1960s and 1970s exploring the many hidden paths, including one from Chapel Hill, around the swamp and back to the horse corral. (Courtesy of Ellen Hydorn Campbell.)

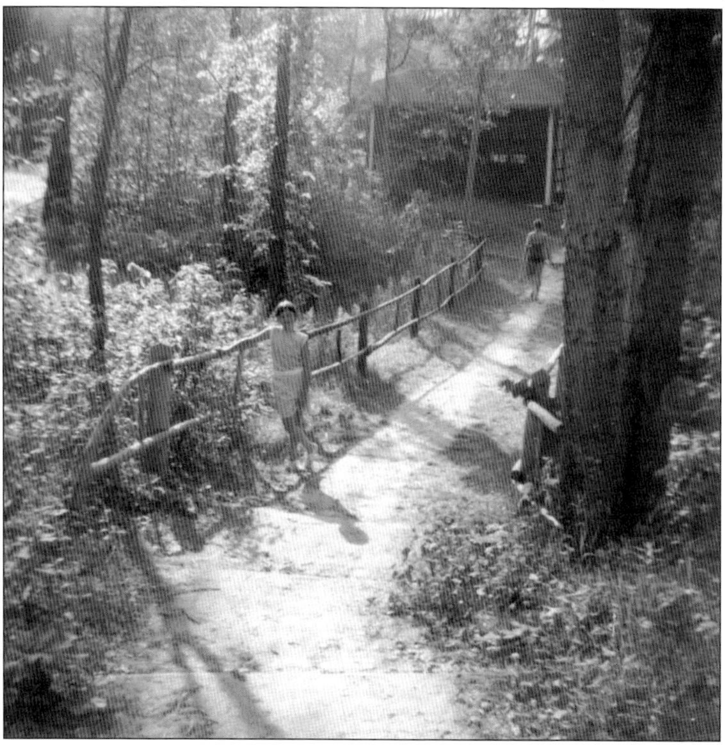

By 1960, the stairs that led to the lake had been improved with a rail fence and wider landings so the girls could safely find their way—sometimes in the dark—to the brownie. These midnight trips were usually made with a flashlight and a buddy. (Courtesy of Ruth Wiesen Krzewinski.)

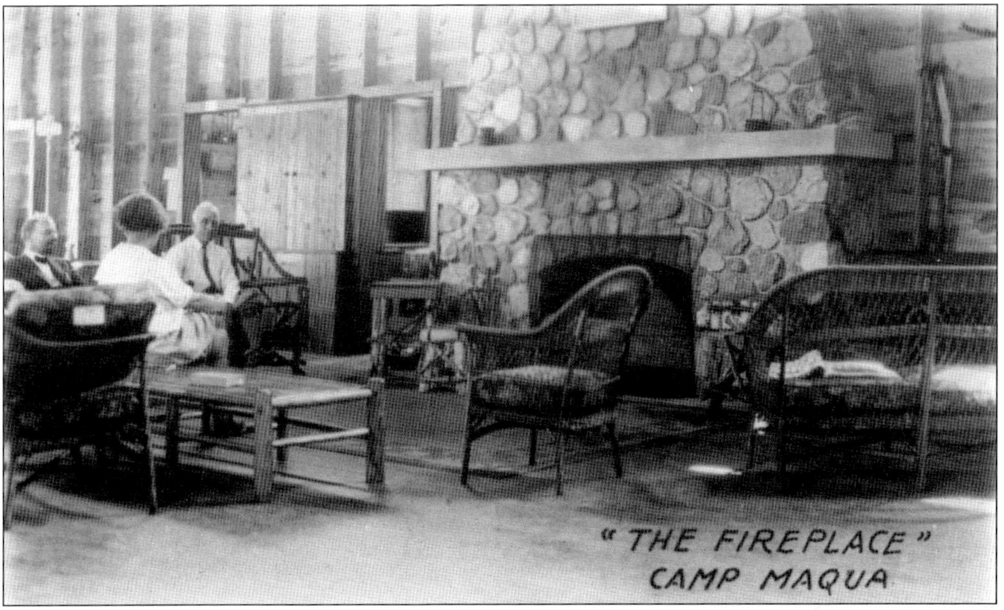

This immense fieldstone fireplace was built inside the lodge for $392.42 and was dedicated to Dr. Mary Williams, who was primarily responsible for the founding of Camp Maqua. It was the focal point of the entire structure and served as a gathering spot for fires on cold and rainy days, as well a place to roast marshmallows, perform skits, and sing songs. Below, four girls knit as they relax on two paddle-armed maple couches in front of the fireplace. Two more girls play jacks, while one avid reader is stretched out with one of the many books loaned to the camp by the Bay City Library. (Courtesy of YWCA Great Lakes Bay Region.)

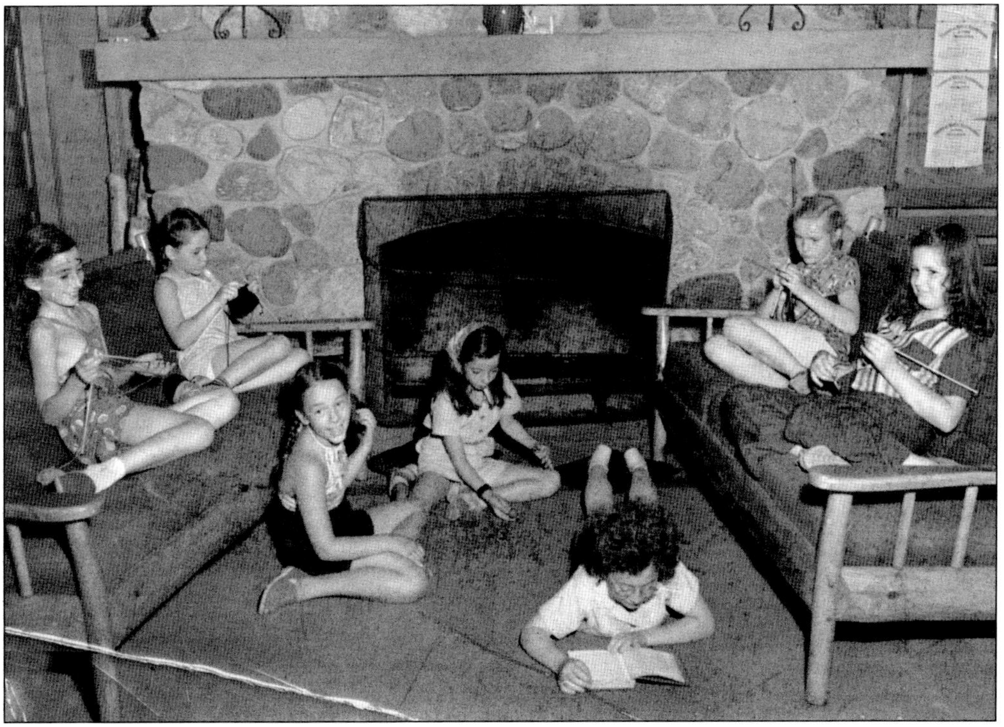

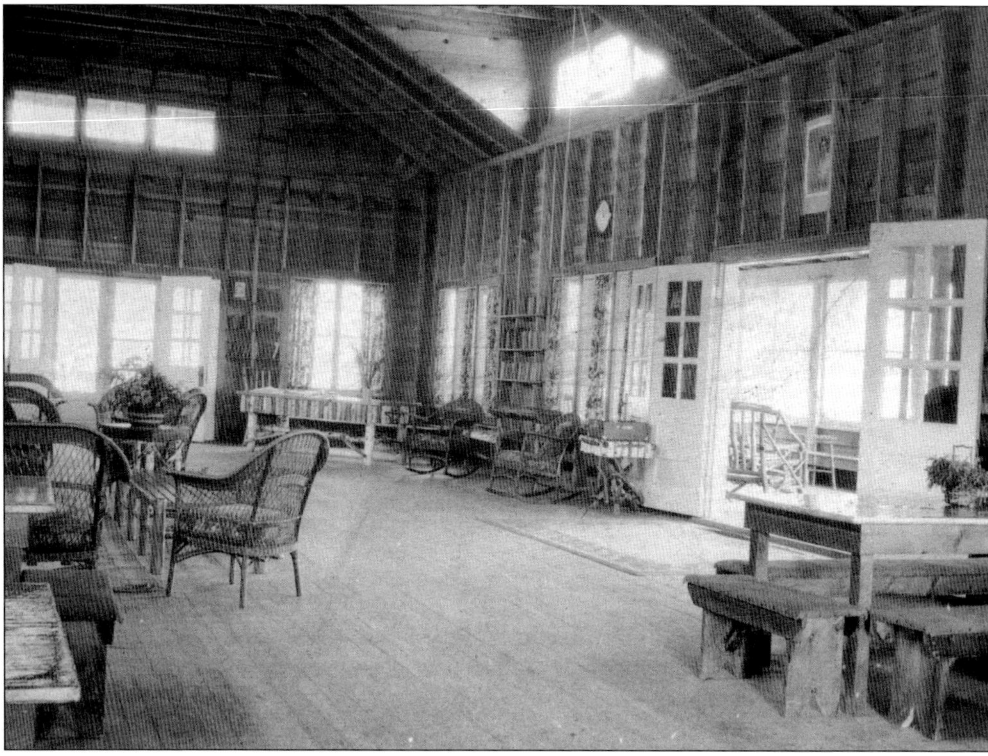

In 1938, Habitant log furniture was purchased for the lodge from a company in Bay City. Large settees, wingback armchairs, and other pieces graced the living area near the fireplace. The photograph above, taken in the 1920s, has a view of the sitting area as it looks onto the lakeside porch. The photograph below, from 1946, looks toward the west entrance and clearly shows the piano, rustic birch chandelier, and an entrance to a room on the left, which served as a business office. The foreground table was typical of the dining tables and was covered in linoleum. (Courtesy of YWCA Great Lakes Bay Region.)

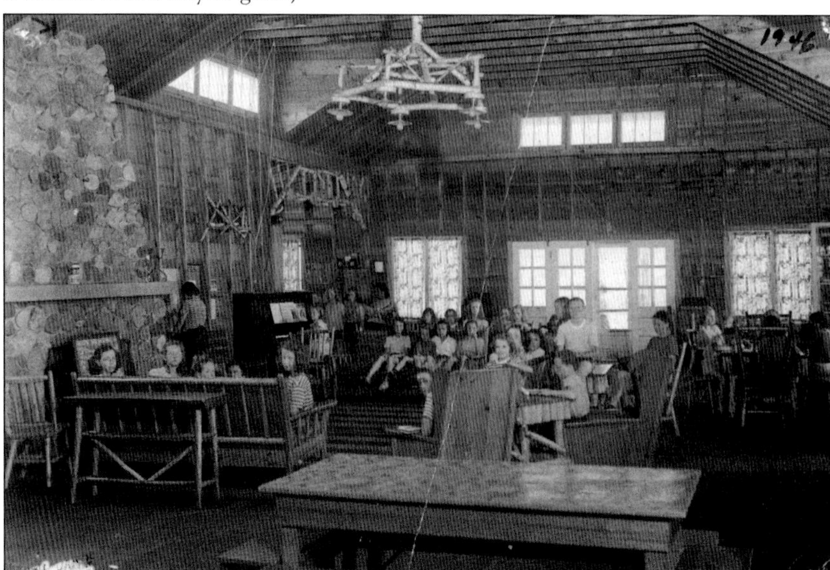

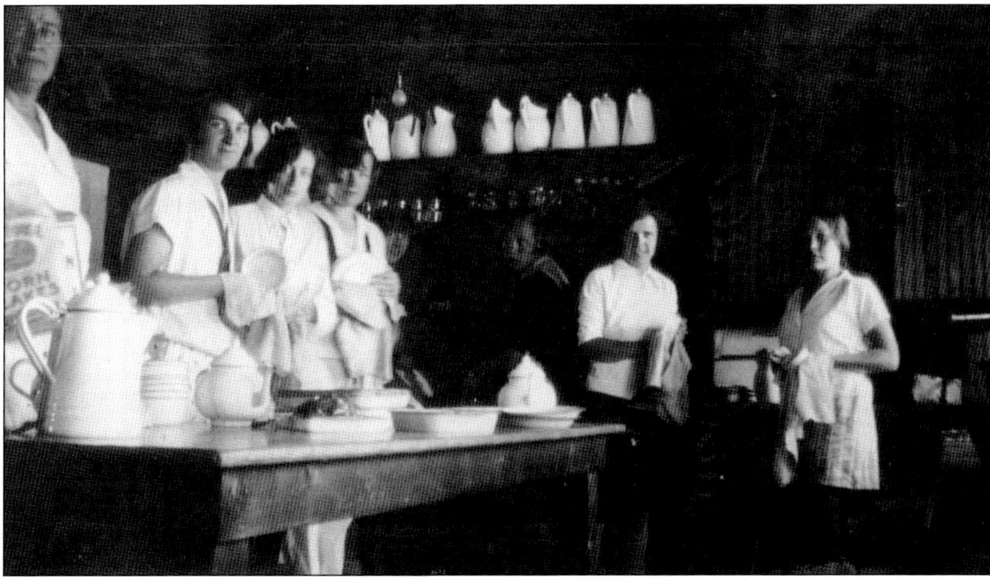

An undated news clipping boasted about the benefits of camping activities, as well as "simple, plain food of sufficient variety and excellent quality . . . milk and cream from an improved farm near the camp, and fresh fruit, vegetables and eggs from neighboring farmers." Cooks were often hired from local schools, and a dietician was on-staff to follow the health standards of the day. In this 1920s photograph, Corn Flakes and milk pitchers create a great kitchen breakfast scene. (Courtesy of YWCA Great Lakes Bay Region.)

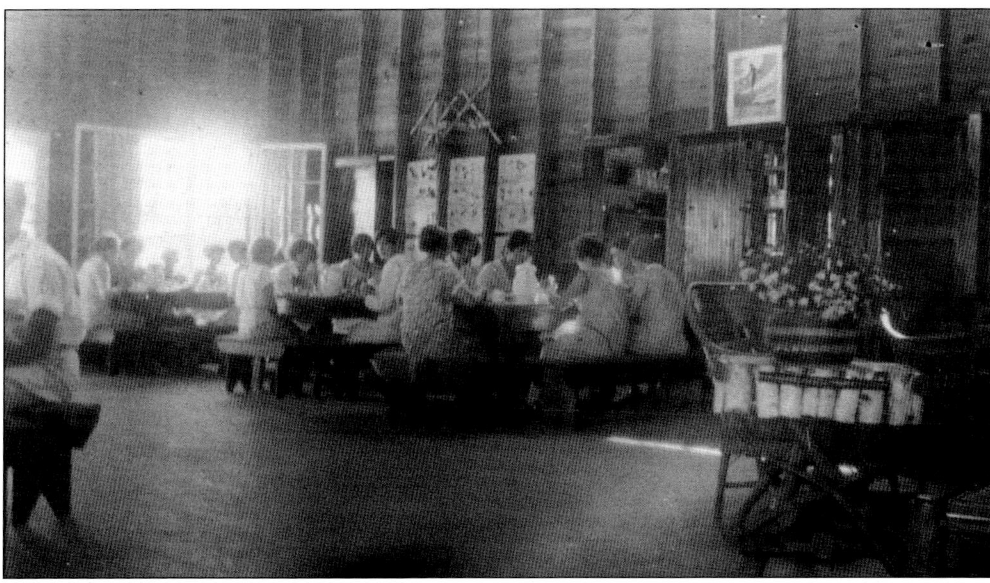

According to camper Geraldine Folkert, who attended Camp Maqua from 1942 to 1947, the lodge began and ended the campers' day and was the gathering place. Manners were learned, new foods were tasted, and responsibilities were taught. In the early years, the girls washed their own dishes in pans of soapy water at the end of each table until the health inspectors deemed that practice unhealthy. (Courtesy of YWCA Great Lakes Bay Region.)

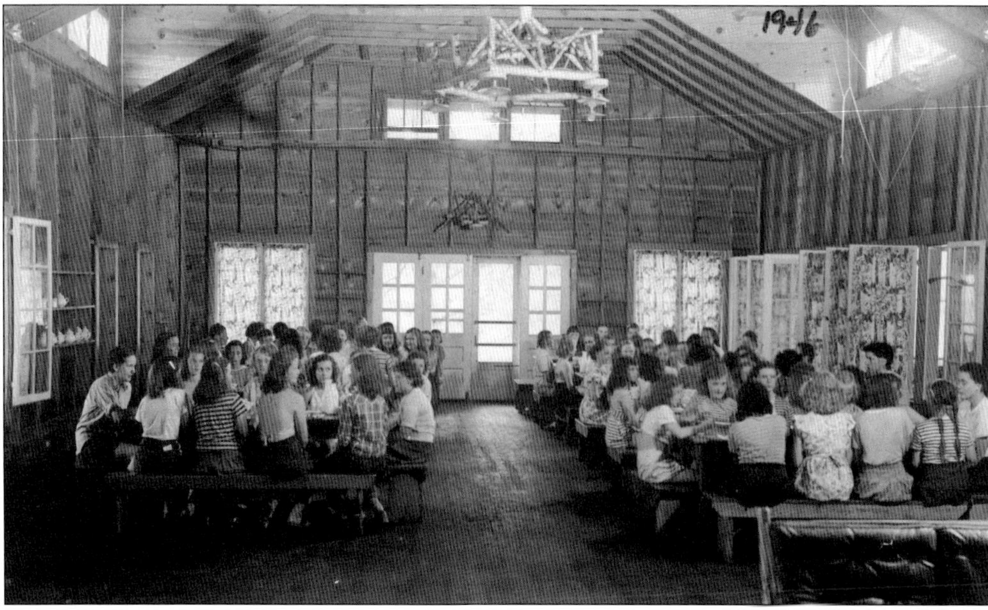

The main dining area consisted of linoleum-covered tables with two large and two small bootstrap benches. Each hut's residents sat together with their counselor. Food was usually served family style and was retrieved from a counter in the kitchen by "hoppers." If elbows were caught on the table, the girls would sing out the offender's name, followed by "strong and able, get your elbows off the table, this is not a riding stable, this is Maqua's dinner table." The above view of the east side was taken in 1946. The view of the west side below, taken in 1940, may have been taken on Visitor's Day, when parents could dine with their campers on the familiar camp dinnerware: white and edged with a green stripe. (Courtesy of YWCA Great Lakes Bay Region.)

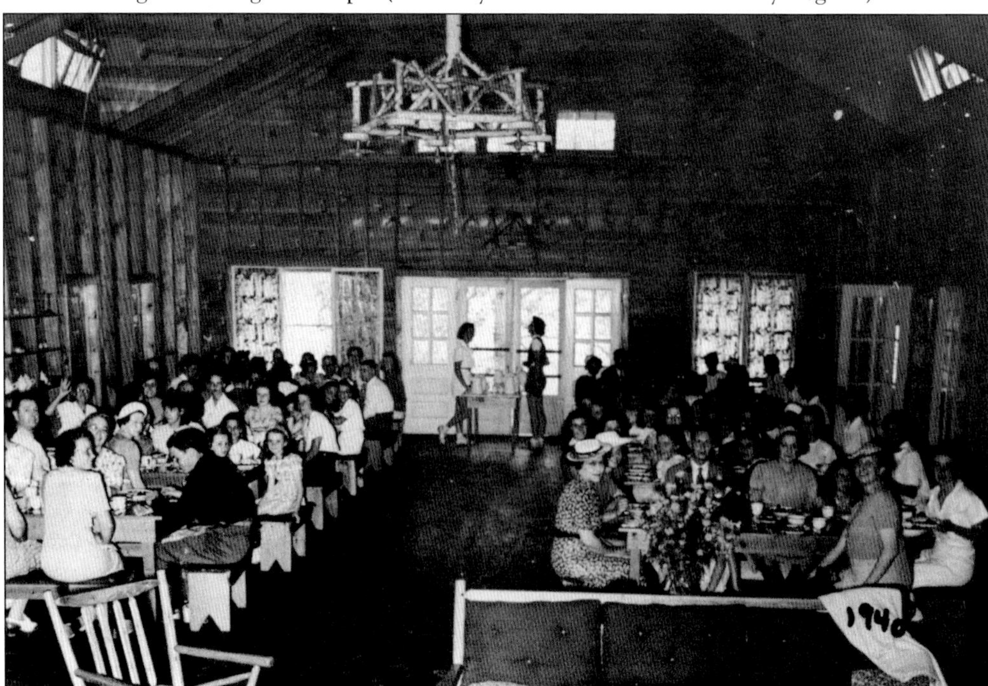

The kitchen was a hot place to work in the summer. Often, the girls would involve in horseplay to cool off, which included a traditional dunking. If one of the coworkers "pulled a boo-boo," then into the lake they went. Betsy Landram was the victim in this July 1957 photograph, with, from left to right, Evelyn Sautter, Karen Wright, Suzanne Pfundt, and Nancy Carter doing the dunking. (Courtesy of YWCA Great Lakes Bay Region.)

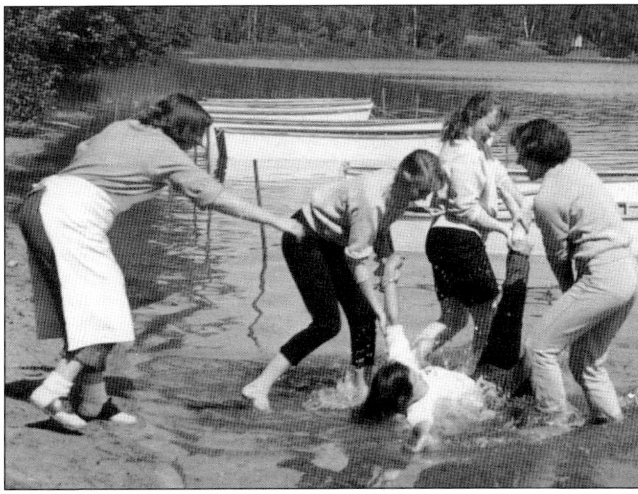

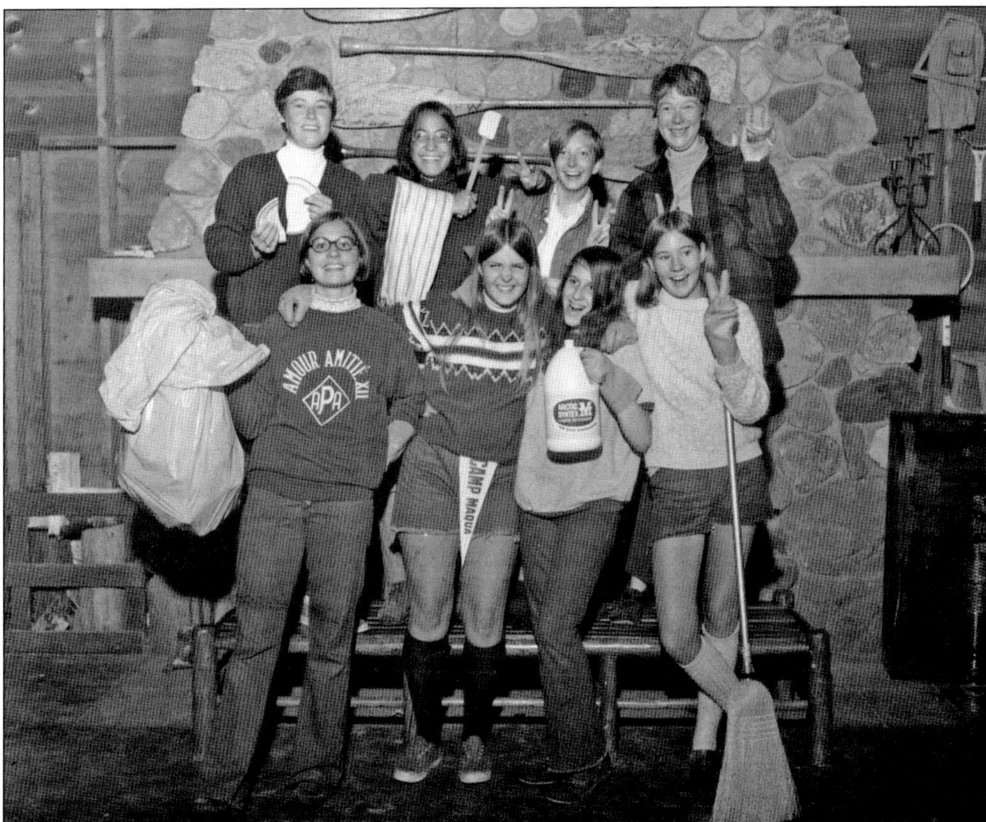

Kitchen aides assisted the cook and her helper before and after meals, assembled meals, served seconds, poured beverages, refilled condiments, and helped clean up. This crew from 1970 consisted of, from left to right, (first row) Marty Stein, B.J. Henderson, Jan Schreiber, and Kathy Baregon; (second row) Judy Moore, Shelley Harris, Chris Lambert, and Barbara Haggart. (Courtesy of Shelley Harris.)

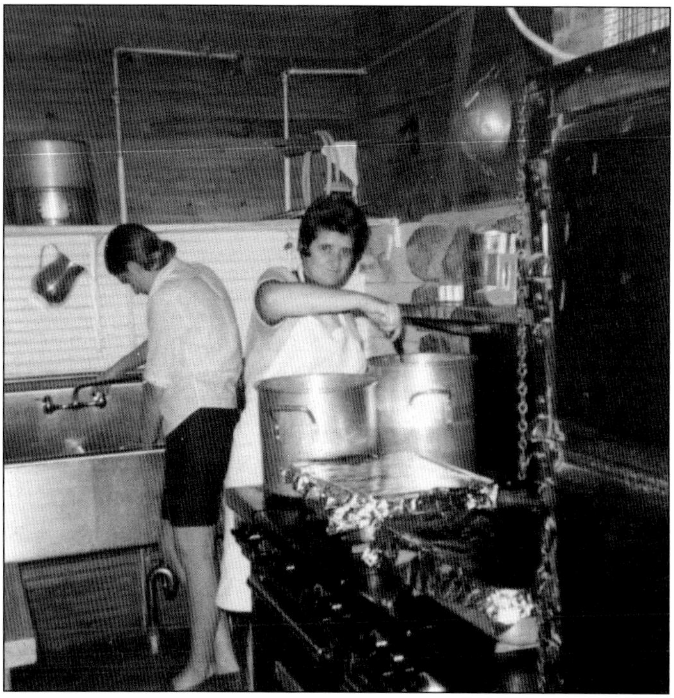

Cooks were often given the weekend off. Anne Obey, a counselor in 1968, assisted director Dorthe Balaskas that summer. Anne had camped for five summers before becoming a counselor, which included a stint as a kitchen aide. She had plenty of practice for cooking and dishwashing. (Courtesy of Barbara Haggart.)

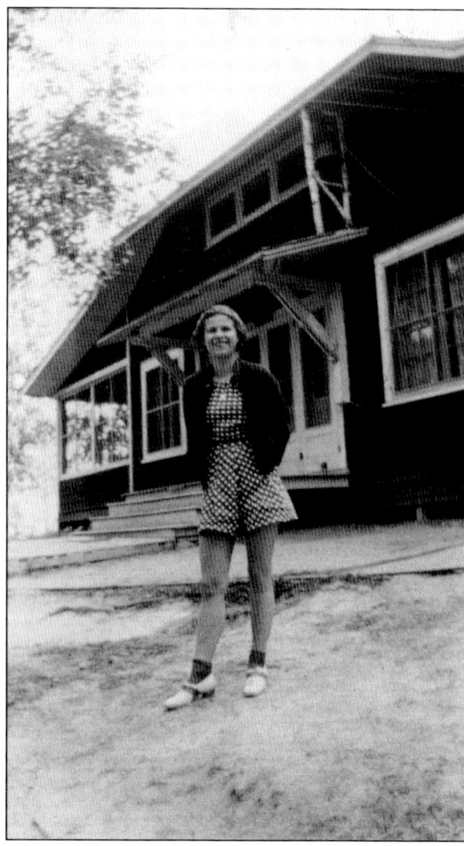

The bell was the "time teller" at camp. Reveille was at 8:00 a.m., and the hoppers had to be ready at the sound of the bell. Two girls from each hut arrived to set the table for their hut for each meal. The bell was high above the main entrance on a birch stand in the early 1930s, but in later years it was moved to ground level. (Courtesy of YWCA Great Lakes Bay Region.)

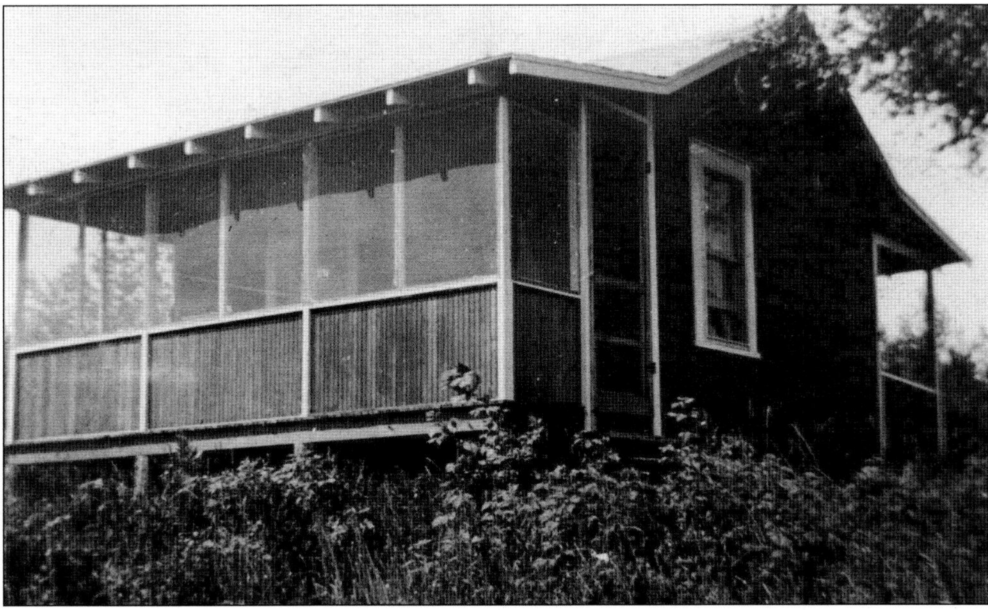

Otto Sovereign, owner of the Alladin Building Company in Bay City, was a benefactor of the camp and donated many of the cabins, including the cook's cabin. The above rear-view photograph from the 1925 archival album shows the screened-in porch where the cook could rest after a long, hot day in the kitchen. An added bonus was a private bathroom. In 1970, the cabin was used by the kitchen aides, and in later years it was used as a nature center. (Courtesy of Shelley Harris.)

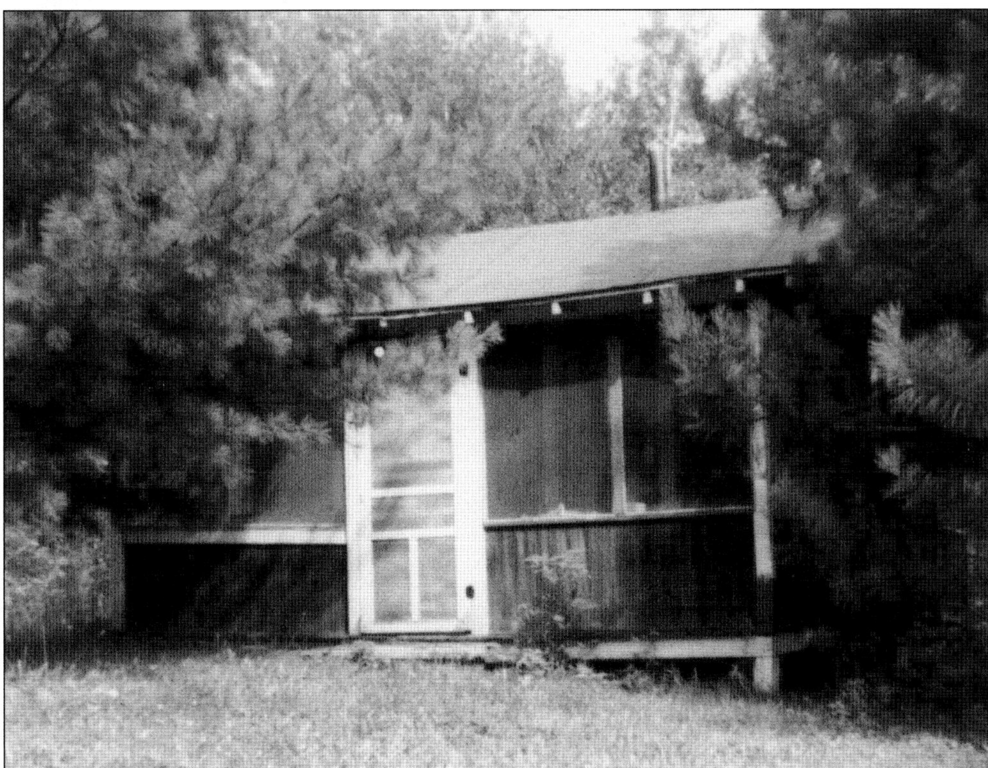

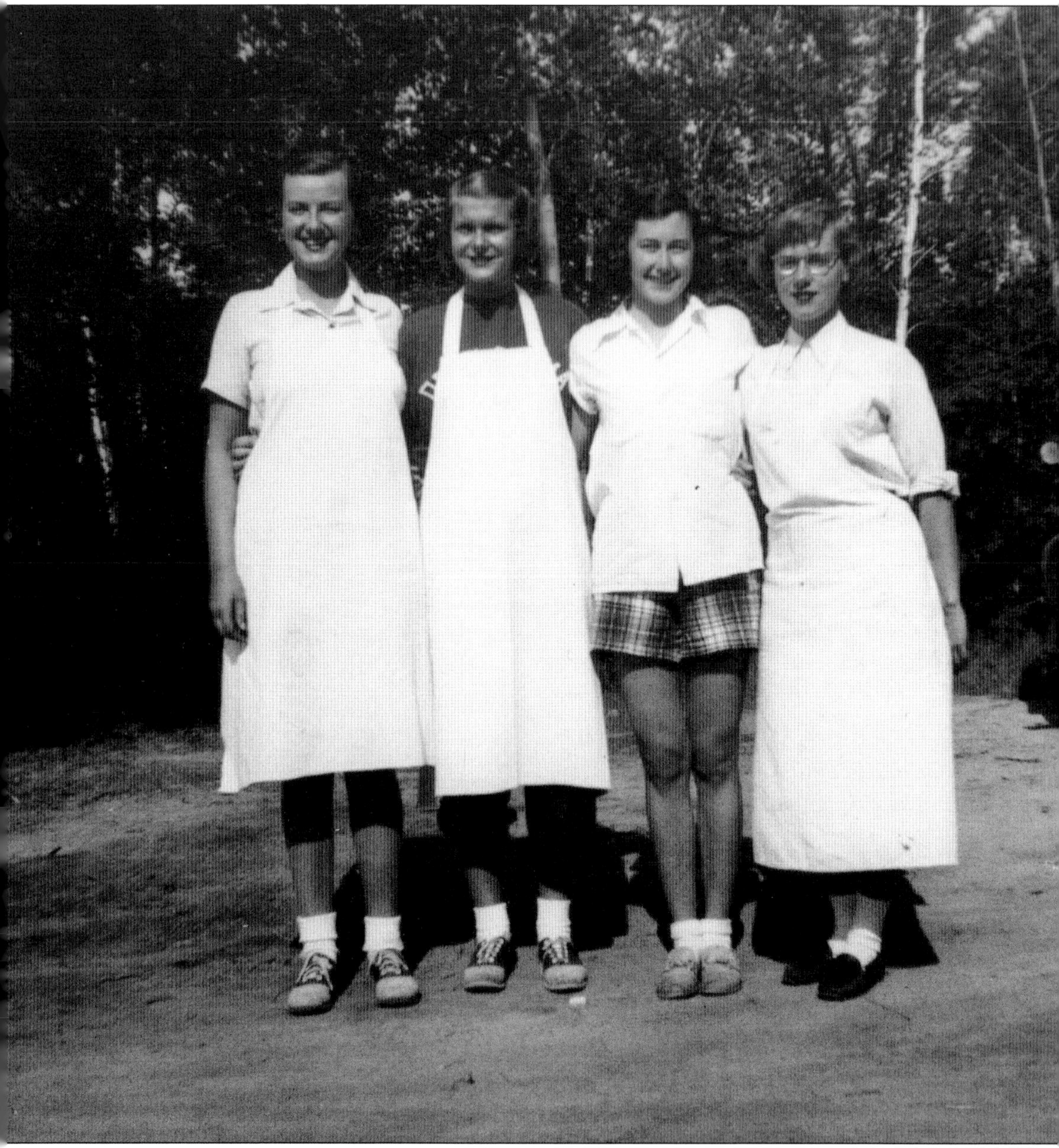

Pictured in 1951 from left to right, kitchen aides Marty, Ginny, Joan, and Susie step outside the hot kitchen wearing their white aprons to cool off and smile for the camera. The cook, though often in the background at camp, was always toasted in song for her delicious meals. There were only a few cooks whose talents were not appreciated by the girls, and to this day some campers cannot eat a particular food associated with their bad experience. (Courtesy of Sascha Immerman.)

Two

We Are the Girls of Camp Maqua

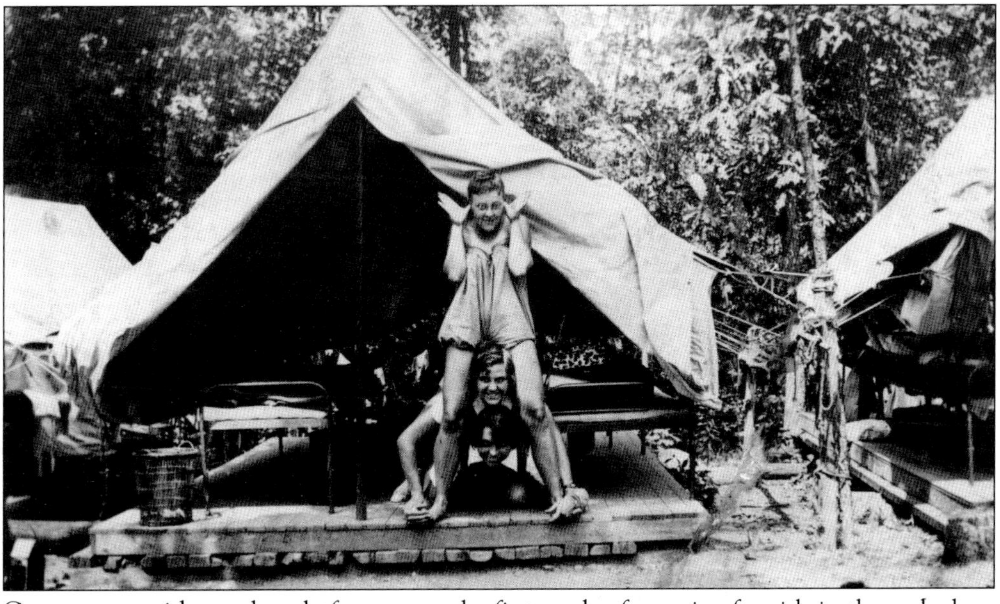

Canvas tents with wooden platforms were the first mode of camping for girls in the early days. This photograph, taken in 1934, shows Mary Madore peeking through her friend's legs. Huts and tents were inspected and had to be "spick and span" for visitors and camp officials. Campers with the highest ratings were allowed to row across the lake and cook their own breakfast on the shore. Mary was an accomplished swimmer and won many events before eventually becoming one of the swimming instructors. (Courtesy of Candy Camerden.)

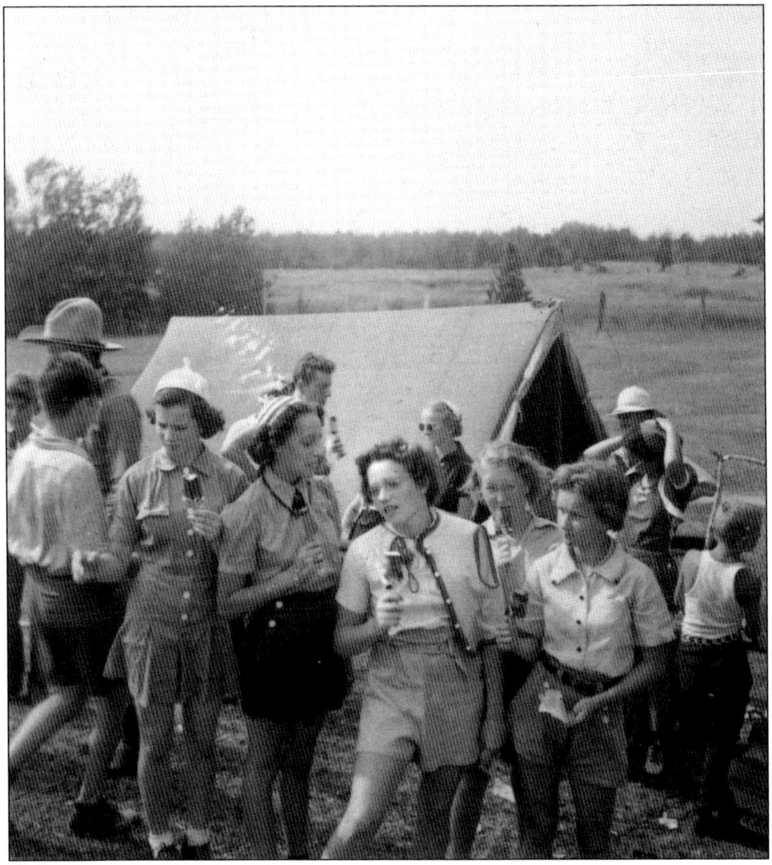

Five girls enjoy a warm day in August 1937 eating ice cream outside their tent at an unknown spot on the property. There were eight cabins that year, and rooms inside the lodge were used by "Employed Girls," who were allowed to come up whenever they wished for a weekend. As the number of registrations slowly increased, more cabins were built to accommodate campers. (Courtesy of YWCA Great Lakes Bay Region.)

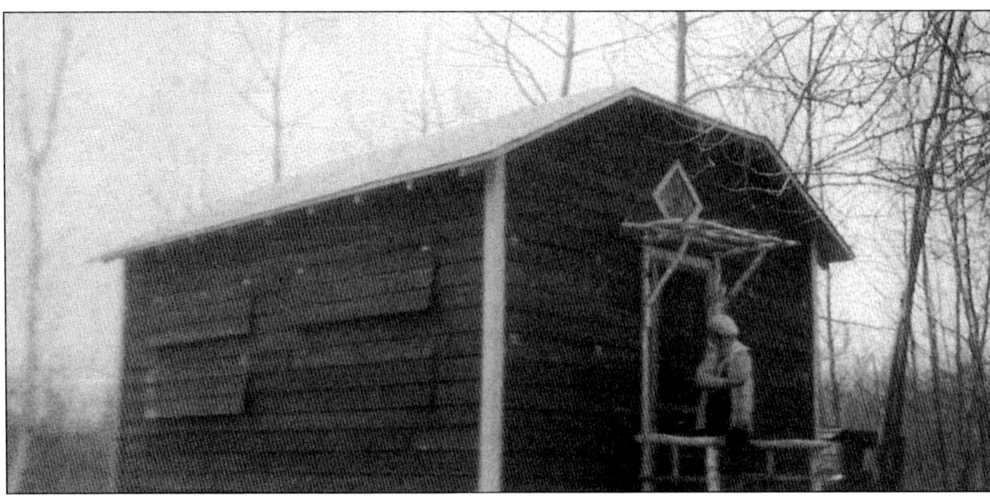

An anonymous visitor from the early 1920s wrote of the cabins, "We go for a walk and follow the road on top of the hill. First we come to another sleeping hut, which we enter by a rustic little porch. Inside we find four double deck cots, a rustic washstand and nearby individual rustic cubby holes for brushes, combs, etc. This hut is typical of all six huts. It has abundant openings for the flooding of the hut with fresh air." (Courtesy of YWCA Great Lakes Bay Region.)

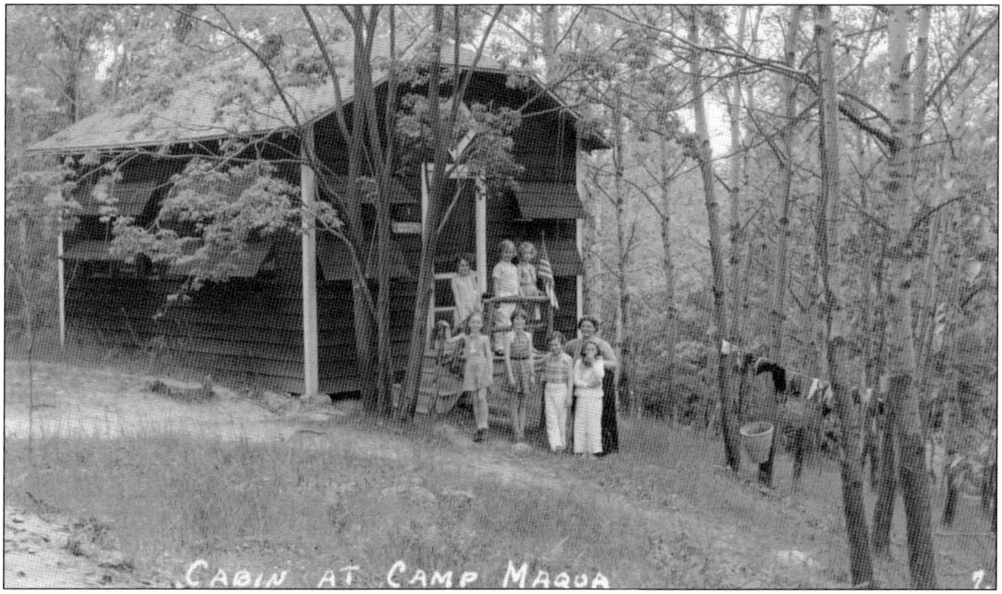

This early postcard of Hut One, with eight campers and a counselor, shows the cabin's hinged, rope-pull windows opened wide over the screens. The brown-stained cabins had white trim and were 14 feet by 18 feet in size. They were built by the Alladin Company and featured eight screened windows for ventilation. (Courtesy of YWCA Great Lakes Bay Region.)

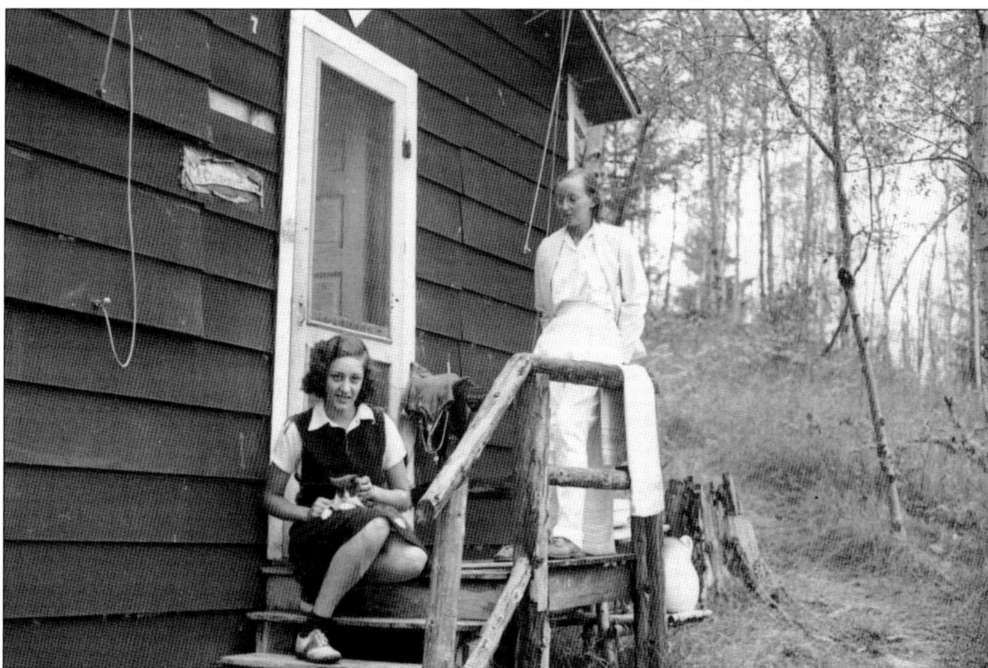

Camp sessions began in late June and ended in late August. There were four sessions, which could accommodate nearly 100 girls who had elected to stay between one and six weeks. The YWCA camp committee formulated the schedule and was responsible for hiring staff, general maintenance and repair concerns, fundraising and expansion, and all financial and publicity issues. (Courtesy of YWCA Great Lakes Bay Region.)

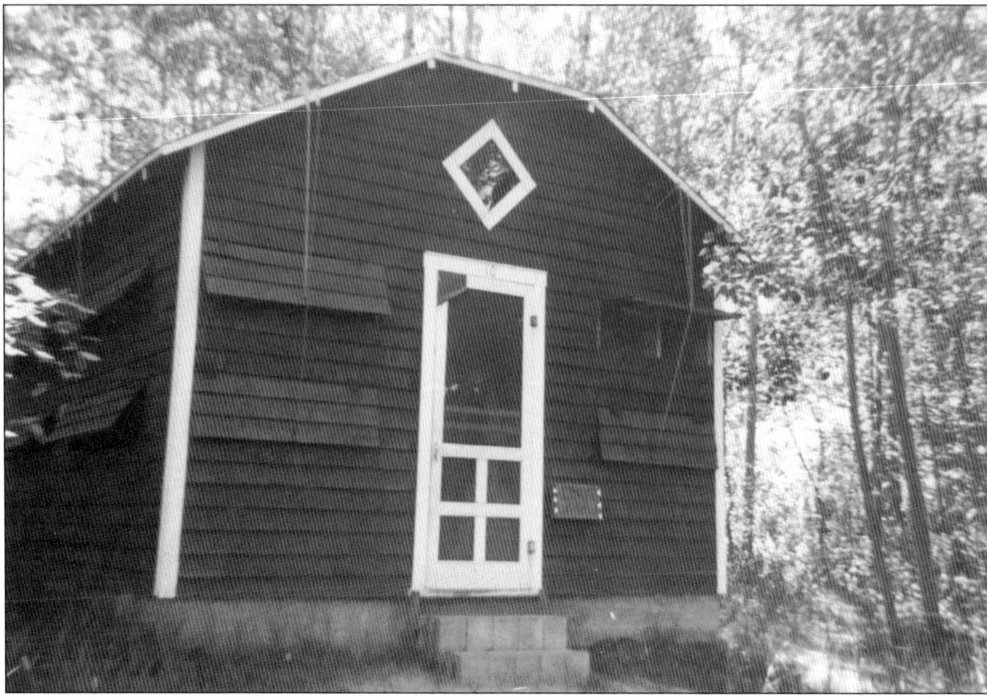

Jenifer Penzien attended camp in the late 1960s and knew that her mother had once bunked in Hut Three, so she searched for the exterior sign that read, "Sleepy Hollow." Although faded after 30 years, Jenifer found the sign. Most huts were numbered, but this hut bears a painted sign with an Indian tribal name. (Courtesy of Ann Ward.)

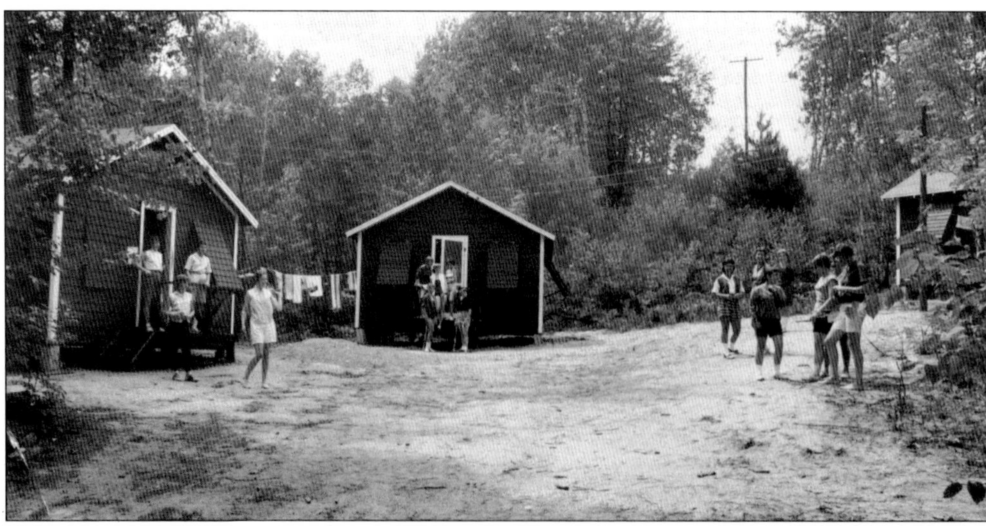

In 1959, three new cabins, each one 16 feet by 20 feet, were built for $4,000. Nicknamed "Senior Village" and lettered A, B, and C, they were built on the knoll south of Hut Six. Painted brown and shingled in green, these three huts were home to older campers and featured new racks for clothing and suitcases. (Courtesy of YWCA Great Lakes Bay Region.)

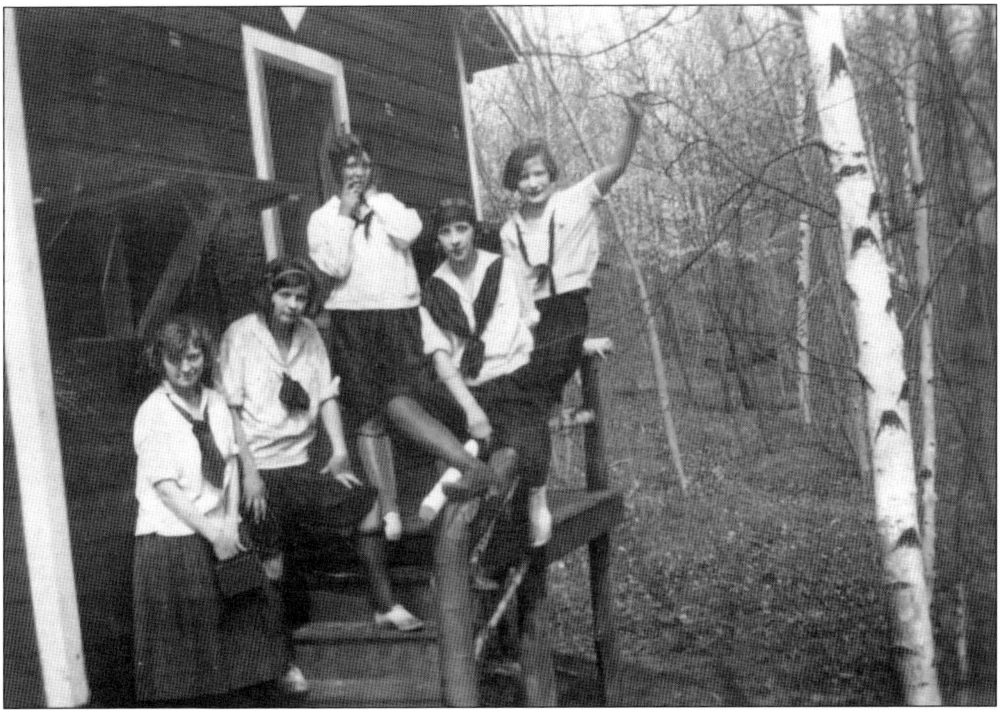

In this photograph from the early 1920s, five campers pose in the fashions of the day. Middy blouses were very popular for girls 14 and younger and were worn with skirts or wool knickers. It was also a favorite style for sports teams, gym, and camp, although it is unclear if this was mandatory dress for camp. (Courtesy of YWCA Great Lakes Bay Region.)

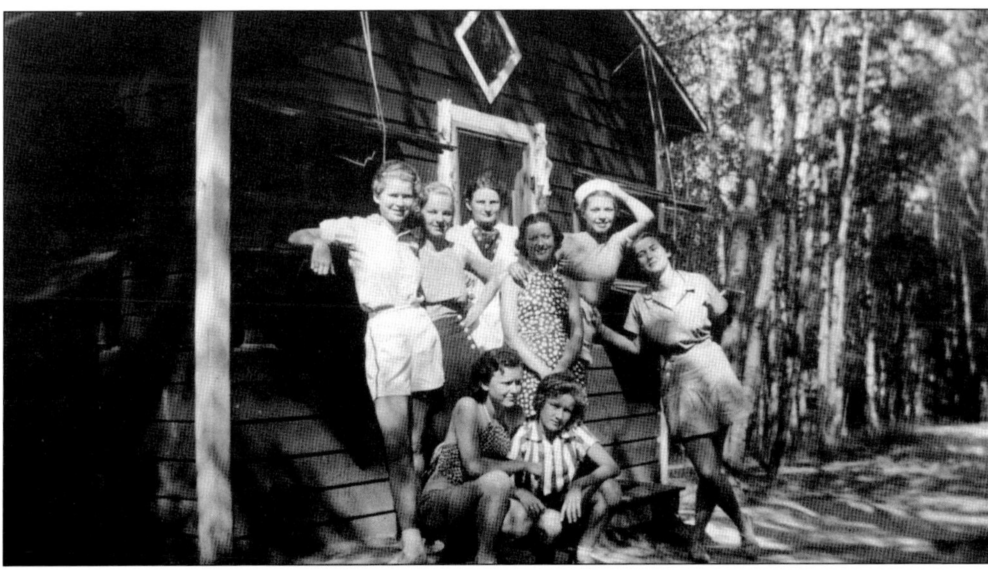

Eight girls occupied each cabin, and whether these girls were campers or counselors, their style reflects the fashions of 1937. Relaxed-fit sailor shorts, with halter-tops and jaunty nautical hats, the girls are all smiles outside their cabin. (Courtesy of YWCA Great Lakes Bay Region.)

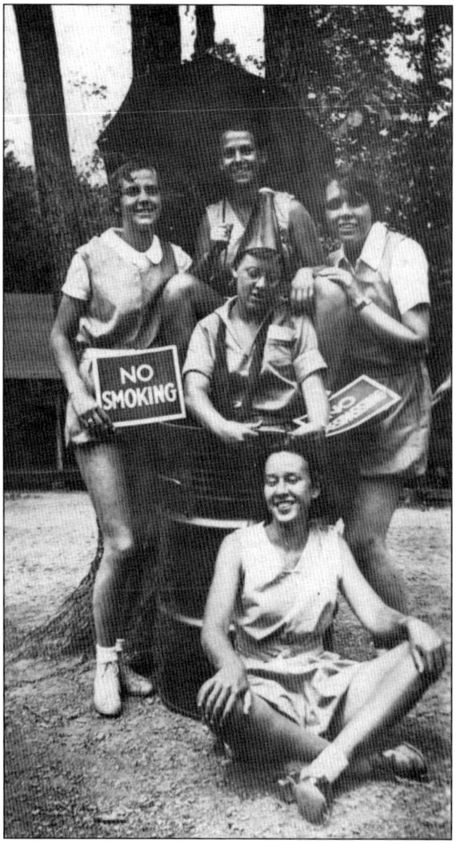

At left, swimming instructor Mary Madore (holding a "no smoking" sign) and friends create an amusing vignette of camp life posing under an umbrella and holding signs while a girl in an oil drum wears a megaphone for a hat. Perhaps they were practicing their skits for the evening entertainment as they posed in their Keds high-top tennis shoes. Below, two campers perch on an oil drum and hide their faces behind a newspaper, only their Keds showing. This style of shoe was popular during the 1930s. (Courtesy of Candy Camerden.)

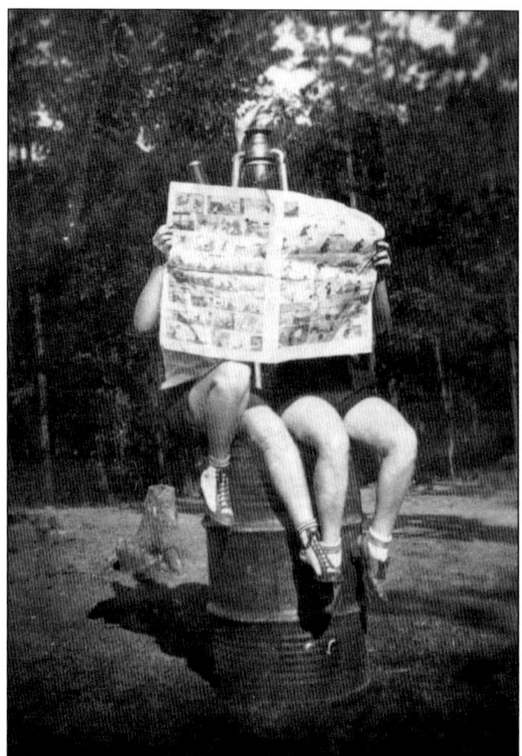

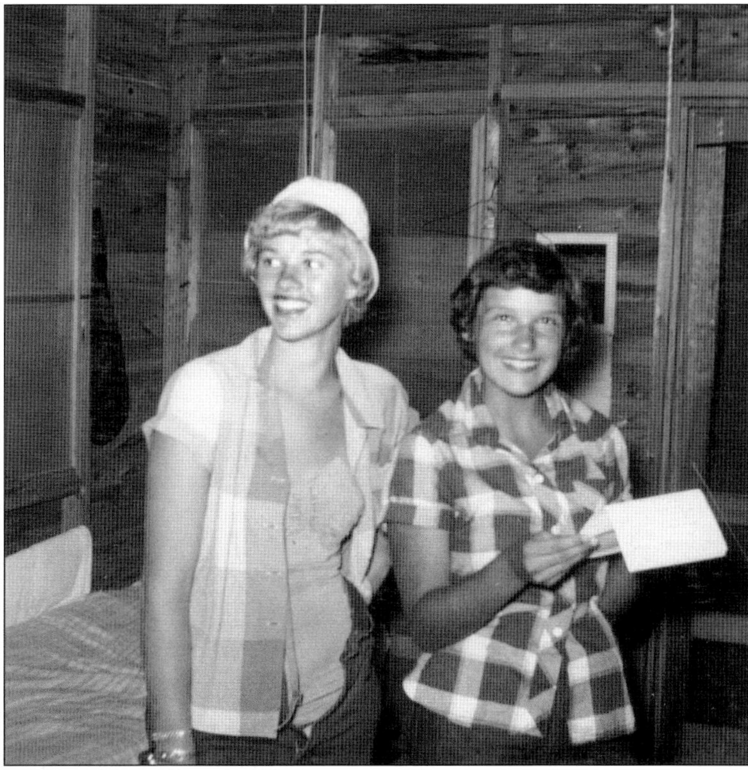

Wearing their plaid "Ship 'n Shore" blouses, good friends Carla Schweinsberg (left) and Bev Lemanski (right) return from a "tinkle in the woods" in 1952—caught laughing as they quickly zipped up their pants. Many campers said they learned that important skill at camp! (Courtesy of Sascha Immerman.)

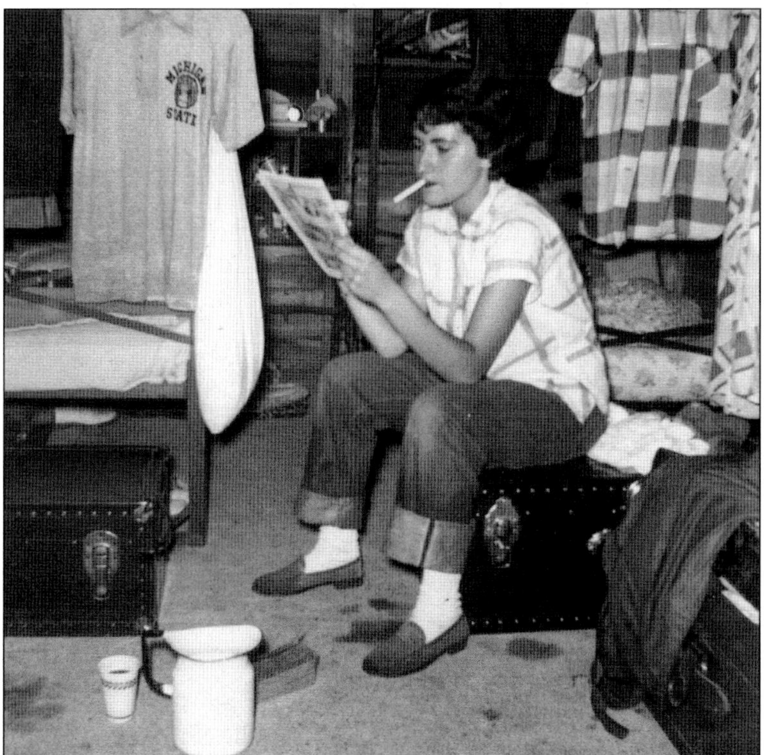

Riding instructor Marsha Immerman is seen here in 1952 perched on her trunk, reading an intellectual newspaper, and smoking a Lucky Strike—her favorite brand. An article in the *Loon* described her as "got a light? was frequently uttered by this small-hipped girl who wore boy's levis." Smoking was not only Marsha's favorite pastime, but that of many. (Courtesy of Sascha Immerman.)

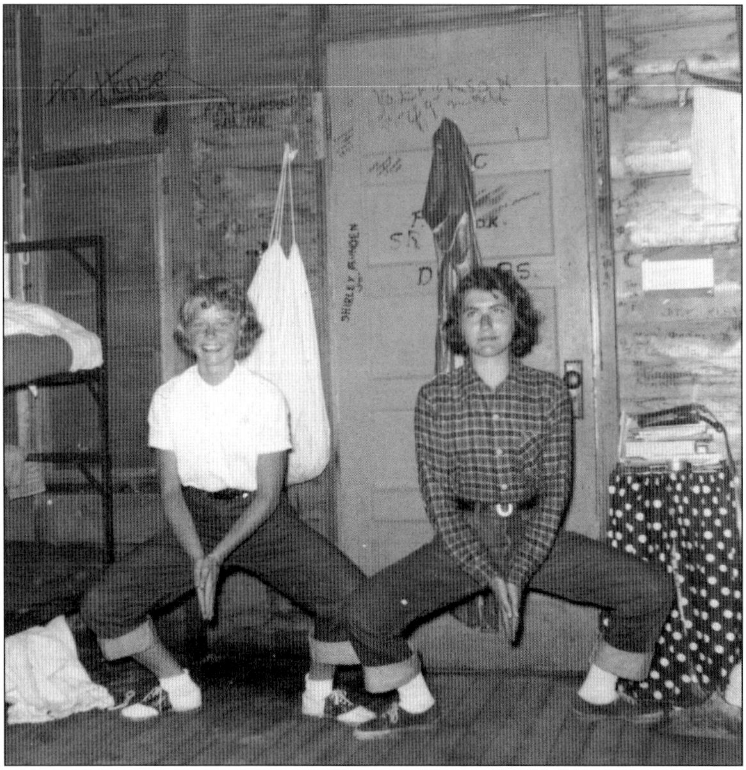

Friends Betty Quillian (left) and Marsha Immerman practice their dance moves after a lesson in modern dance from Gay Gould, which was one of the many activities offered in the summer of 1952. Betty, Marsha, and another friend Molly were so inseparable that the YWCA sent a letter to Marsha's mother requesting she make more friends. (Courtesy of Sascha Immerman.)

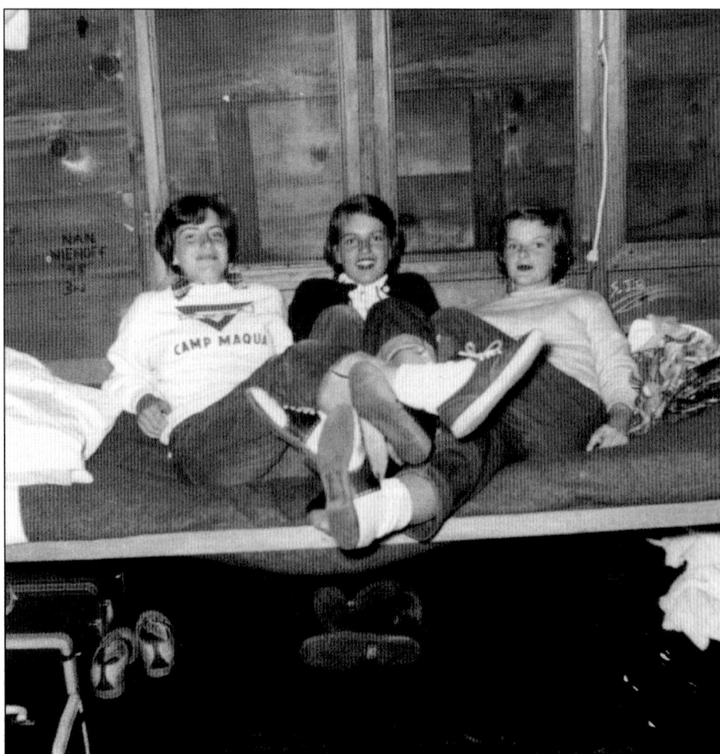

What to do on a rainy day inside the hut? From left to right, Mary Jane Keschman, wearing her Maqua sweatshirt; Molly Olson; and Sally Harris relax on a counselor's bunk. Rainy-day activities inside the lodge often included plays, skits, indoor games, and storytelling. (Courtesy of Sascha Immerman.)

Many girls looked forward to finding the name of their grandmother, aunt, mother, or sister inside their huts. Written either in toothpaste or lipstick, it is unclear when the tradition began. Nancy Mueller (standing on the left) is shown with her bunk mates in 1966, perhaps during rest period after lunch. (Courtesy of Valerie Monto Richardson.)

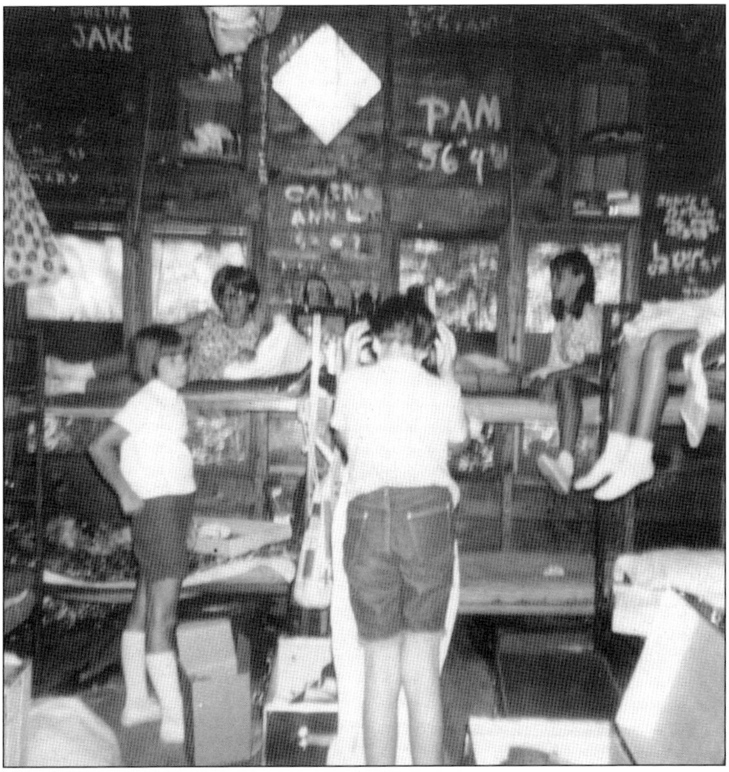

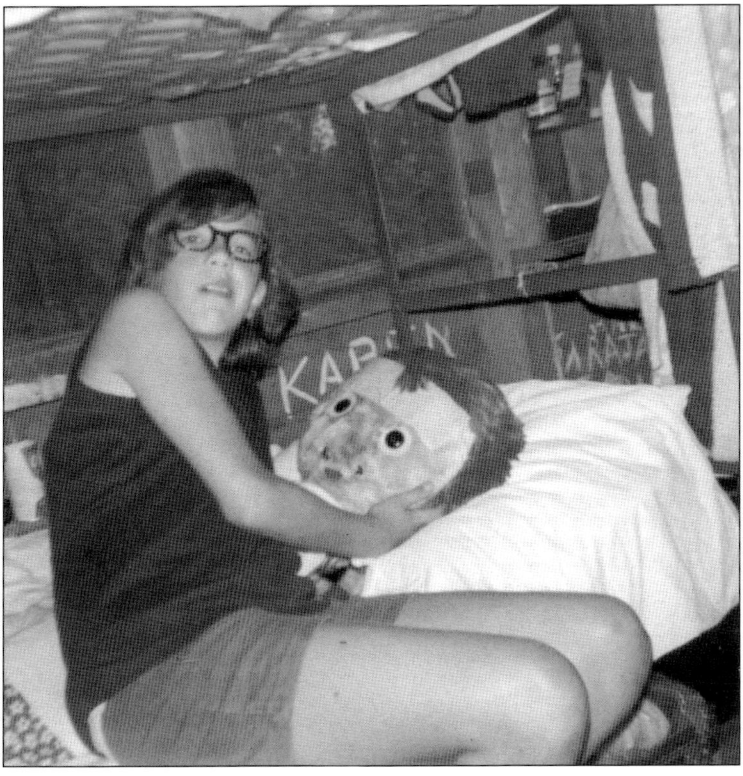

Susie Prieskorn, seen relaxing on her "Tiger" bunk bed, was eight when she first attended camp in 1966. She brought her Raggedy Ann doll, Jo-Jo, but with all the teasing she endured, she left it at home the second year. For many of the girls, the security of a loved stuffed animal was only needed the first year, as teasing was rare and the counselors assisted with homesickness—ensuring that girls did not form cliques. (Courtesy of Karen Magidsohn.)

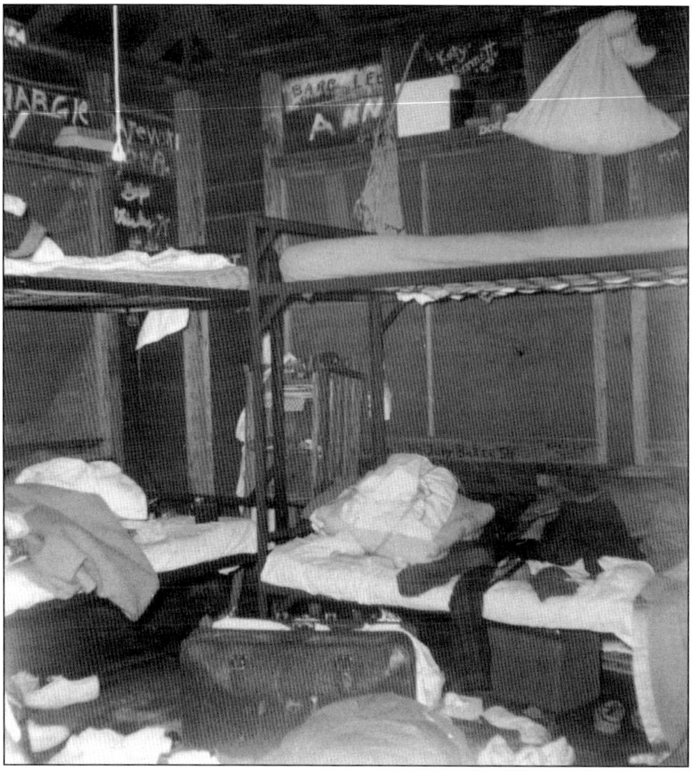

The hut above the boathouse enchanted campers, who were envious of anyone who ever bunked by the water. Located next to the campfire pit, the hut was unique and spacious. Sue Utter and her friends won the cleanest hut award in 1957. "The boathouse was the elite place to be—we were the oldest and boldest." (Courtesy of Sue Utter Seelye.)

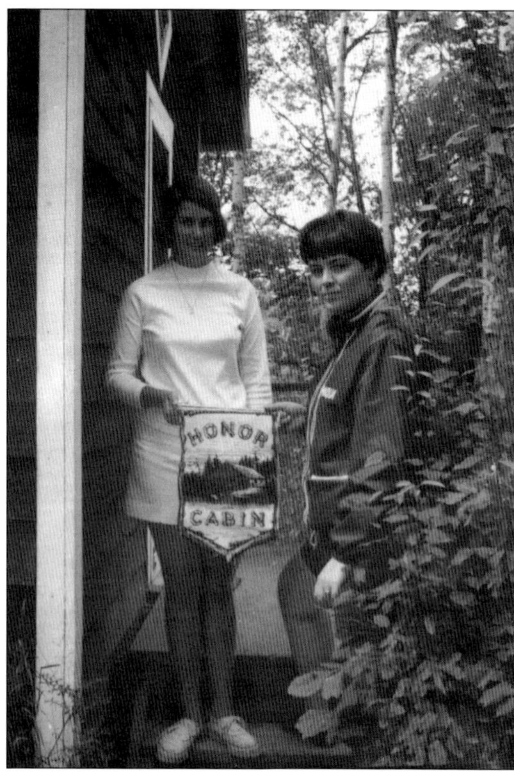

Zoe McGrath (right), a camper in 1956 and 1957, had just graduated from the Henry Ford School of Nursing when she accepted the position of camp nurse in 1968. One of her duties was to inspect all of the cabins for cleanliness. Seen here with Sheila Hanes, they hold the Honor Cabin banner proudly. (Courtesy of YWCA Great Lakes Bay Region.)

For girls who attended more than one session, laundry was an important chore. Some rode in to use the laundromat in Hale, while others hung their wet clothes on a clothesline outside their cabin. Here, from left to right, Ethel Feldman, Pat Kula, Mary Lou Winn, Dody Niedzielski, Shirley Colbert, and Betty Miller clown for the camera. (Courtesy of Pat Kula Reinlein.)

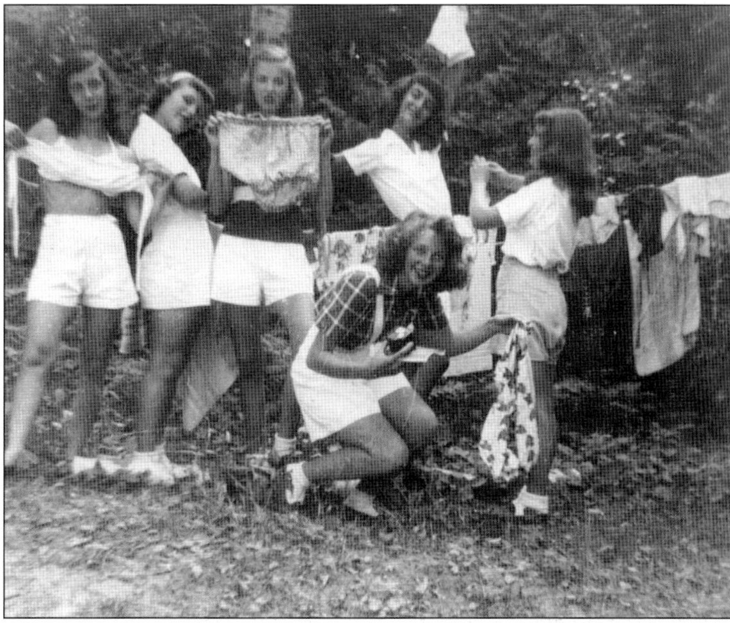

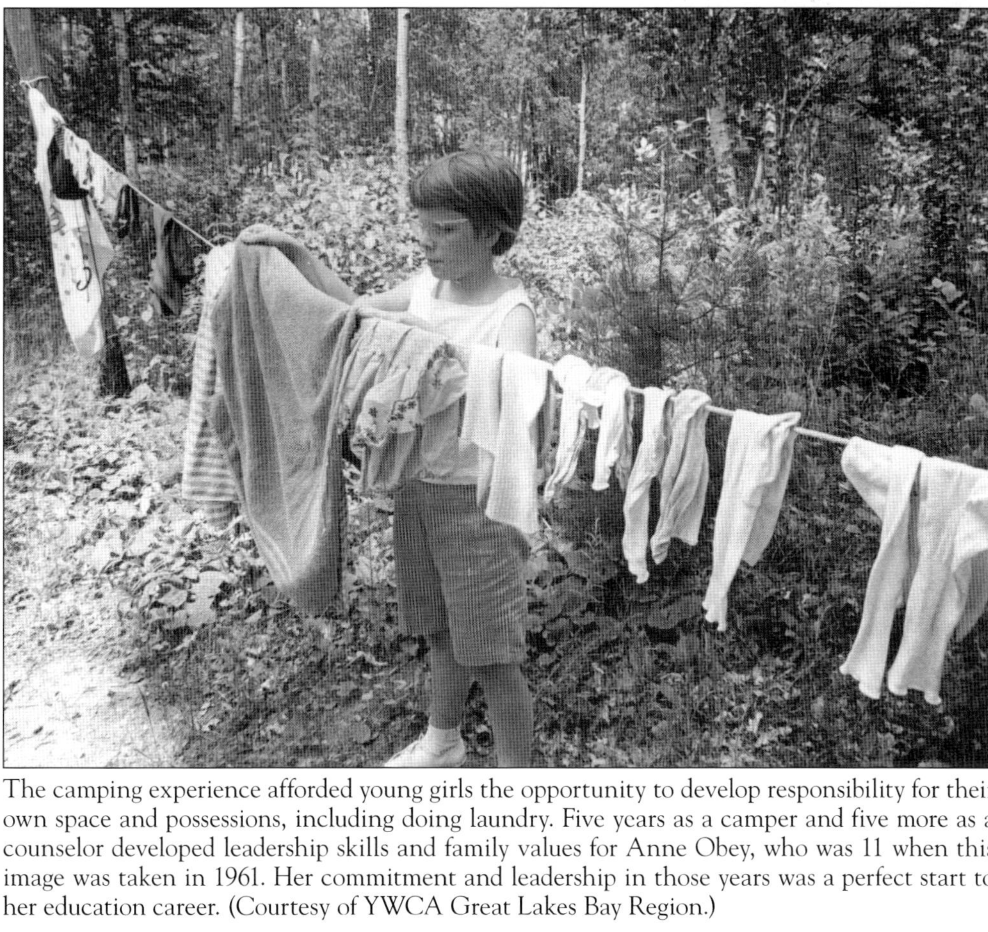

The camping experience afforded young girls the opportunity to develop responsibility for their own space and possessions, including doing laundry. Five years as a camper and five more as a counselor developed leadership skills and family values for Anne Obey, who was 11 when this image was taken in 1961. Her commitment and leadership in those years was a perfect start to her education career. (Courtesy of YWCA Great Lakes Bay Region.)

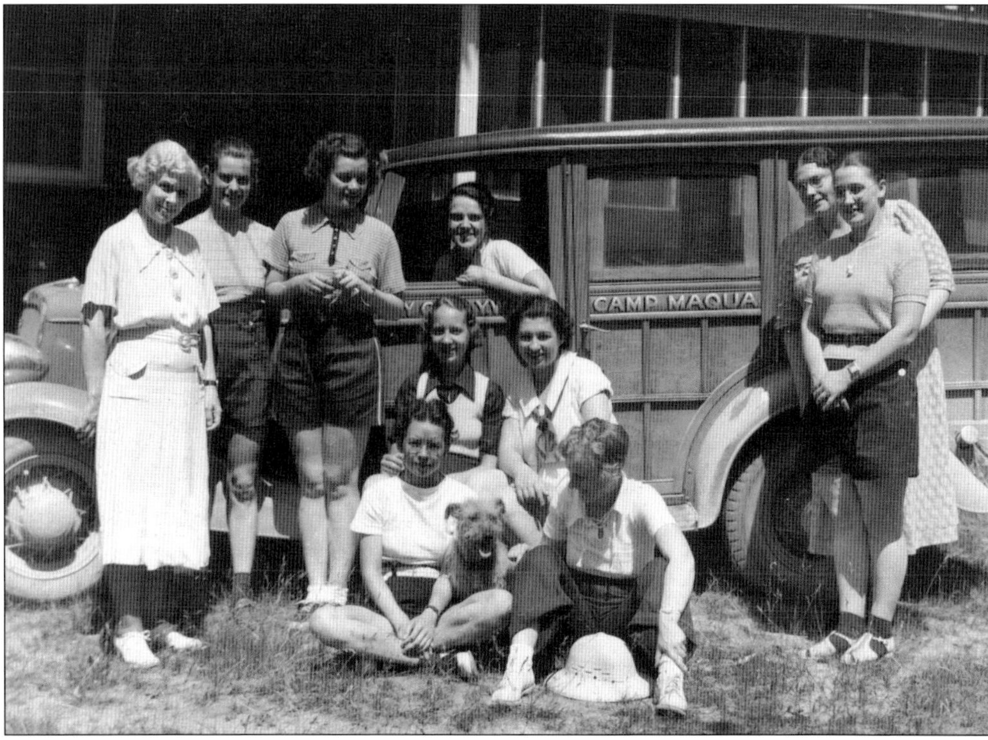

"Remembrance of Camp Maqua August 11-25," wrote Jeanette Simon on the back of this photograph from 1937. Seated in the front row with Tucker, the "periodic pet," are Nadine Bell and waterfront director June Morrell; seated on the running board are Alice Knepper (left) and Leona Merkel; standing from left to right are Mrs. Norris R. Wentworth (camp hostess), Mary Hayes, Mary Ellen Eddy, camp nurse Thelma Mosey, and unidentified; camp director Ruth Buckwalter is seated inside the Ford Deluxe station wagon. (Courtesy of Brenda Boettger.)

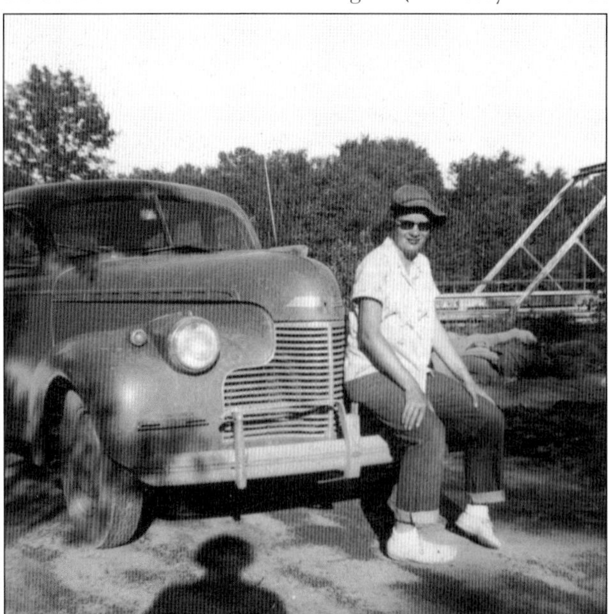

A camp vehicle was a necessity for many reasons: loading and unloading suitcases and luggage upon arrival and departure, transporting campers and staff to church, picking up supplies in town, or getting campers help in case of an emergency. A truck was best for these trips and was especially useful for hauling supplies to overnight camping outposts. Mary is seen here with "Leapin' Lena" in 1952. (Courtesy of Sascha Immerman.)

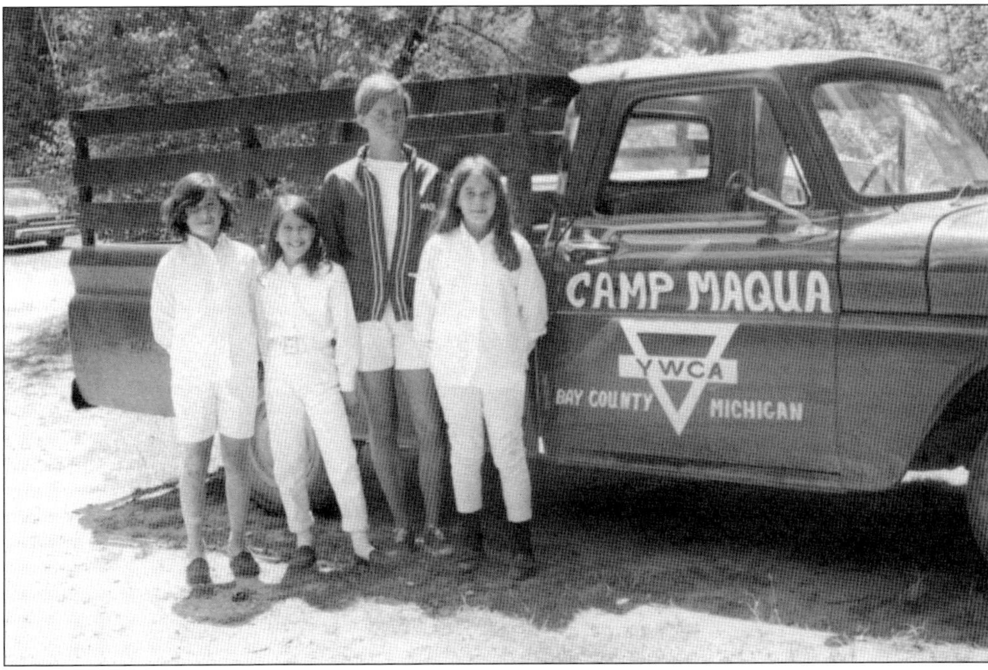

Over the years, vehicles were borrowed, loaned, or donated to the camp. The YWCA camp committee raised funds for the station wagons and pickup trucks, which were expensive to maintain. Counselor Barb Stover poses here in front of the camp truck, with, from left to right, Pamela Hartz, Karen Magidsohn, and Lori Rosenbaum. (Courtesy of YWCA Great Lakes Bay Region.)

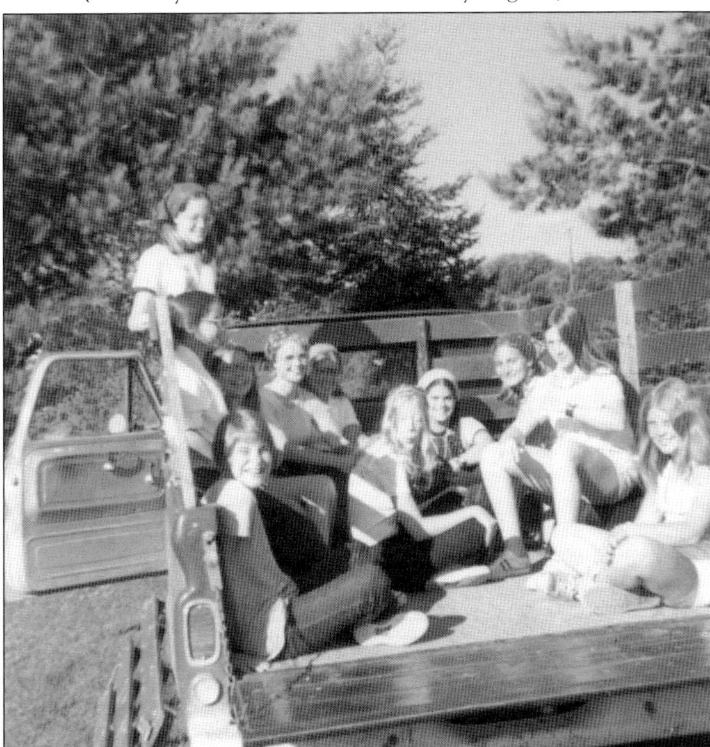

Loaded in the back of the camp truck in 1974, campers Kim Sohigan, Dawn Gerzishon, Dawn Levin, Jackie Foelkert, Ann Jennel, Dedde Watton, Jamie Trerice, Sarah Smith, Ann Sinclair, Dee Foelkert, and Sandy Shepard pose for Carol Hulett, the health director who shared the health cottage with Edna the cook that summer. (Courtesy of Carol Hulett.)

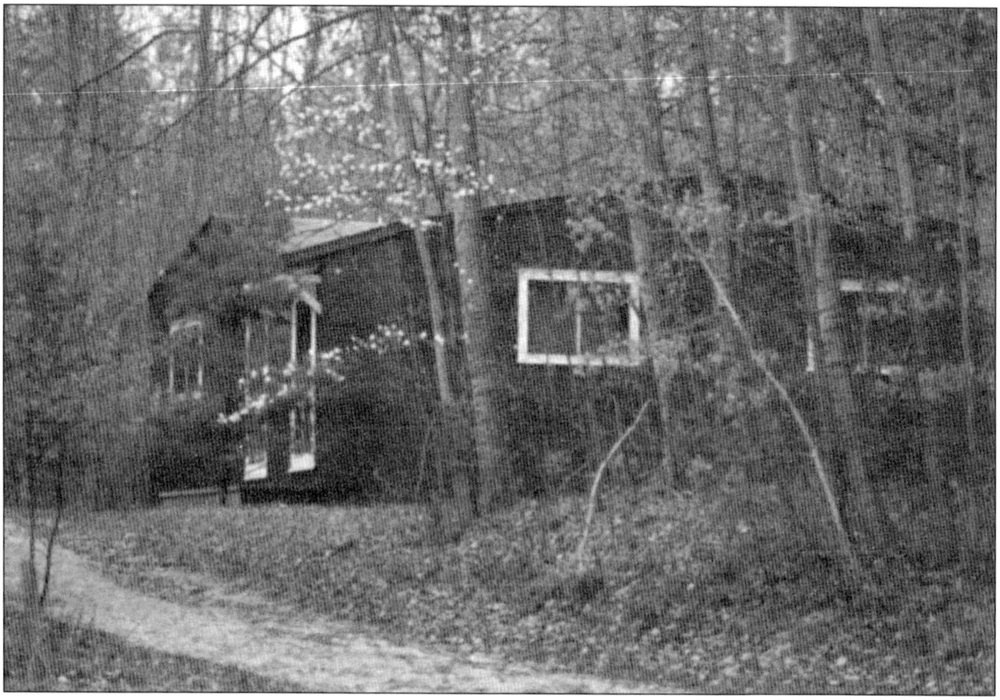

The prefabricated Infirmary building was purchased from the Alladin Company and was 20 feet by 26 feet, with a bathroom and bedroom for the camp nurse. Physicals, the administering of medication, and cabin inspections were among the nurse's duties. A camp doctor was appointed but was never in residence. The nurse handled 100 girls per session, who suffered ailments ranging from allergies and homesickness to broken bones and serious illnesses. (Courtesy of Amy Johns Ikler.)

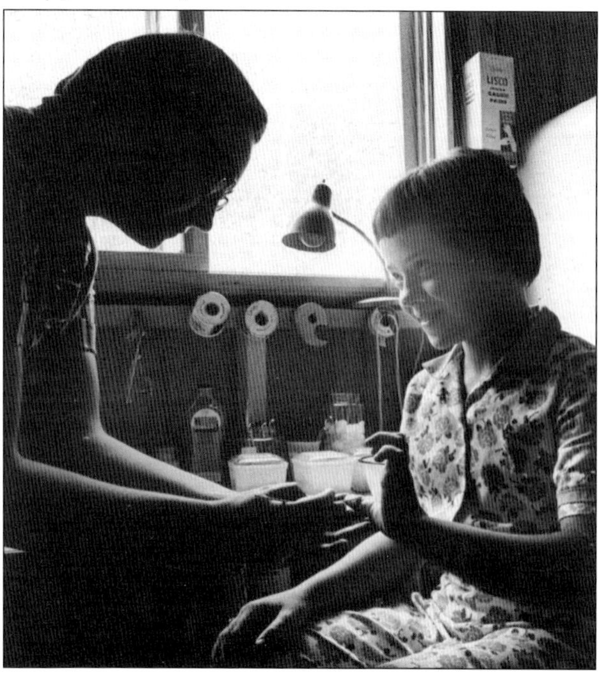

The camp nurse attends to a camper inside the new Infirmary in 1961. Poor posture and underweight girls were the primary concerns for the nurse of the early 1920s, according to an article. Some of the girls had weak arches that had to be strapped, while others were ordered to shed weight. In later years, the girls were weighed before camp started and many lost weight due to increased activity. (Courtesy of YWCA Great Lakes Bay Region.)

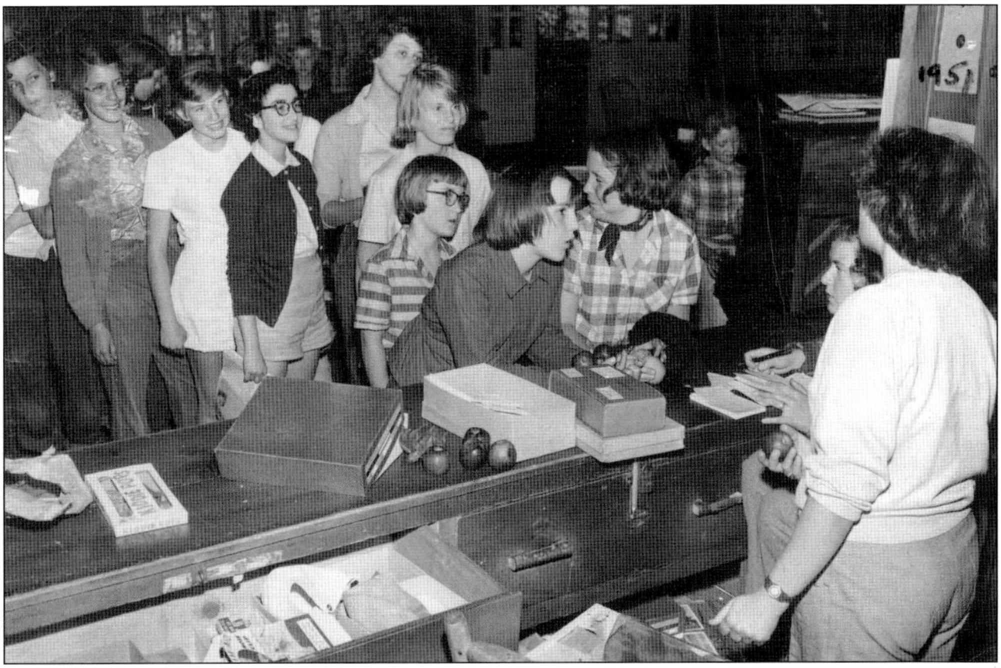

Parents deposited money into the campers' accounts to spend on sundries. Here, a line-up of girls in 1951 are all smiles as they decide what to purchase. This rustic counter inside the lodge operated as the camp store before another building was erected. Postcards, stamps, stationery, candy, ice cream, and camp memorabilia were among the favorite purchases. (Courtesy of YWCA Great Lakes Bay Region.)

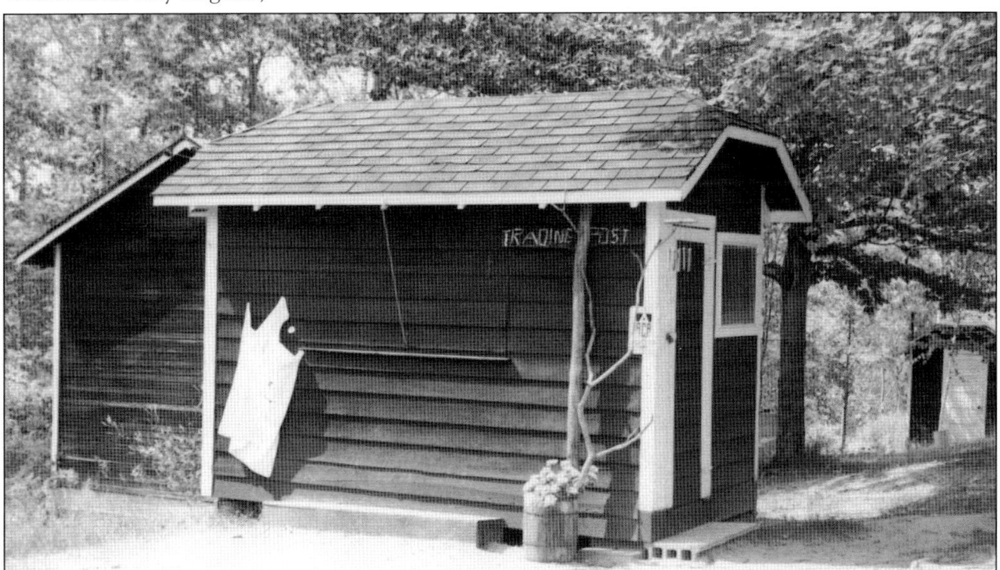

"I was always overdrawn at the camp store," said 1960s camper Kim Wynne-Parry. "My parents would put money into my account and inevitably my Dad would have to settle up at the end of camp. It was a treat, but it was also a good way to teach us about spending." This image was taken in 1967 while the store window was closed. (Courtesy of YWCA Great Lakes Bay Region.)

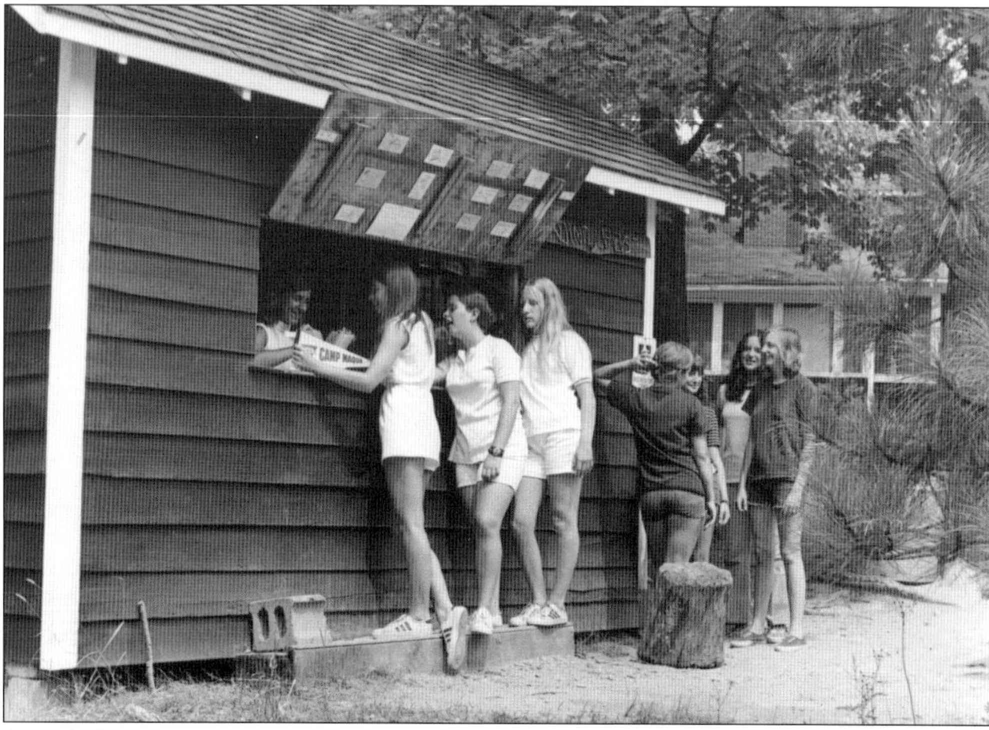

Open for business! A camper purchases her Maqua pennant while Marcia Michelson (second from left) and Debra Osher wait their turn in line. Catching up with friends was half the fun while waiting to purchase, and Lori Gottlieb (left) and Chris Lambert (right) catch up with two friends in the background of this photograph from 1970. (Courtesy of YWCA Great Lakes Bay Region.)

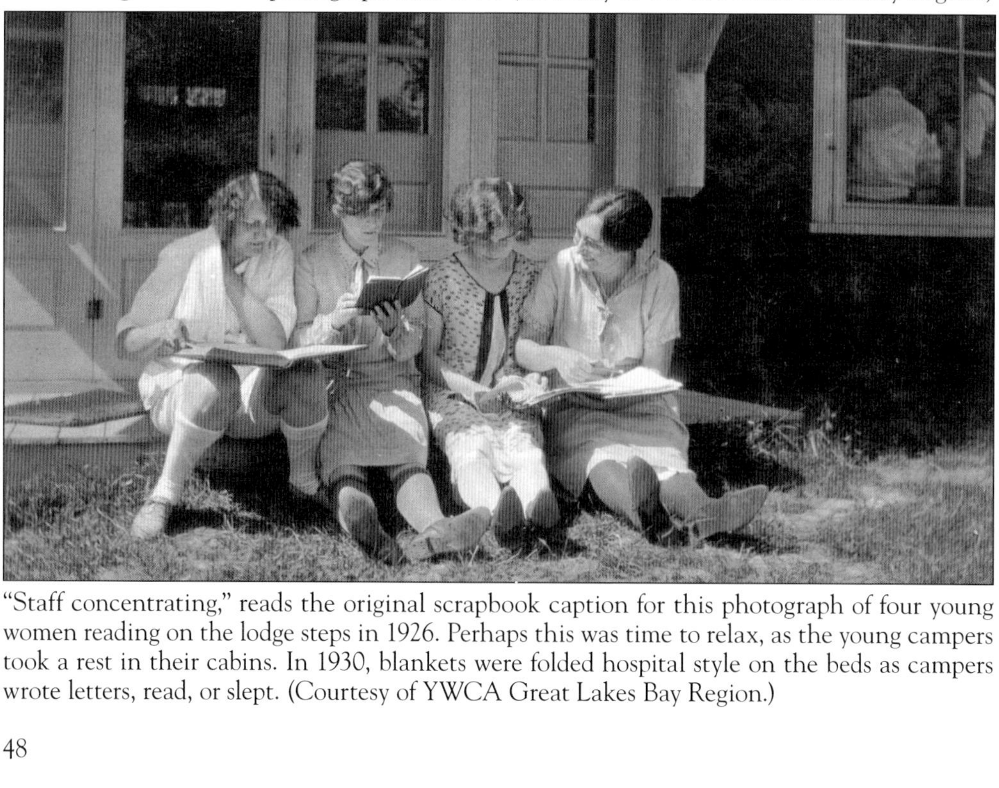

"Staff concentrating," reads the original scrapbook caption for this photograph of four young women reading on the lodge steps in 1926. Perhaps this was time to relax, as the young campers took a rest in their cabins. In 1930, blankets were folded hospital style on the beds as campers wrote letters, read, or slept. (Courtesy of YWCA Great Lakes Bay Region.)

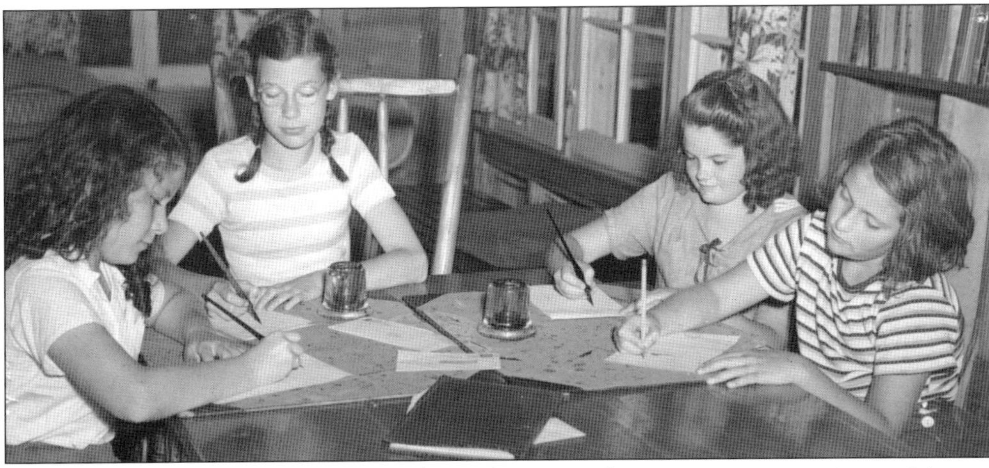

Four young campers take time to write letters home, maybe even on camp stationery. Many of the campers, like Janet Dixon, still have cherished camp letters to their parents. In 1951, Janet's handwriting was childlike, with a carefully controlled letter formation and an uneven slant, but the following summer she had more fluid and consistent penmanship. (Courtesy of YWCA Great Lakes Bay Region.)

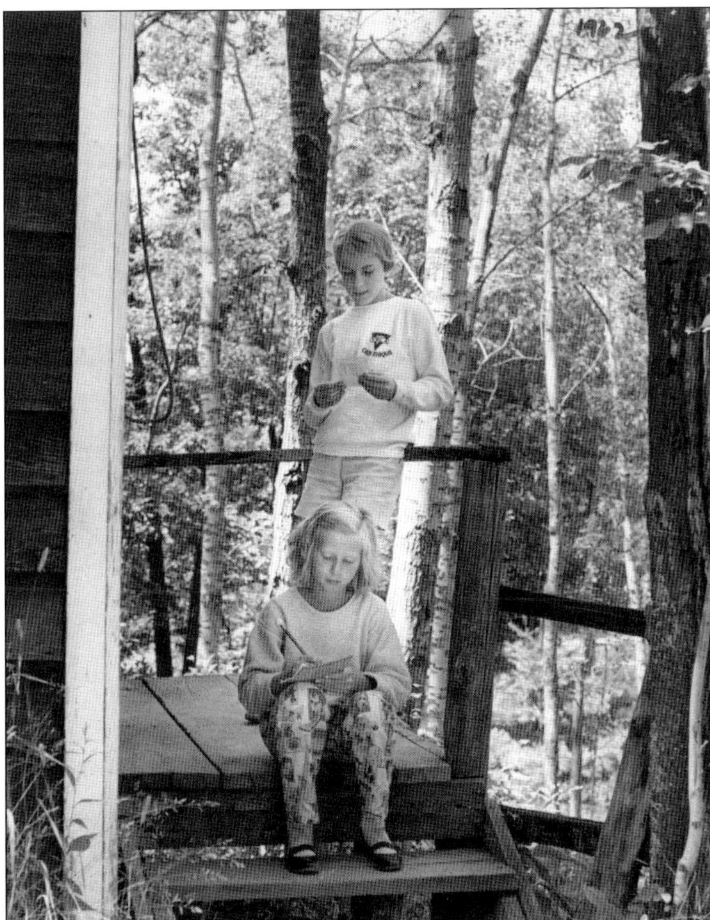

In 1962, Carol Selinsky sits on the steps outside her hut as Brenda Butler (in her new Maqua sweatshirt) reads a postcard. Mail call was the highlight of the day, as parents often sent care packages from home, as well as letters that were appreciated by homesick girls. (Courtesy of YWCA Great Lakes Bay Region.)

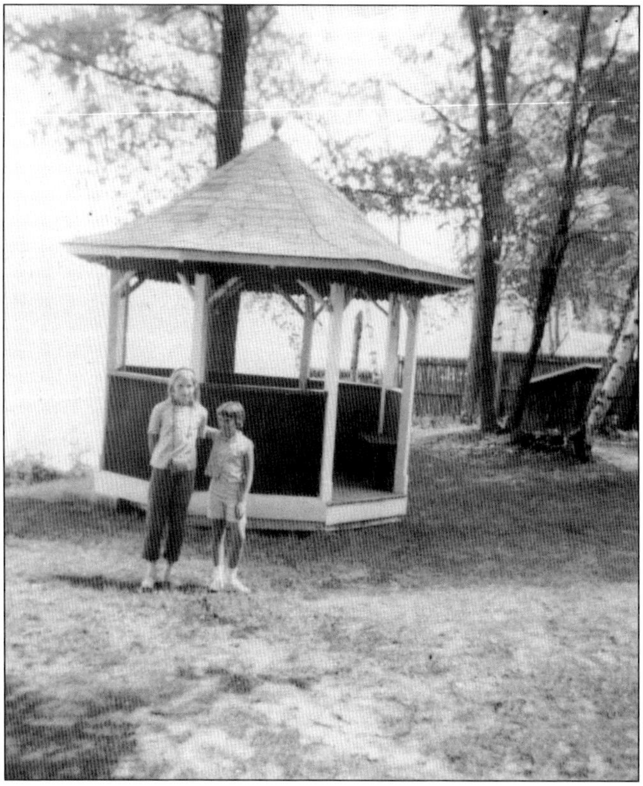

There were very few places where girls could escape a group setting despite the peacefulness of Loon Lake. The gazebo, sometimes called the band shell, was built in the late 1950s or early 1960s. It sat close to the fence that separated the camp from a development near the shoreline. At left, Cindy Rose (right) is shown with another camper. Below, Gail Schultheiss is pictured with her brother Mark and father, Carl, in 1966. Gail camped from 1966 to 1968 and her father, who was "super involved," passed away in 1967. Many found camp a wonderful escape from pressures like new siblings, family responsibilities, divorce, and death. (At left, courtesy of Cindy Rose Belanger; below, Gail Schultheiss Scherer.)

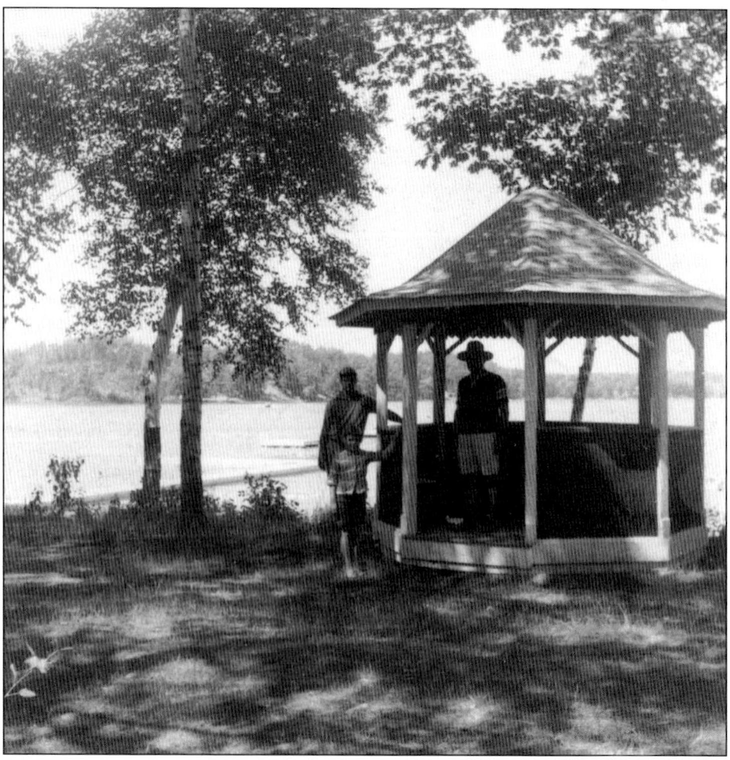

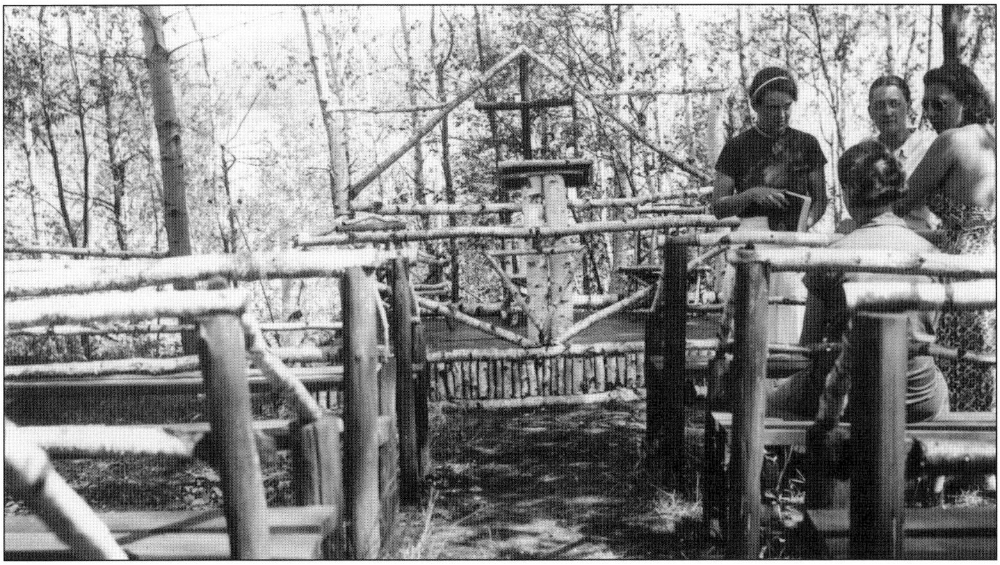

According to ledgers and minutes from the 1930s, the construction of the outdoor chapel at Chapel Hill occurred in 1933. Children helped clear the ground and collected saplings for the altar, while a podium was constructed from birch logs. Services did not take place until the following summer. (Courtesy of YWCA Great Lakes Bay Region.)

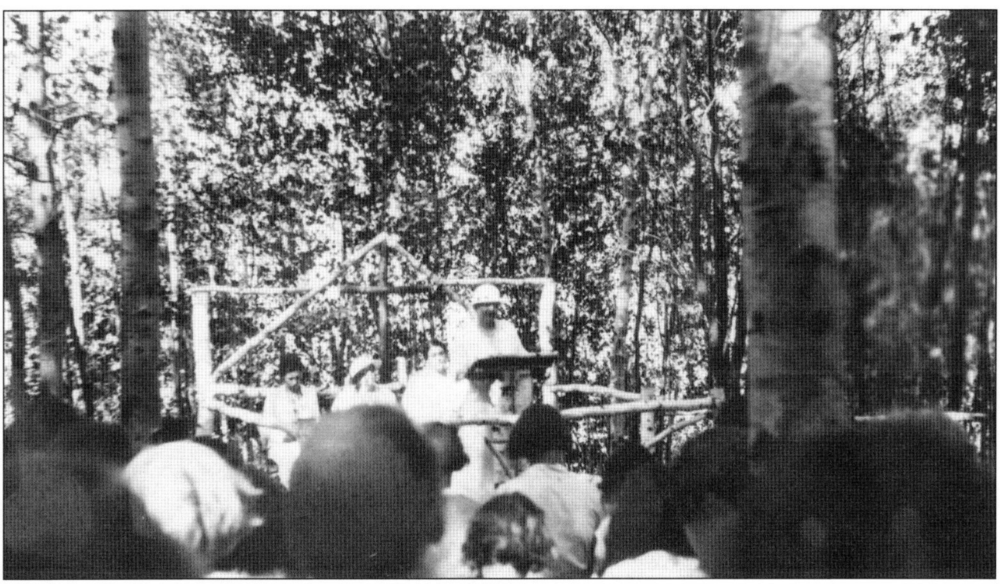

This c. 1934 postcard shows the dedication ceremony of Chapel Hill. Director Wilma Lewis, camp doctor Lorna Feng (from China), staff member Alice Forbes, and YWCA president Mrs. F. Hewitt were present for the event. One attendee wrote of the event, "We could judge by her inspirational words how much she loved camp and how much time she has devoted to its development." (Courtesy of YWCA Great Lakes Bay Region.)

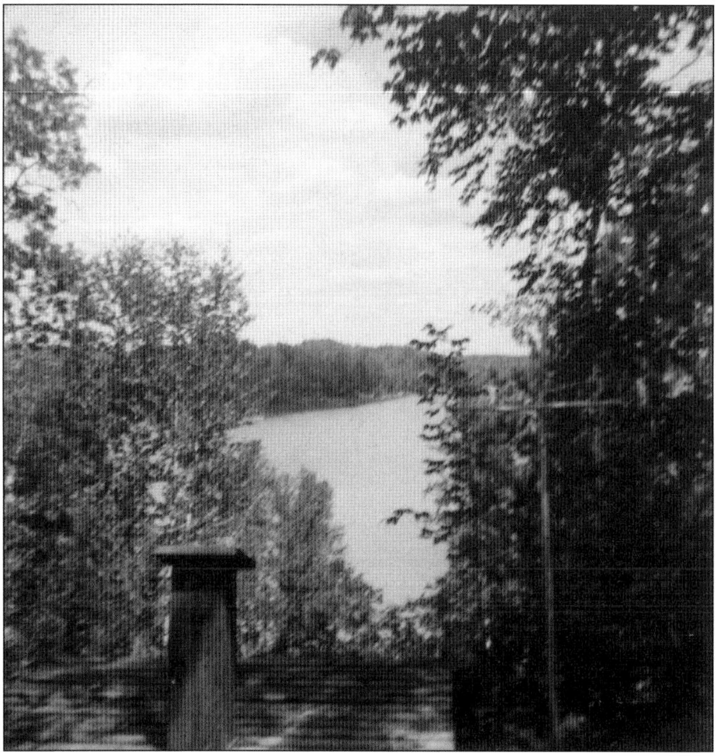

"Before an altar built of birch logs, etched against a blue vista of sky and lake and standing on a hilltop where green trees form a thickly wooded background for the natural amphitheater, Camp Maqua visitors will bow heads in the dedication ceremony at the out-of-door chapel this afternoon," states a weathered article from 1934. This photograph is from 1966. (Courtesy of Valerie Monto Richardson.)

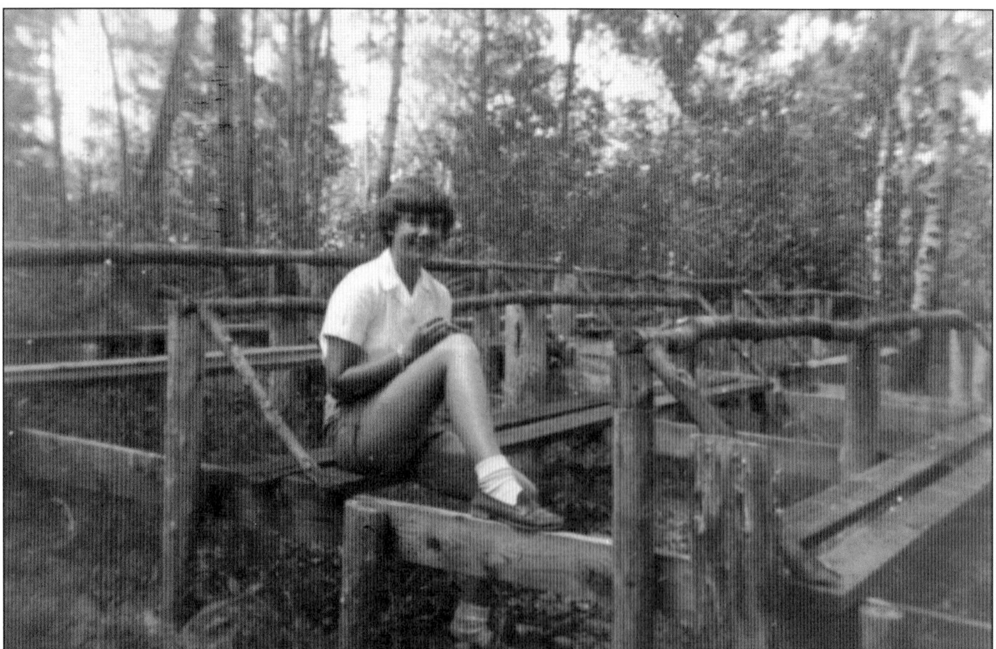

Here, Judy Rowden sits on a log bench at Chapel Hill in the early 1950s. This was a perfect spot to reflect in nature, and it made more of a spiritual impression on many of the girls because of its natural setting. For Tracy Topping, a camper from the mid-1960s, Chapel Hill was the place where she felt closest to God. (Courtesy of Judy Rowden Sauve.)

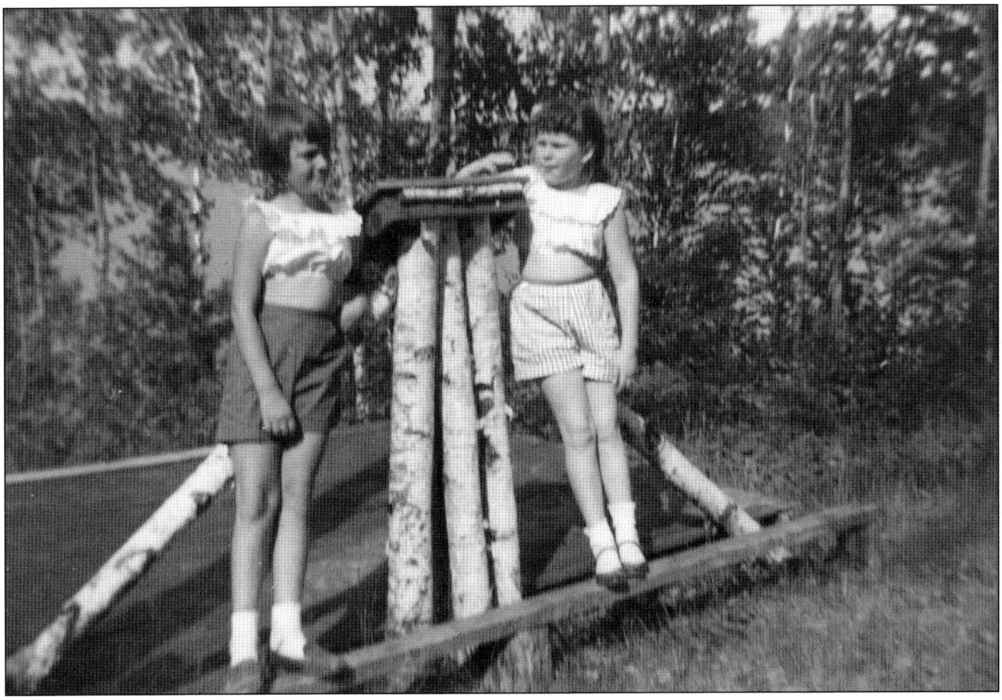

Cheryl Sierocki (left) poses with Pam Watson in 1956 beside the birch podium at Chapel Hill. Girls of all faiths filed quietly up to the hill, dressed in their Sunday whites, or sang the Chapel Hill song. The Catholic girls usually missed out on this ritual, as they attended Mass at a nearby church. (Courtesy of Pam Watson Roberts.)

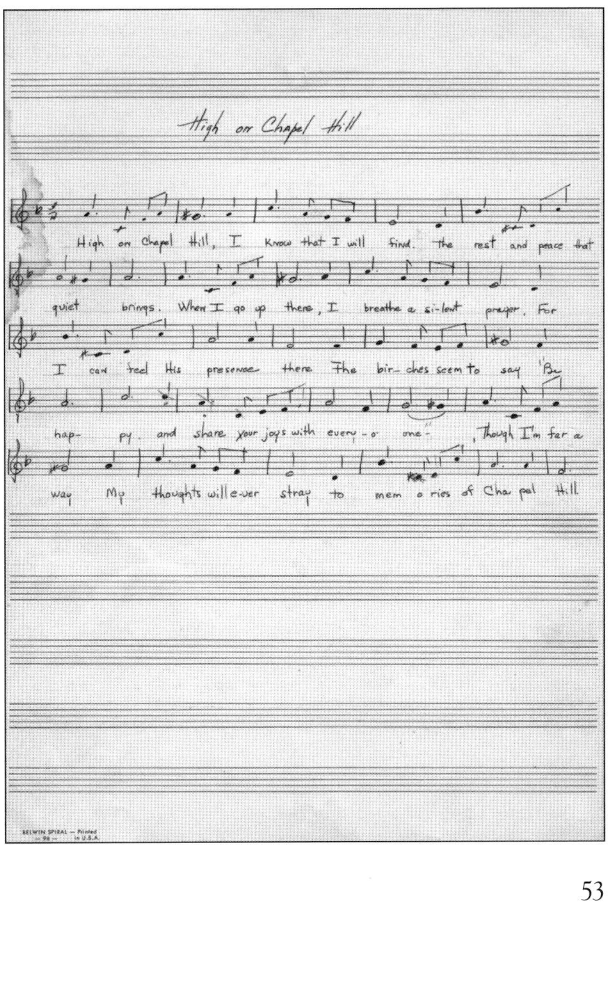

Nadine Bell, a counselor on staff in 1934, wrote the song "High On Chapel Hill," which was published and gained enough popularity that it was heard frequently on the radio. It also became a favorite among campers. It is unclear whether this old spiral-bound musician's notebook, with the hand-lettered song belonged to Nadine. (Courtesy of Barbara Haggart.)

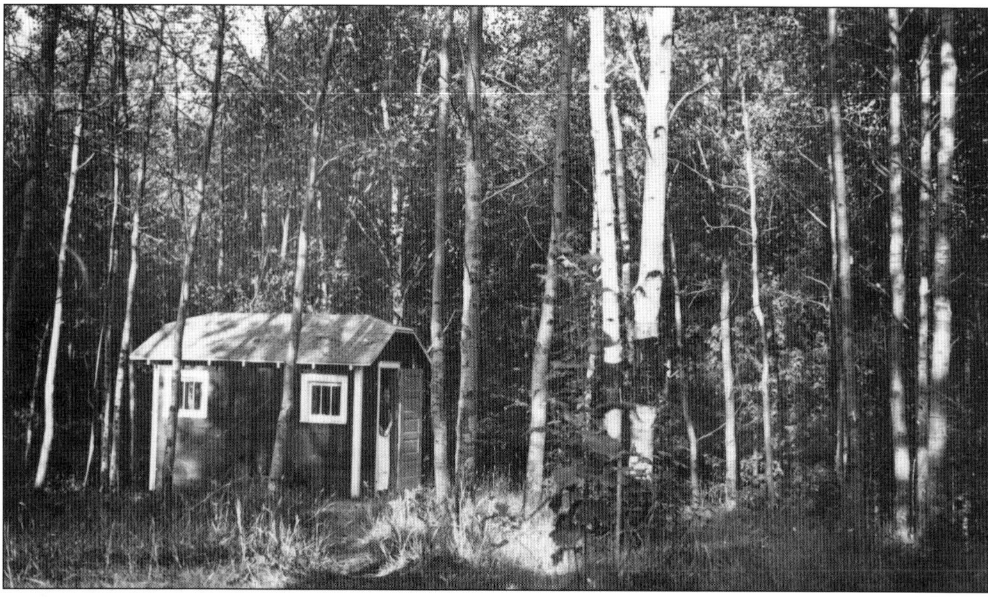

Shown in the mid-1930s, this primitive camp outhouse was constructed of wood and had no flush toilets. Affectionately called a "brownie" by the girls, it was never a place they wanted to venture to—especially in the night. Even armed with a buddy and a flashlight, any rustle or sighting of an animal terrified the campers. (Courtesy of YWCA Great Lakes Bay Region.)

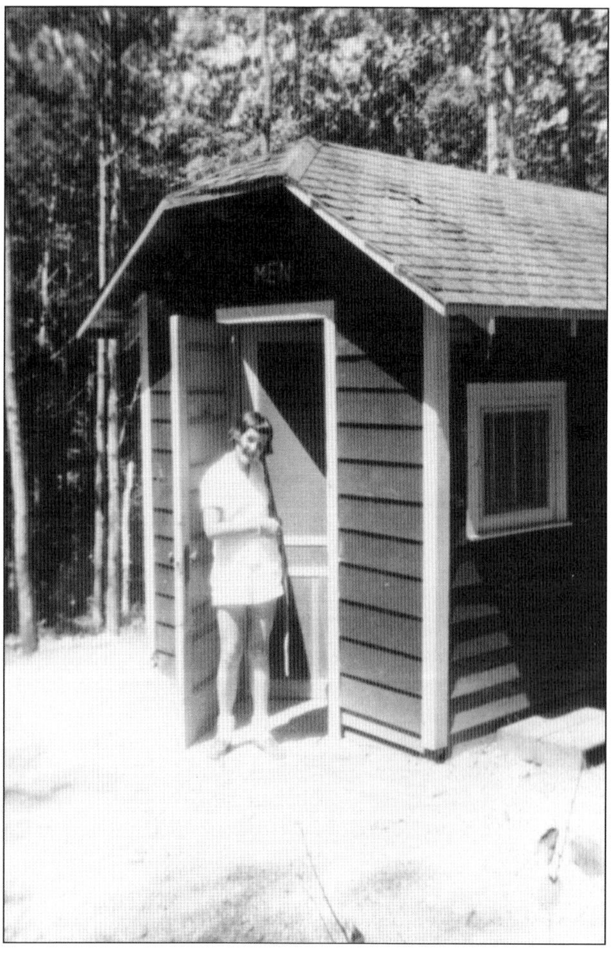

Cleaning the latrines was the least favorite chore of any camper, and part of that duty included coming up with ideas for improving the facility. Always a big expense, the brownies were converted to privies in 1951; Bobbi Hale poses outside of one before the conversion. Campers had memories of spiders, water on the floor, and signs instructing campers how many squares of toilet paper to use. (Courtesy of Sascha Immerman.)

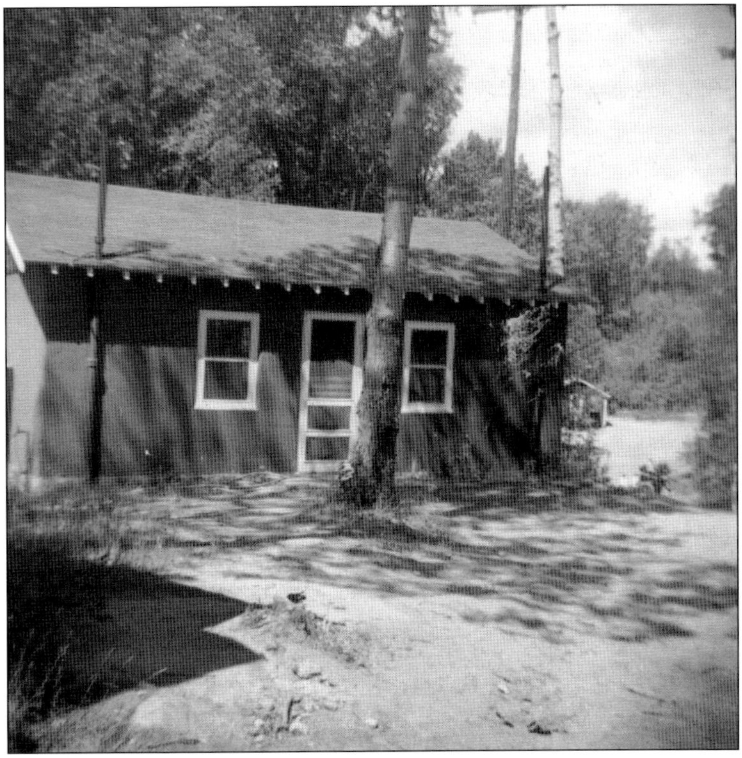

With no shower facilities on hand, bathing in the lake or scrub dips were common, but in 1952 "the pride of the camp" was this cement block brownie. Built with donations, it was situated on the road between the lodge and the lake. In 1966, another facility was built near Senior Village with hot showers. (Courtesy of Ruth Wiesen Krzewinski.)

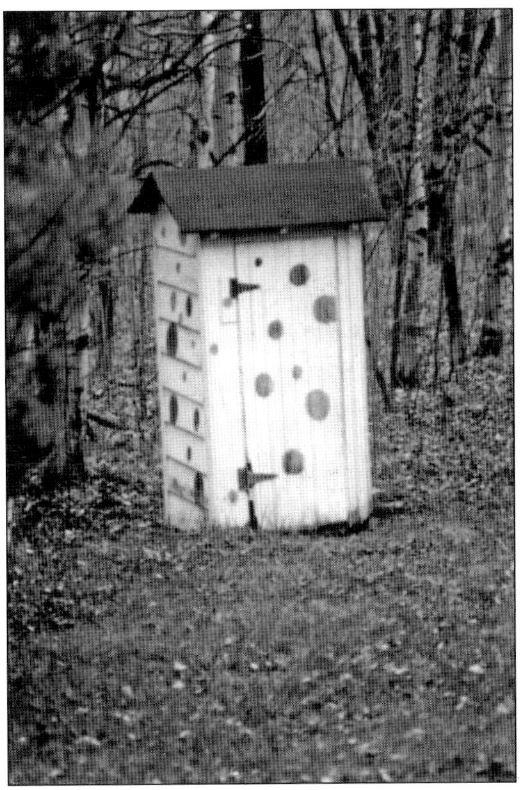

Director Dorthe Balaskas reinstated the primitive camping program in 1964. This little outhouse sat in the woods for the primitive campers, including Priscilla Johns. The rustic one-hole setup meant that campers had to clean up with lye and seal the building to deter flies. It was Priscilla's idea to paint it orange with a racing stripe, but later campers decided polka dots were more trendy. (Courtesy of Amy Johns Ikler.)

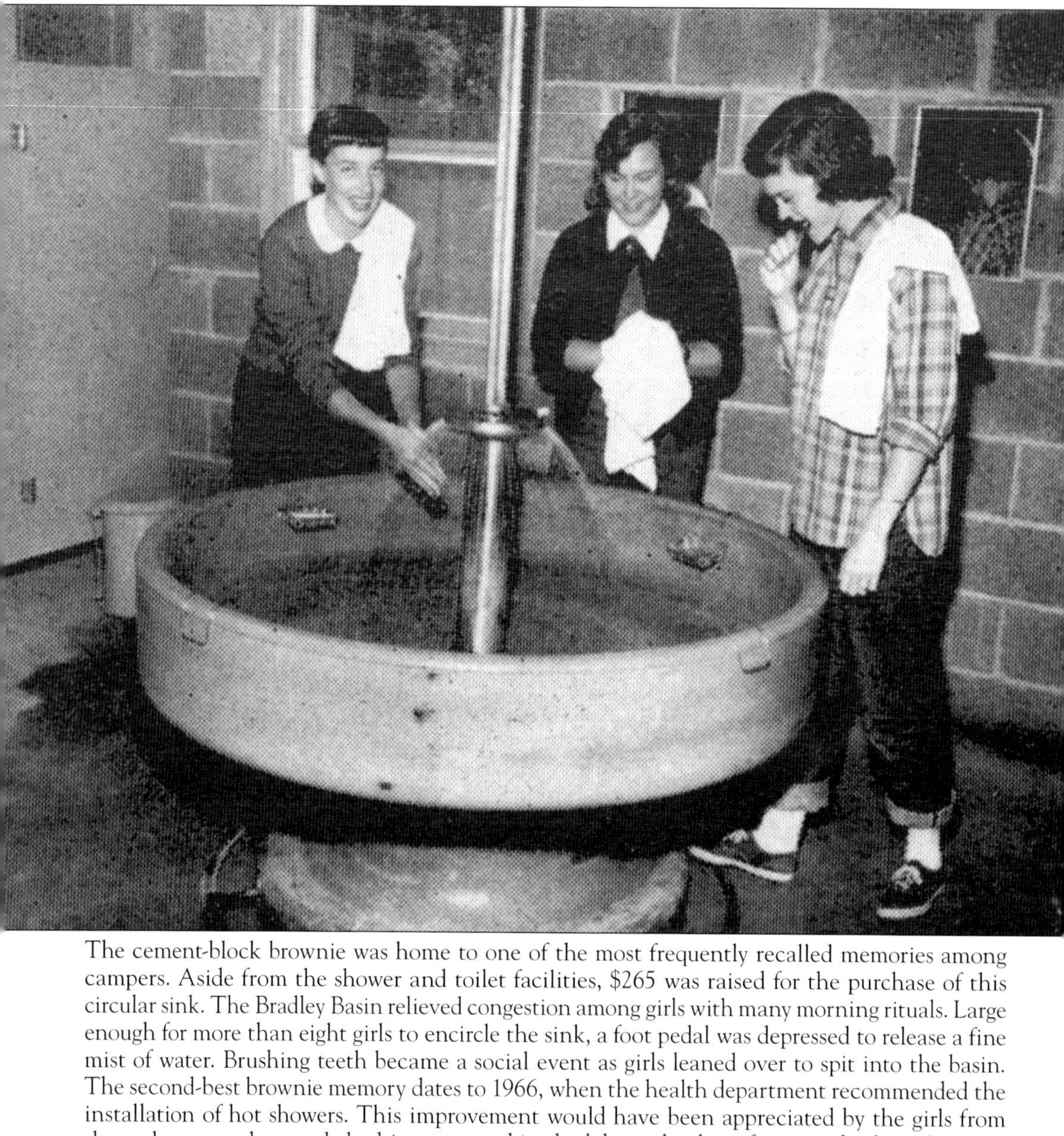

The cement-block brownie was home to one of the most frequently recalled memories among campers. Aside from the shower and toilet facilities, $265 was raised for the purchase of this circular sink. The Bradley Basin relieved congestion among girls with many morning rituals. Large enough for more than eight girls to encircle the sink, a foot pedal was depressed to release a fine mist of water. Brushing teeth became a social event as girls leaned over to spit into the basin. The second-best brownie memory dates to 1966, when the health department recommended the installation of hot showers. This improvement would have been appreciated by the girls from the early years, whose only bathing occurred in the lake with a bar of soap and a fear of passing males. (Courtesy of YWCA Great Lakes Bay Region.)

Three

Of Saddles, Skits, Leeches, and Lanyards

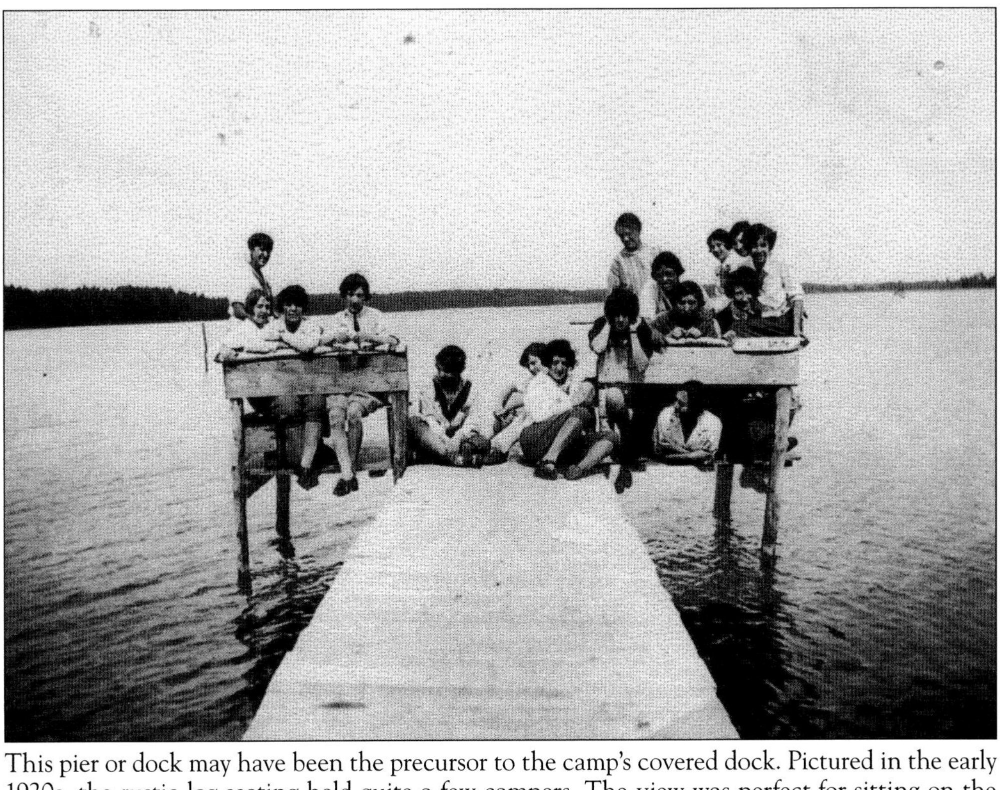

This pier or dock may have been the precursor to the camp's covered dock. Pictured in the early 1920s, the rustic log seating held quite a few campers. The view was perfect for sitting on the spring-fed, 400-acre lake. When this photograph was taken, there were very few homes on Loon Lake. (Courtesy of YWCA Great Lakes Bay Region.)

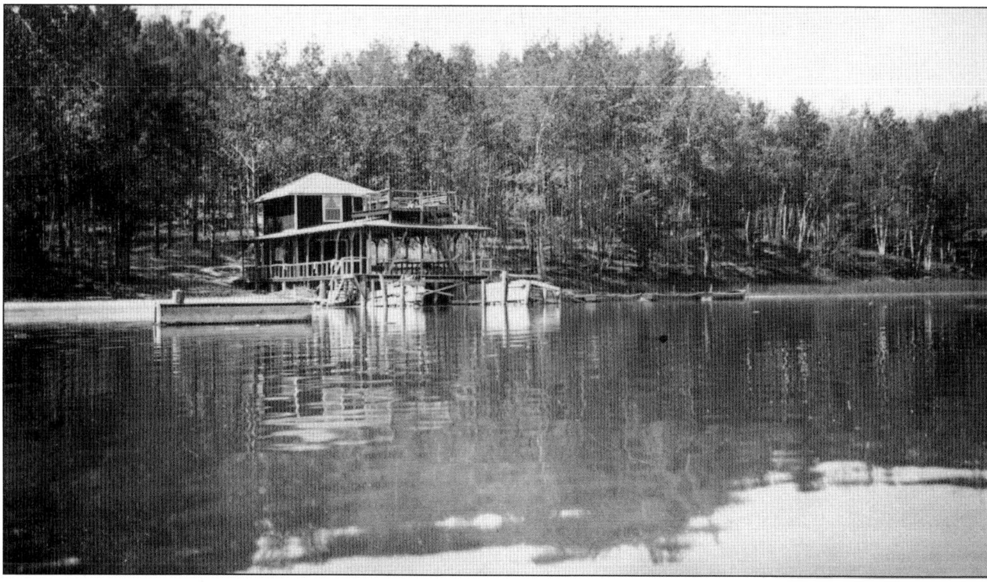

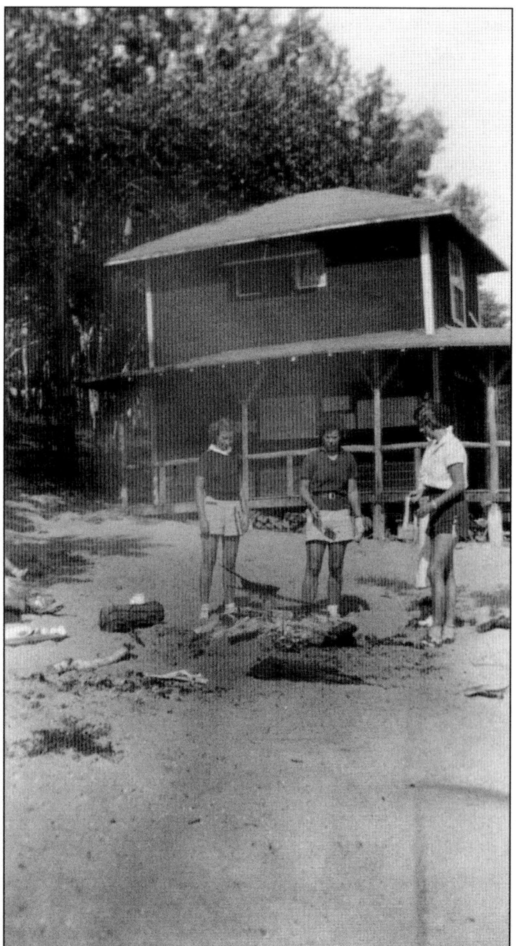

The boathouse was built in 1927 under the direction of Mr. C.T. Clark, who chaired the construction committee. The second story was another dwelling for overflow campers, with a covered pavilion that extended over the wooden pier. According to news clippings, this area was added to the boathouse for recreational activities. (Courtesy of YWCA Great Lakes Bay Region.)

Here, three campers or counselors attend to a campfire beside the east side of the boathouse in the 1930s. The walls of the lower level were a perfect place to put the "buddy board," safety procedure requirements for certification in lifesaving, and bulletins relevant to water safety. The waterfront was always the main attraction for campers, with its sandy beach and clear water. (Courtesy of YWCA Great Lakes Bay Region.)

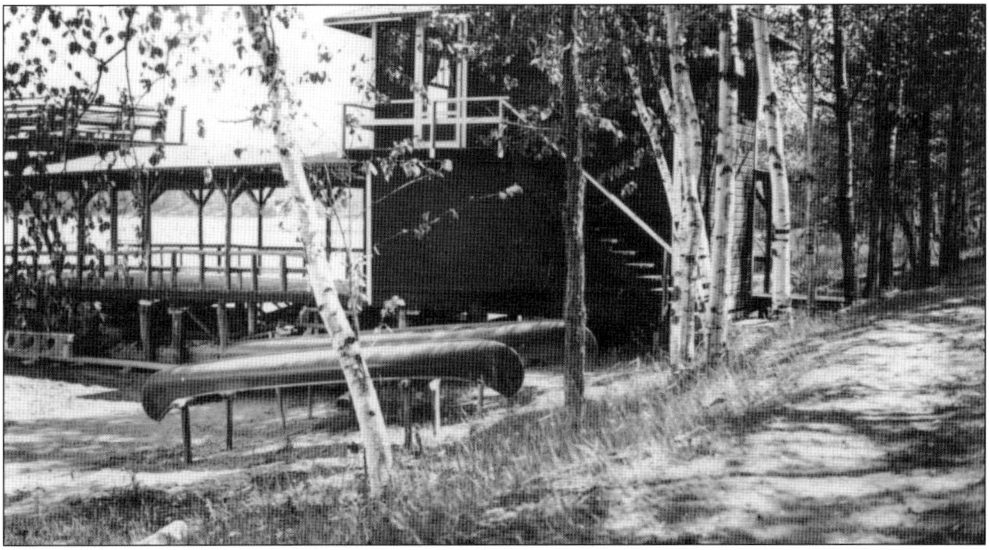

A stairway led to the hut above the boathouse. Girls loved to stay here, and with the sounds of the waves lapping the shore and the view of the dark night sky filled with stars, it was a coveted spot. This c. 1937 photograph gives a view of the structure's west side. In 1942, the boathouse was reinforced and several new windows installed in the upper room, along with 10 new beds. (Courtesy of YWCA Great Lakes Bay Region.)

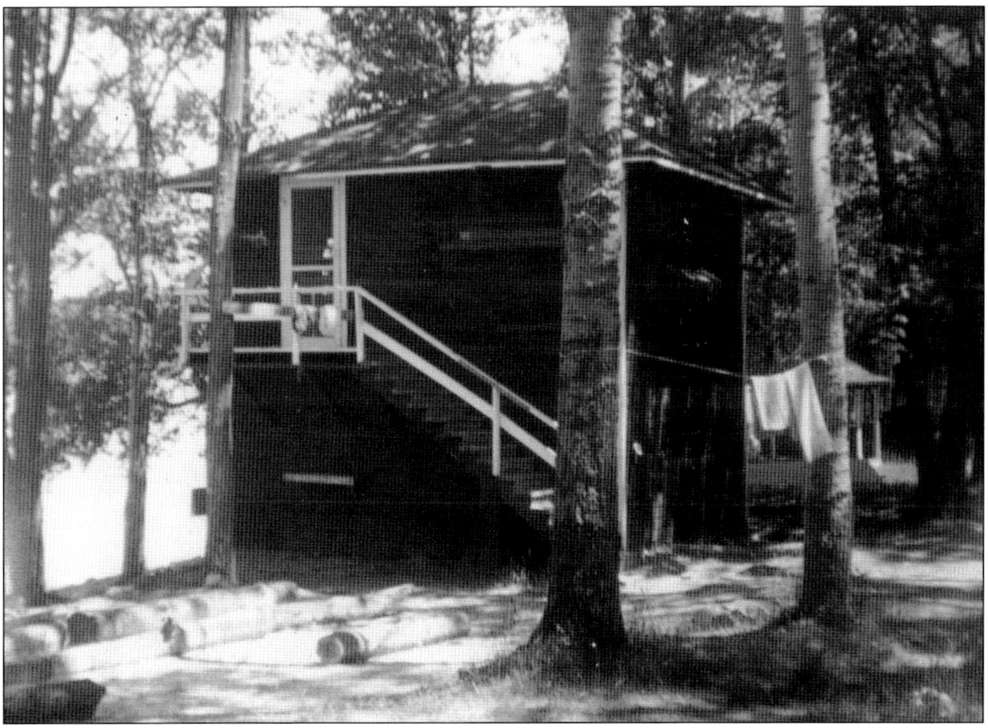

The lower level of the boathouse, with its wooden-plank floors, was the storage area for all things waterfront. Canoe paddles, flotation boards, life jackets, and boating items were hung on the walls. On rainy days, Red Cross training was held inside. During the off-season, sailboats were de-rigged and stored, along with the *Snipe*. (Courtesy of Sue Utter Seelye.)

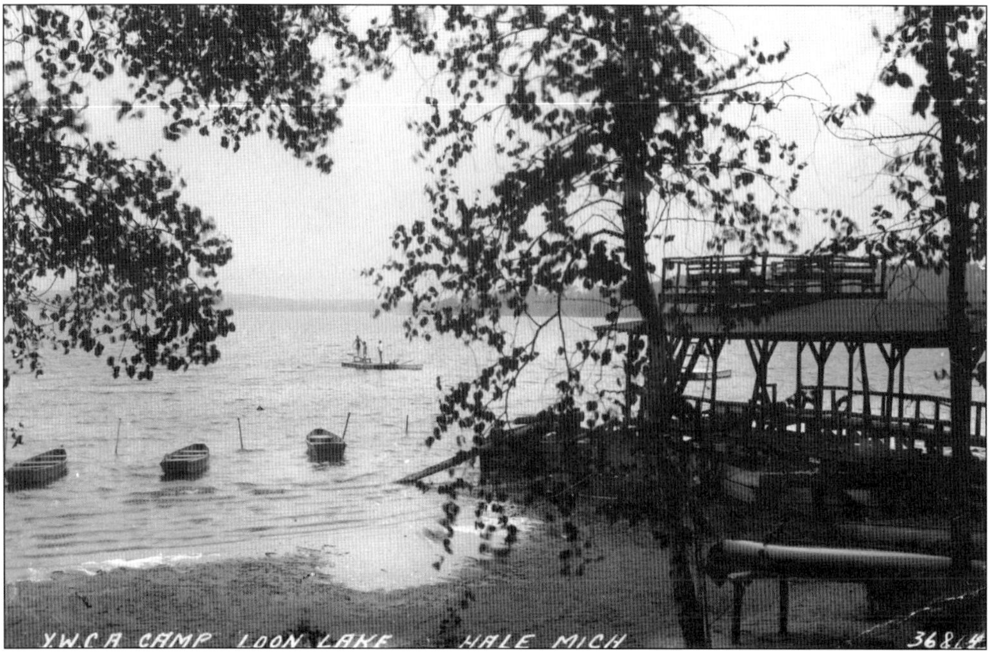

This undated postcard, with a view of the boathouse deck, shows the swim raft and several girls readying to dive. It is unclear when this rustic structure was removed, but notes from a 1951 committee meeting note, "Removed front half of platform-ruined by lake ice." (Courtesy of YWCA Great Lakes Bay Region.)

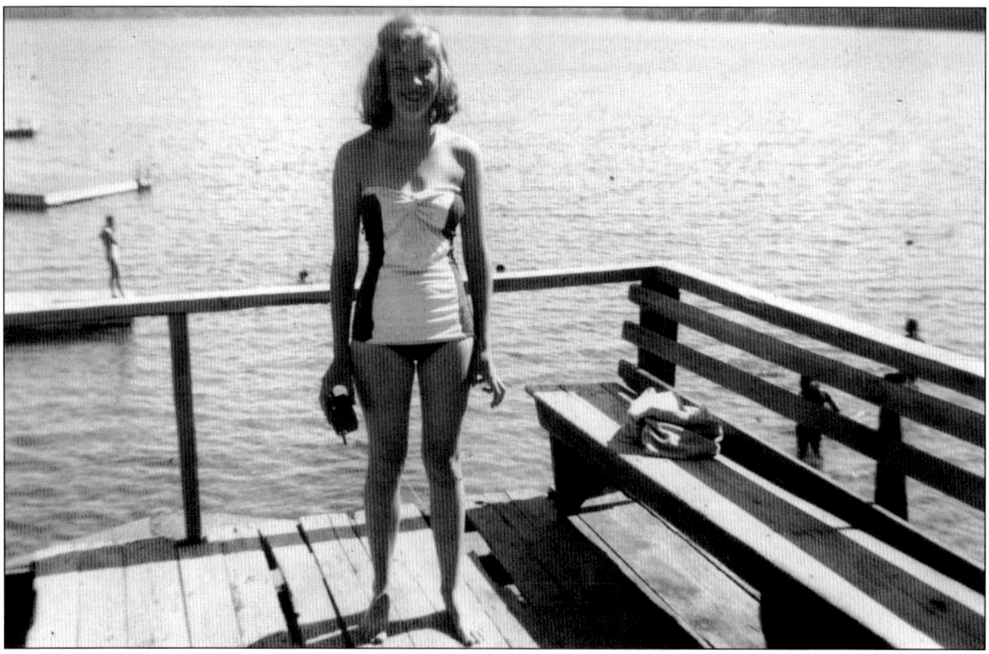

A young staff member poses in 1949 atop the boathouse deck. It was the ideal spot for sunbathing or sleeping under the stars on a warm night. It also had the best view of the dock, the rafts, and any boys from Camp Mahn-go-tah-see—who frequently rowed past the girls' camp. (Courtesy of Judy Rowden Sauve.)

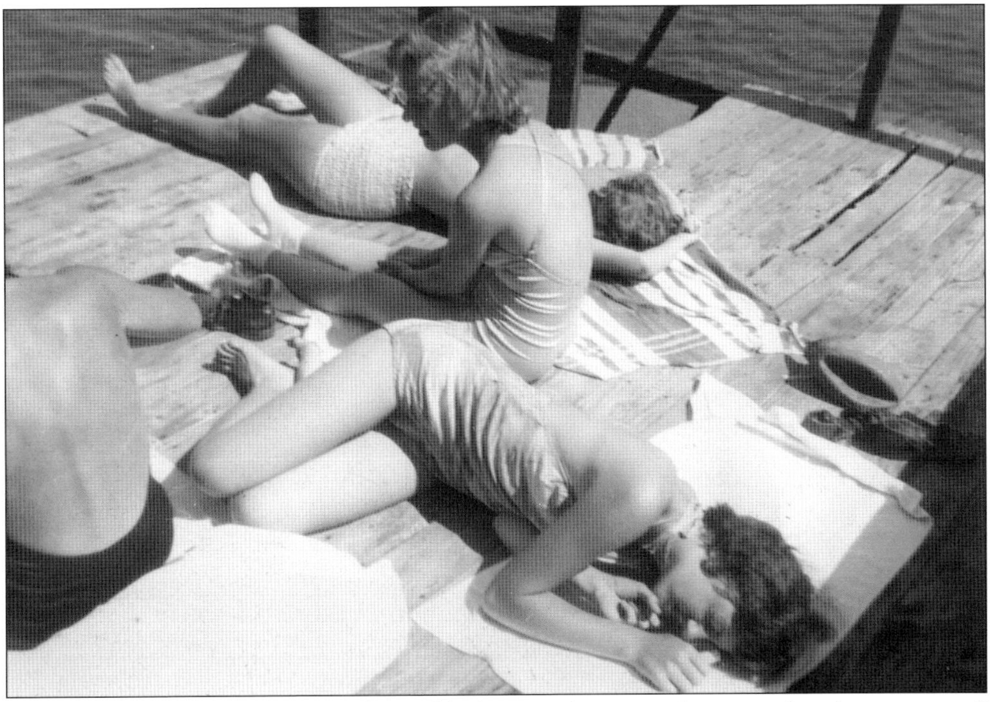

"I think we swam a couple times a day and had time to lay out in the sun and work on our tans," recalled 1940s camper Margot Hamburger, whose favorite spot was the boathouse sundeck. In later years, the young girls slathered on baby oil laced with iodine, Sea and Ski, Coppertone, or Bain de Soleil, which turned them brown as berries. (Courtesy of Judy Rowden Sauve.)

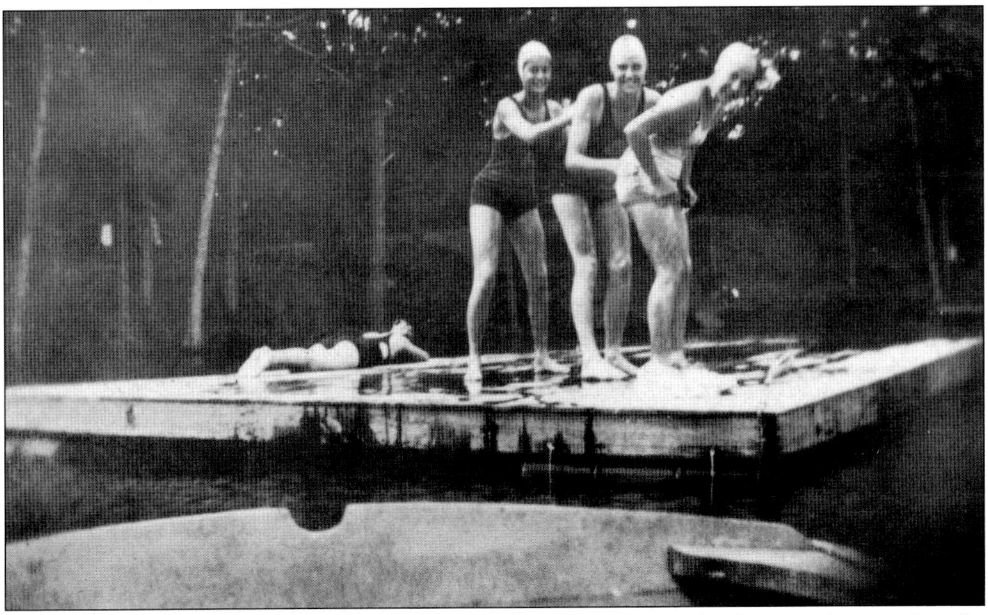

Mary Madore, the swimming instructor in the early 1930s, is pictured in between her two friends, ready to jump or dive from the raft. Her name, along with Mary Jo Stegall and Edna Young, is among those placed on a shield of lake swimmers in 1934. Edna swam two miles on Loon Lake in 47 minutes and 30 seconds, and Mary Jo received an honorable mention. (Courtesy of Candy Camerden.)

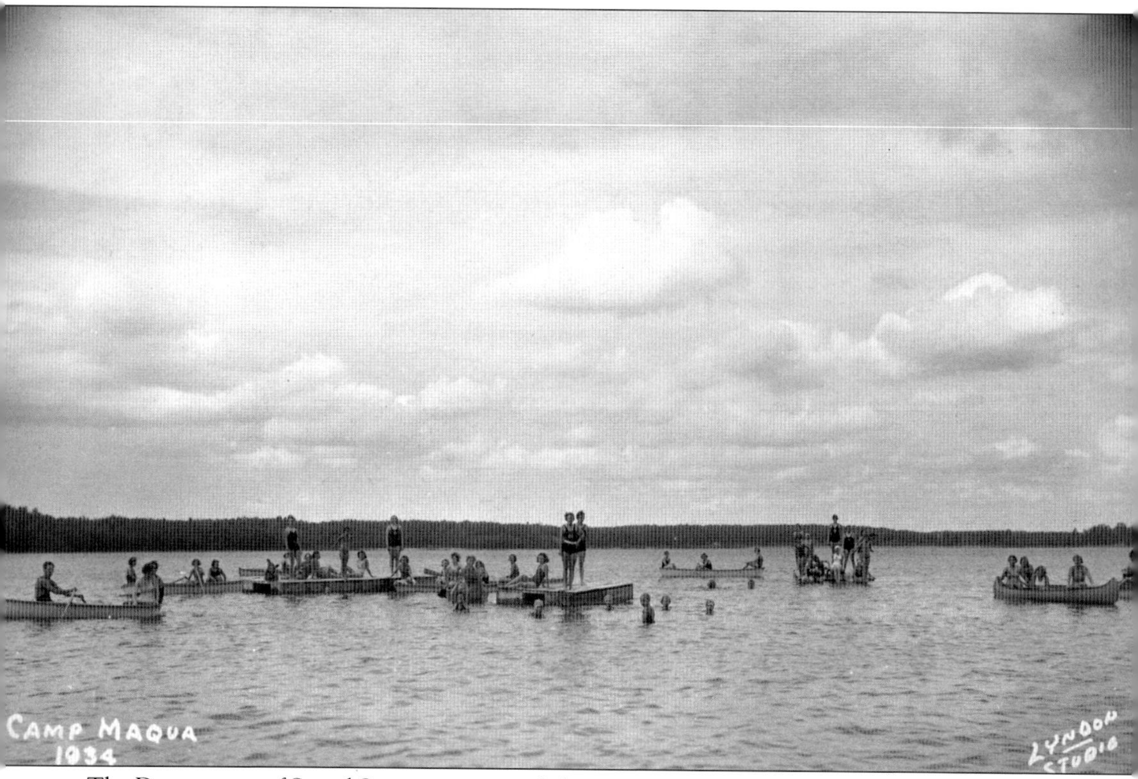

The Department of Social Services inspected the campgrounds, facilities, and programs each year so that the camp could be licensed in Michigan. Swimming was always the main activity, and the waterfront had excellent supervision under the guidance of certified water-safety instructors. In the early years, campers swam three times a day. Many had learned to swim before attending, but an equal number learned at camp and obtained their Red Cross certificates in lifesaving. Older girls swam across the lake accompanied by a rowboat for safety. This photograph from 1934 sets a lovely scene for boaters and bathers. (Courtesy of YWCA Great Lakes Bay Region.)

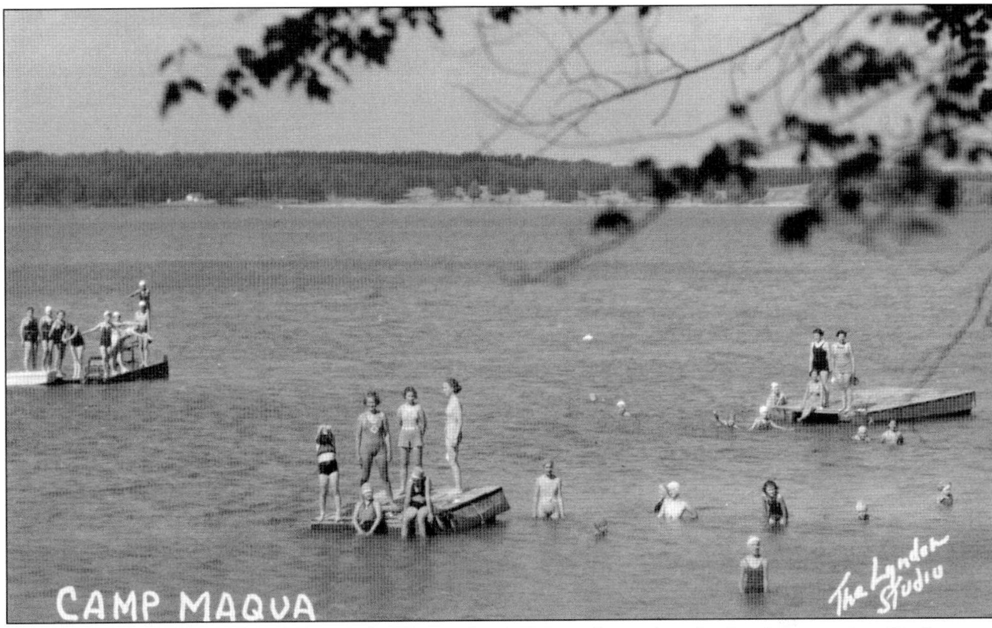

This undated postcard appears to be from the 1930s judging by the bathing attire. Rafts were placed according to swimming level, with the first being for red-cap swimmers, the second for green, and the third for blue. Different years required different criteria to pass the tests, but in the late 1930s girls were required to flip a canoe in the middle of the lake and climb back in to earn a blue cap. (Courtesy of YWCA Great Lakes Bay Region.)

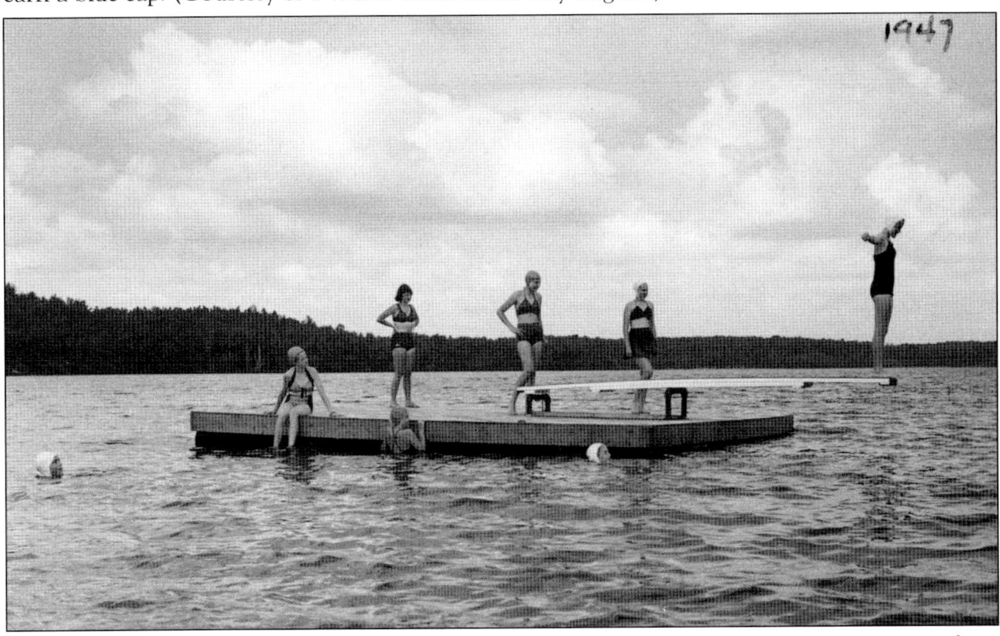

Judy Crissey, a 1950s camper, learned to swim through the YWCA in Bay City. "We went from beginner to advanced and took synchronized swimming using the local high school pools in the winter, so I was able to do all the water activities the first year of camp. In order to pass I had to be able to swim to the raft or the length of the dock." This raft photograph was taken in 1947. (Courtesy of YWCA Great Lakes Bay Region.)

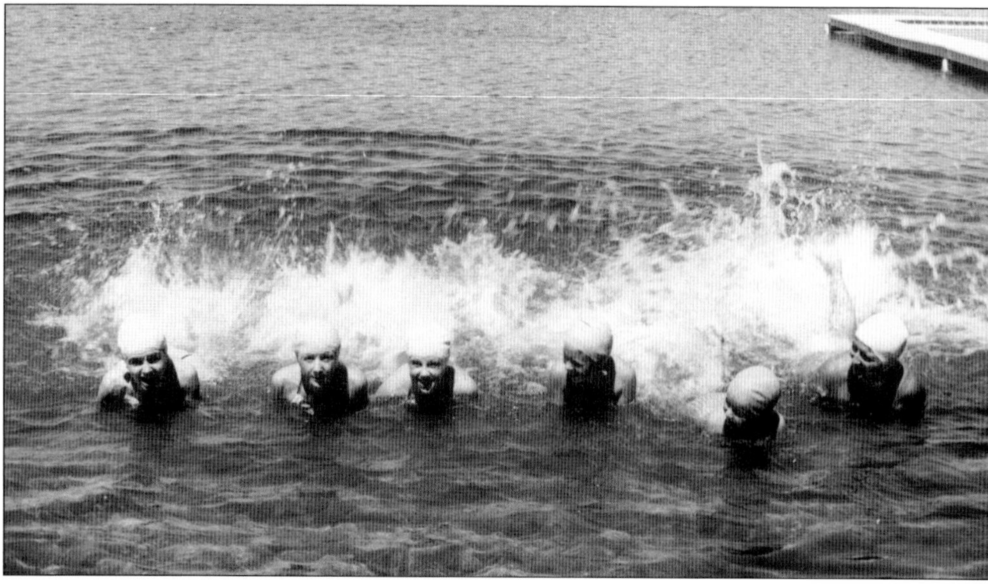

The girls were tested at the beginning of the session to determine their swimming abilities. An incentive to pass to the intermediate level was to be able to graduate from the shallow water, where all the leeches lurked. Campers were more afraid of the "bloodsuckers" than the water! This photograph from 1954 could be of one of the synchronized classes for advanced swimmers. (Courtesy of YWCA Great Lakes Bay Region.)

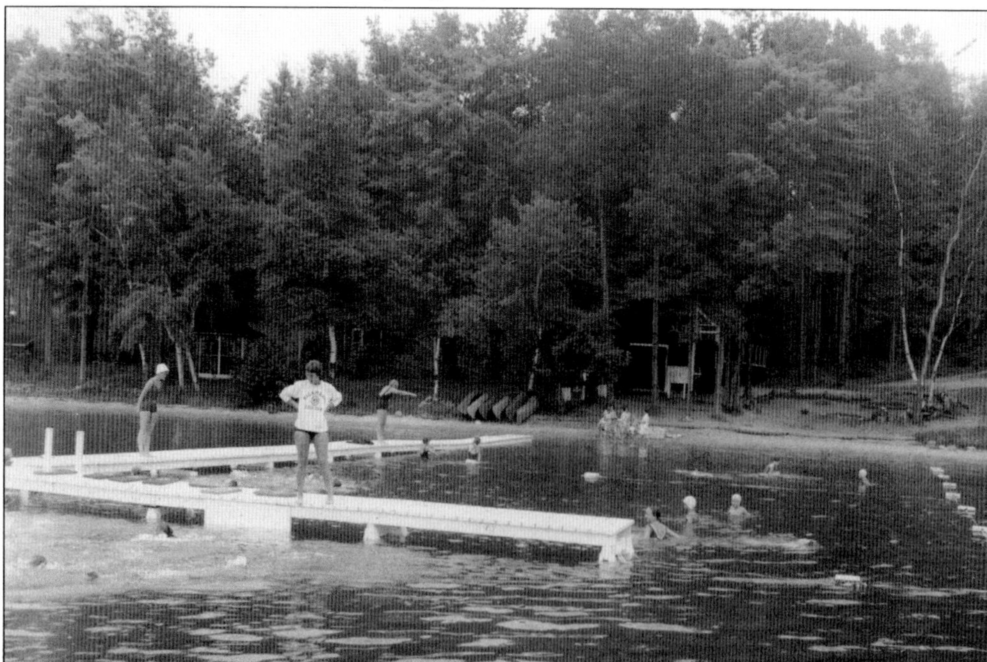

The Imperial Oil Company donated oil drums for floating rafts and docks in 1933, which were later replaced with Styrofoam. The *L*-shaped dock in this 1962 image defined the swim area for all levels except the advanced swimmers, who could swim out to the raft. The fire pit, boathouse, craft hut, and band shell can be seen onshore. (Courtesy of YWCA Great Lakes Bay Region.)

Here, from left to right, Gail Schultheiss, Vicki Sand, and Nancy Jacobs pose in front of the boathouse in 1967 just before their swim time. Gail was the only girl in her family, which lived in a neighborhood with "way too many boys," so the girl time was a treat. Despite knowing how to swim, her first day was spent in the beginner area. (Courtesy of Gail Schultheiss Scherer.)

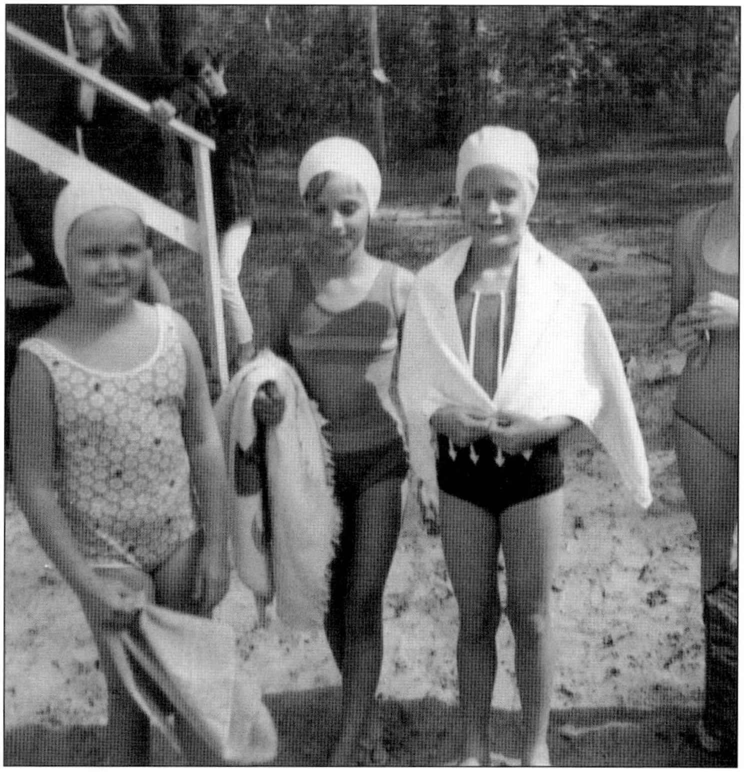

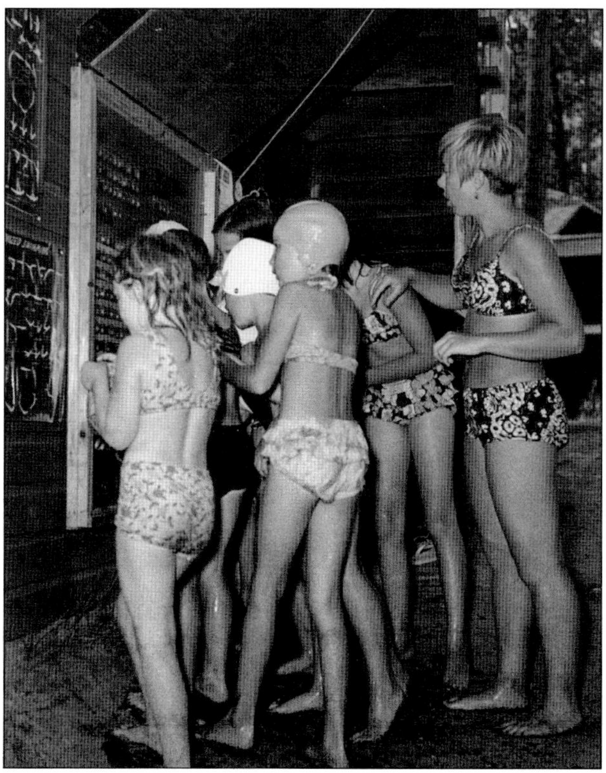

Nancy "Scoots" Sautter, waterfront director, is pictured here in 1969, with some of her pupils by the buddy board. The tag system indicated whether a swimmer was in or out of the water. Periodically, a whistle was blown, and the girls would either exit the water or hold their buddy's hand high in the air for a head count by staff. (Courtesy of YWCA Great Lakes Bay Region.)

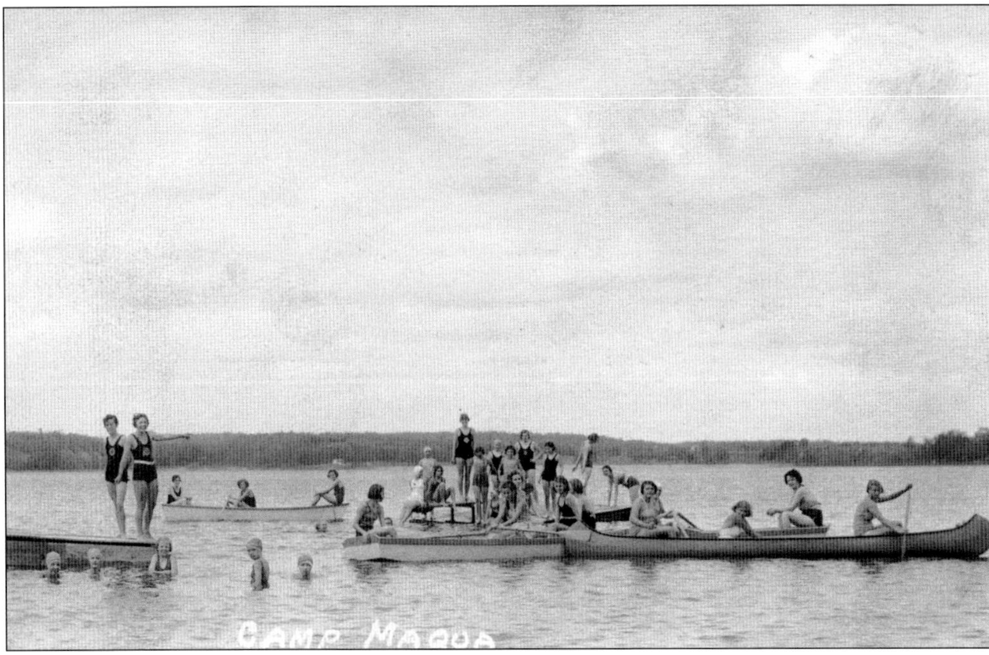

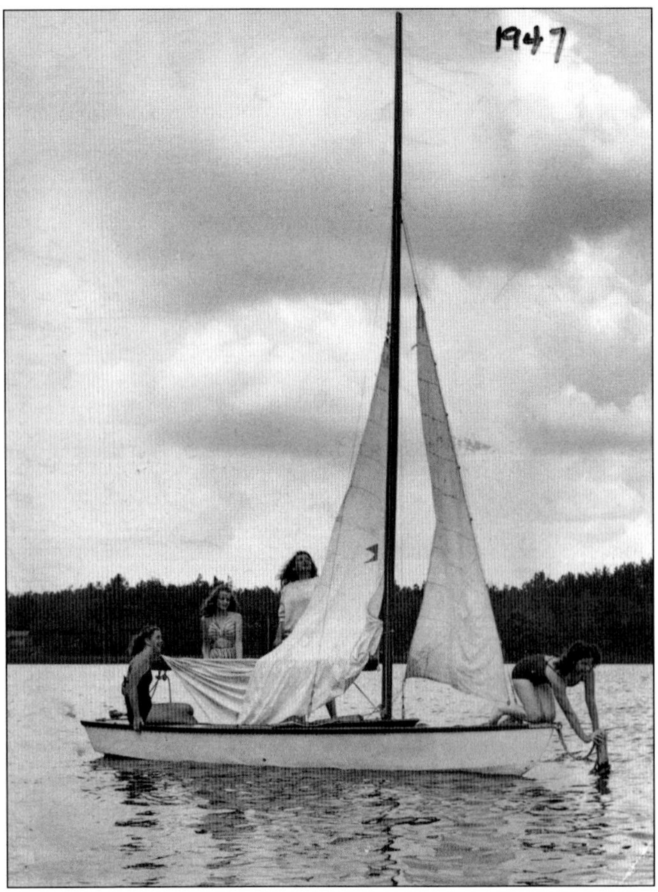

In 1934, campers were invited to paddle or row across the lake to the boys' camp, Mahn-go-tah-see. According to an early article, they stopped midway, at the Recreation Hill inlet, for supper with hikers before continuing on to see "moving pictures" and return home before dark. This postcard is from the early 1930s. (Courtesy of Candy Camerden.)

Sailing was always a popular activity, but only the girls with advanced skills were able to use the boats, which were often loaned to camp. This photograph, taken in 1947, shows four campers unfurling the sail. Pictured from left to right are Julie Ford, Virginia Webb, Barb Jacoby, and Sally Reason. (Courtesy of YWCA Great Lakes Bay Region.)

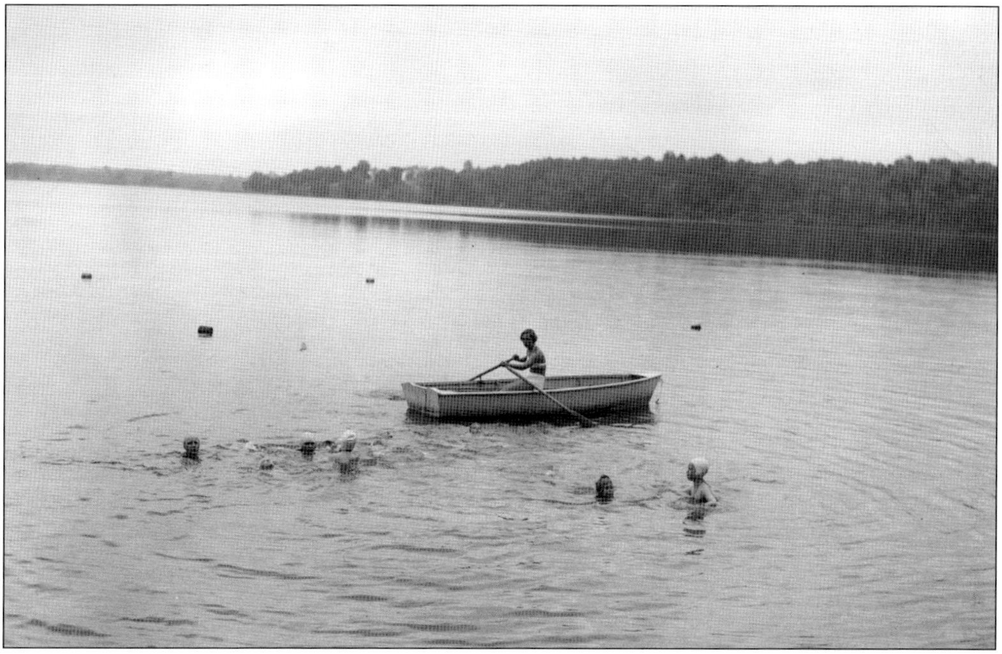

Penny Mitchell, a 1950s camper, could not wait until she was old enough to swim across the lake. "You had to be a decent swimmer, so that you wouldn't drown when you swam across. The rowboats went ahead of you and you were very careful," she recalled of her cool sixth-grade experience. Girls in this 1948 image demonstrate a lake crossing. (Courtesy of YWCA Great Lakes Bay Region.)

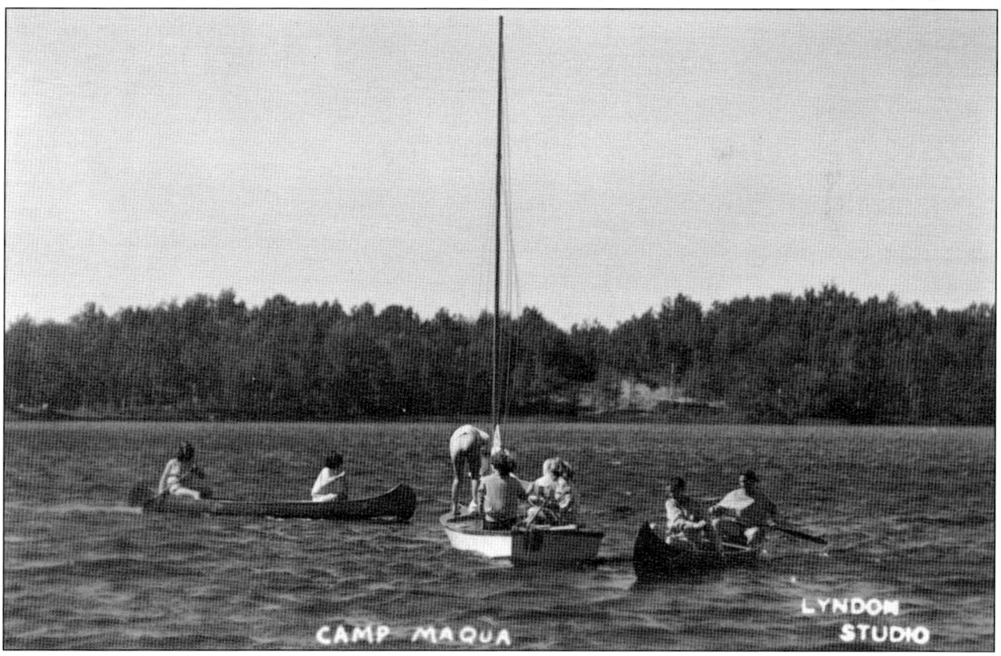

The sailboat *Snipe* had a reputation of tipping mast down and, on one occasion, rolled repeatedly—pitching sisters Nan, Pat, and Judy O'Tool into the water before they were able to right it. Nan had a reputation for teaching a period of sailing with no sails, waiting for the arrival of replacement sails. This postcard is dated to 1946. (Courtesy of Pat O'Tool Smith.)

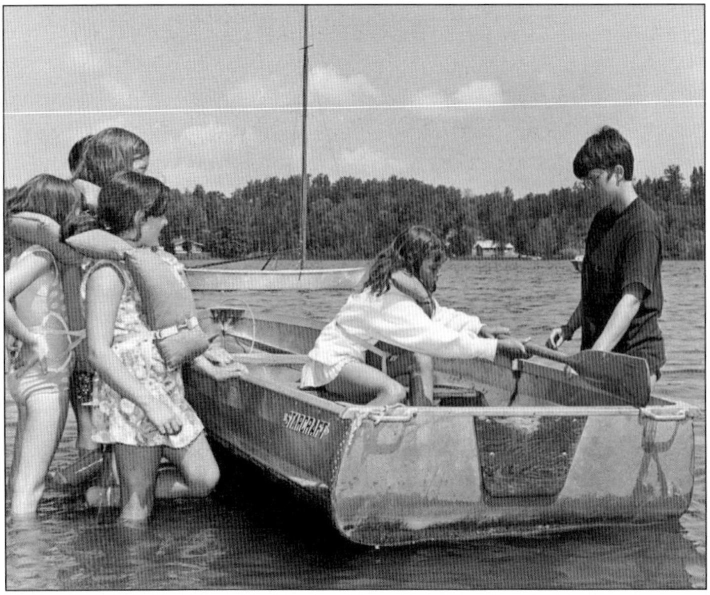

Boating instruction demanded responsibility and good judgment, as well as an understanding of the safety rules of small craft. Staff was hired carefully to ensure that girls were able to maximize their experience with rowing, canoeing, advanced canoeing for overnights, kayaking, sailing, tubing, and even swamp adventures. This 1967 photograph shows a class in session. (Courtesy of YWCA Great Lakes Bay Region.)

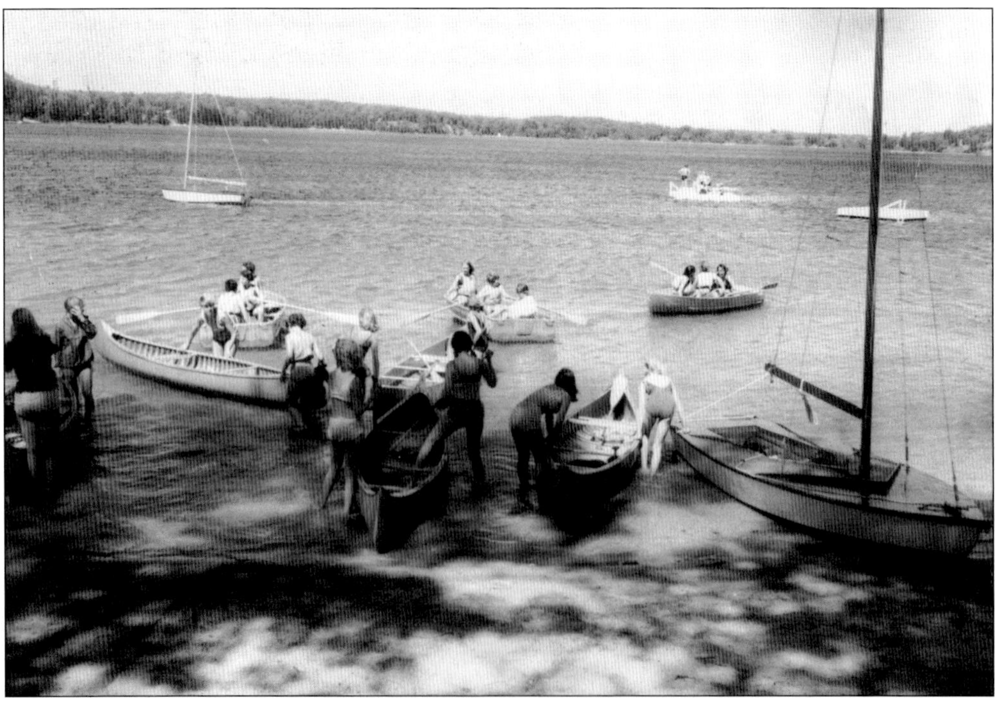

This image of all the watercraft on the shore is from 1965. Tales of canoe tests, which often involved lifting the canoe, navigating to the middle of the lake, and tipping it while fully dressed, were legendary. The drills enabled the girls the practice needed to climb back into the boats for emergency purposes, but the "gunnel pumping," or teetering back and forth on the boats, was the favorite pastime. (Courtesy of YWCA Great Lakes Bay Region.)

“The coolest thing was the Kiltie sisters, who brought up their own sailboat to camp. There seemed to be enough wind to even sail the thing and it was a big deal to get the rigging up,” recalls camper Cara Prieskorn of the summer of 1967. Sue Kiltie was a junior counselor and taught canoeing and sailing. Her father bought her a 13-foot, aqua blue Chrysler Lonestar LS-13. She learned to sail on the camp’s *Raven*, which was 14 feet long, and she was only 15 years old when she began her three-year reign teaching the basic skills of sailing. According to a director’s report, Sue taught in an enjoyable and understandable manner and was considered an asset to the program. The boat was never damaged or capsized unless she was teaching capsize recovery. Sue (below) spent a great deal of time sailing across the lake, as her summer boyfriend was at the boy’s camp. (Courtesy of Susan Kiltie.)

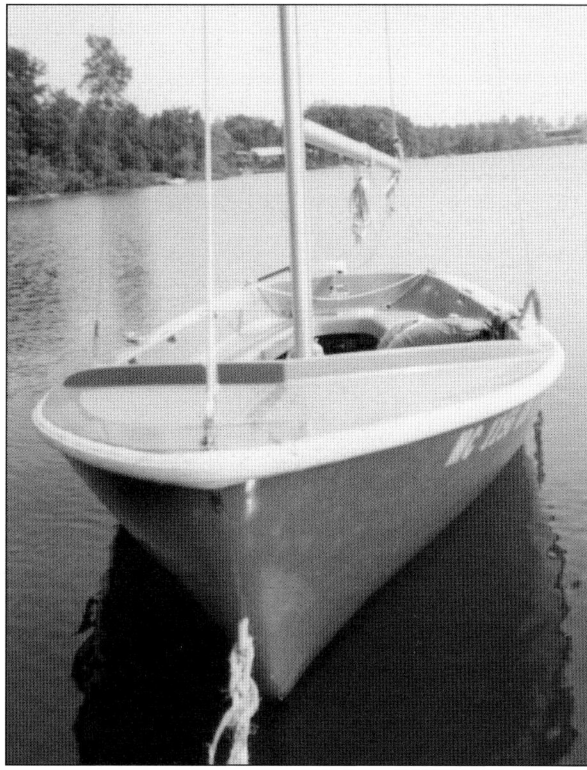

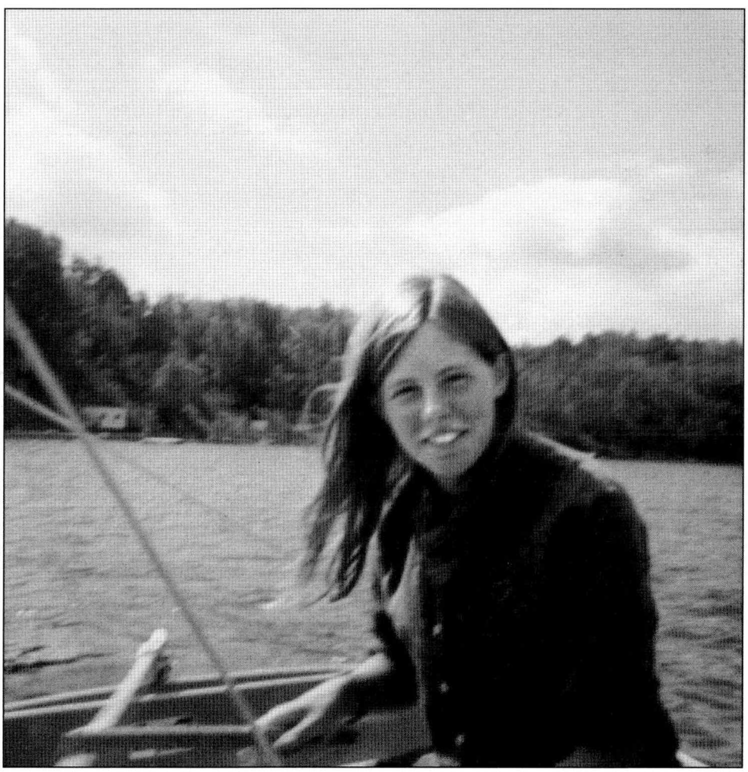

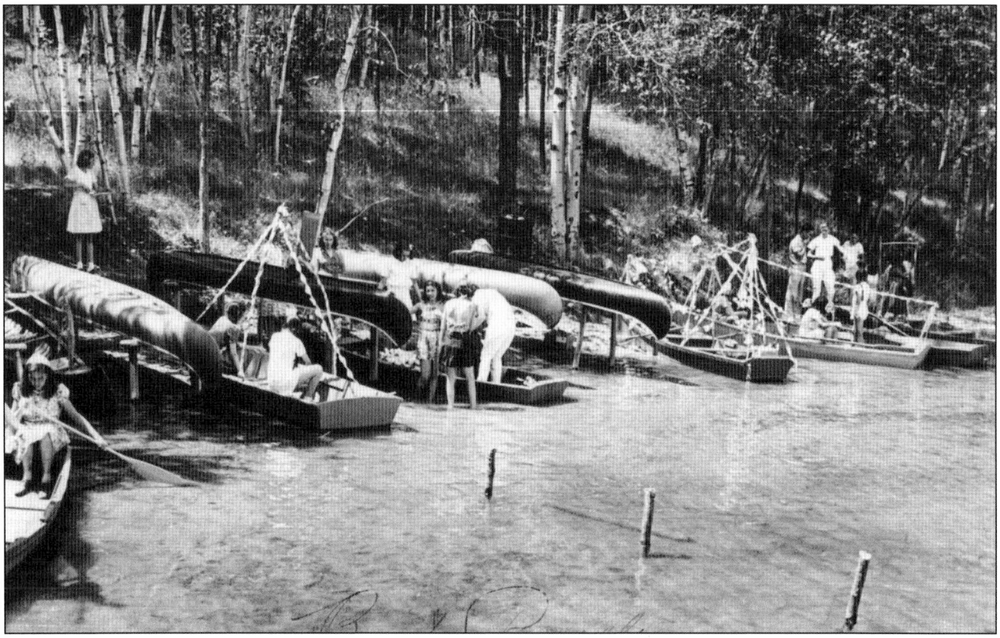

Clippings from a July 30, 1935, news article describe the water carnival, which was probably similar to these two undated photographs. "All the boats were bedecked in gallant trimming for the boat regatta of the Water Carnival, which began with the coronation of the Water Queen, Helen Beckett by Mrs. Volmey Young of Bay City." Boats paraded past a judge's stand, decorated as gondolas and Lady of the Lake yachts, and one carried the queen with a red and gold cape over her white bathing suit. The waterfront directors were Sylvia Johnson and Esther Middlewood, who supervised the festivities. (Courtesy of YWCA Great Lakes Bay Region.)

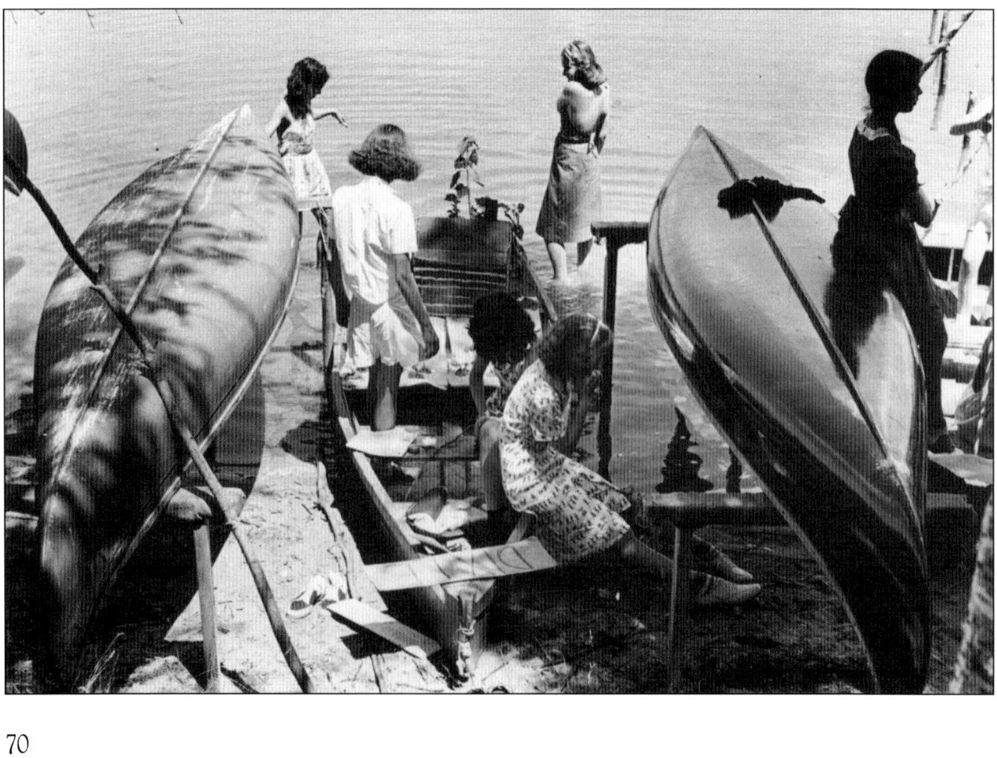

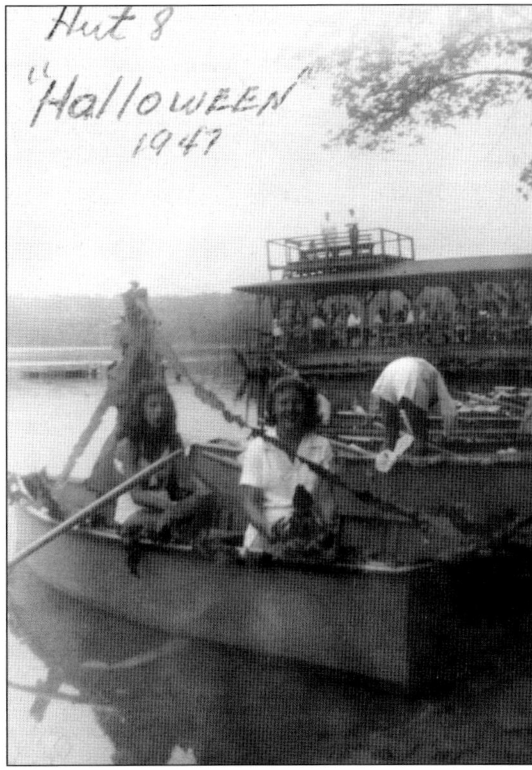

At right, Ethel Feldman (left) and Pat Kula (right) are seated in their Halloween-themed rowboat, with the elaborated boathouse pavilion in the background. Nine huts participated in the 1947 Water Carnival with holiday themes. "Easter Bonnet" was the theme of the gaily decorated boat below, but another boat, decorated in a Fourth of July theme with girls holding giant firecrackers, was the winner. Canoe races, swim exhibitions, and a water ballet were featured as part of the program. Lifesaving techniques were demonstrated by Geraldine Folkert and Julie Ford for their part of the program. (Courtesy of Pat Kula Reinlein.)

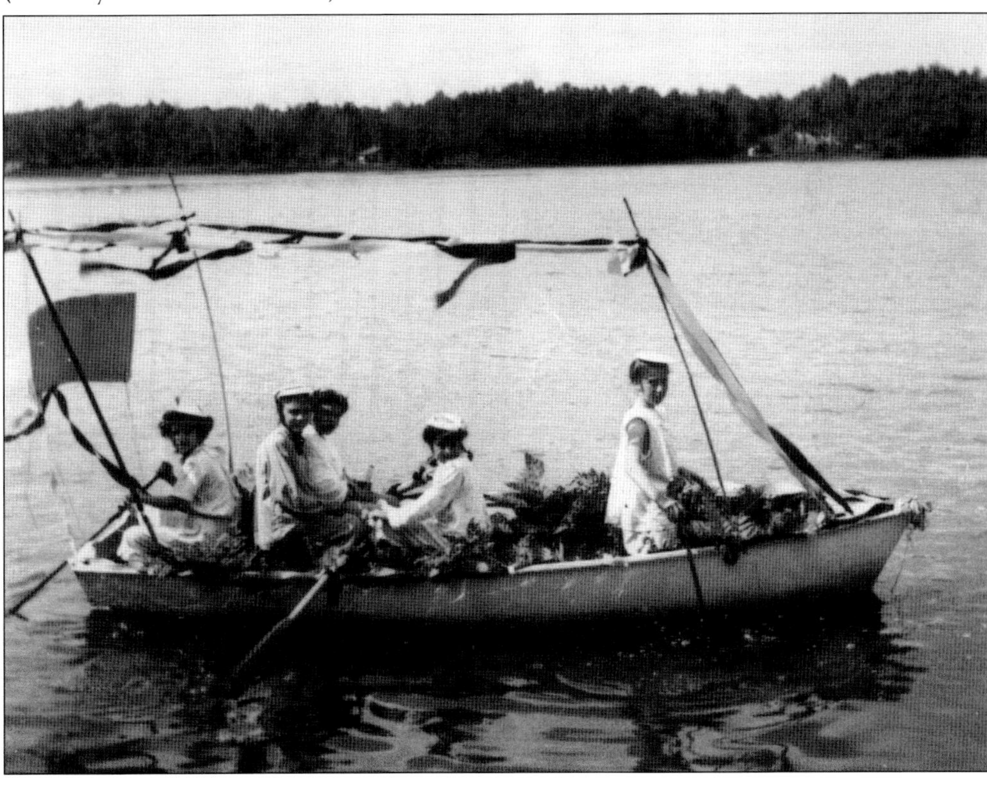

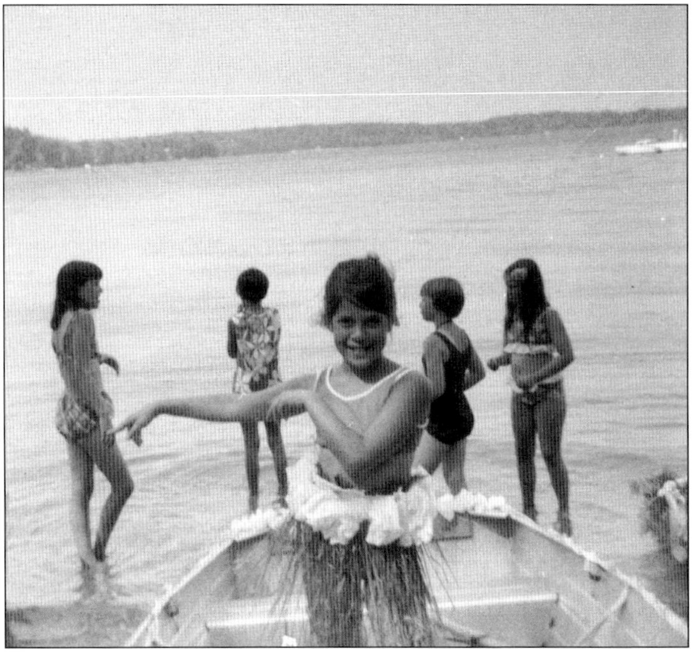

"That would be me," wrote Karen Magidsohn in 1968 on this photograph of herself as "Luau Girl" aboard one of the Regatta boats. Just 10 years old, she was selected by her bunkmates to be the Hawaiian girl on their themed boat. Who would have guessed that this little girl would end up camping and staffing for the eight best summers of her life? (Courtesy of Karen Magidsohn.)

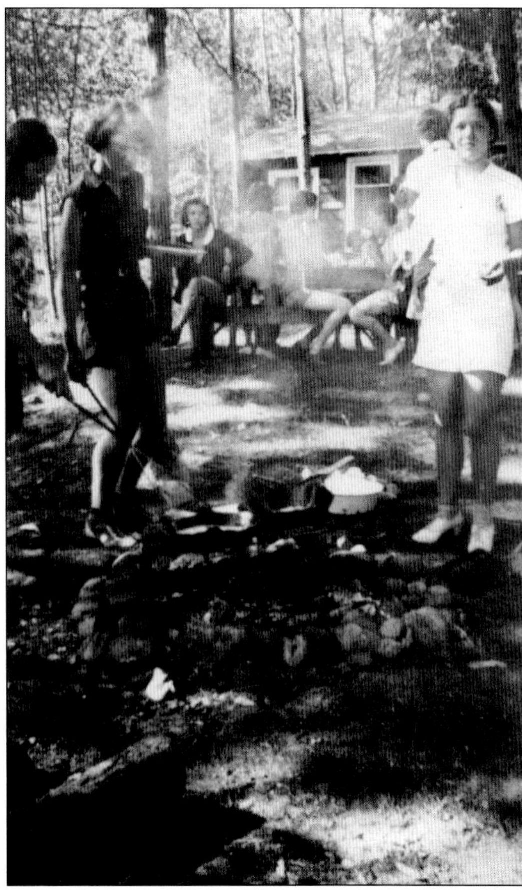

"The gang started out in blithe spirits enough, but at the end of the journey it was only the roaring fire and marshmallows that kept their spirits from sagging," states a *Loon* entry from August 1925 after an overnight hike. This photograph from the mid-1930s was taken in front of the craft hut, where a campfire was started for a favored activity. (Courtesy of YWCA Great Lakes Bay Region.)

Foil dinners were also a popular meal over the campfire. Carol Hulett served as the camp health director in 1974 and can be seen here preparing "hobo dinners" made with meat and vegetables. Dilly Dogs, Squaw Corn, Pioneer Drumsticks, Angels on Horseback, Banana Boats, Peach Toast, and Little Pig Potatoes were all fun campfire meals. (Courtesy of Carol Hulett.)

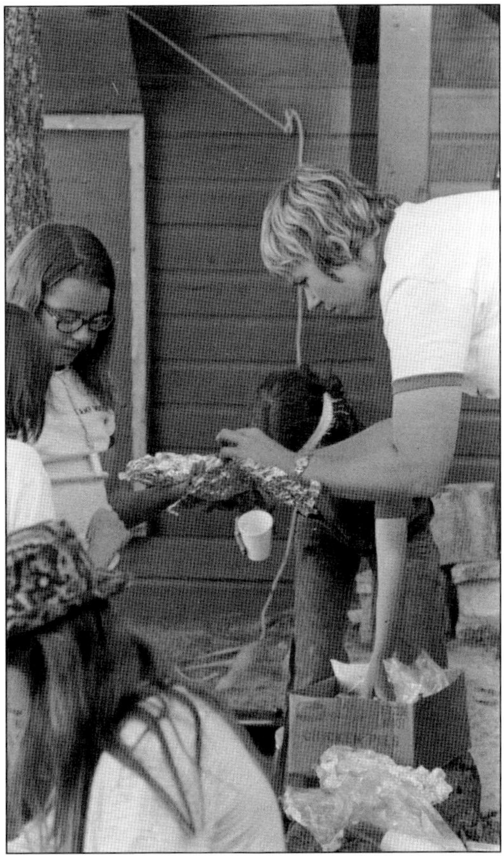

In the 1961 camp craft unit, girls practiced their new lashing, rope, tool, and fire-building skills. They learned to lash furniture from fallen wood and to carve Tiki figures or Lummi sticks. Bark was peeled off of one-foot-long sticks, which were then whittled and carved for rhythmic chanting, stunts, and singing. (Courtesy of YWCA Great Lakes Bay Region.)

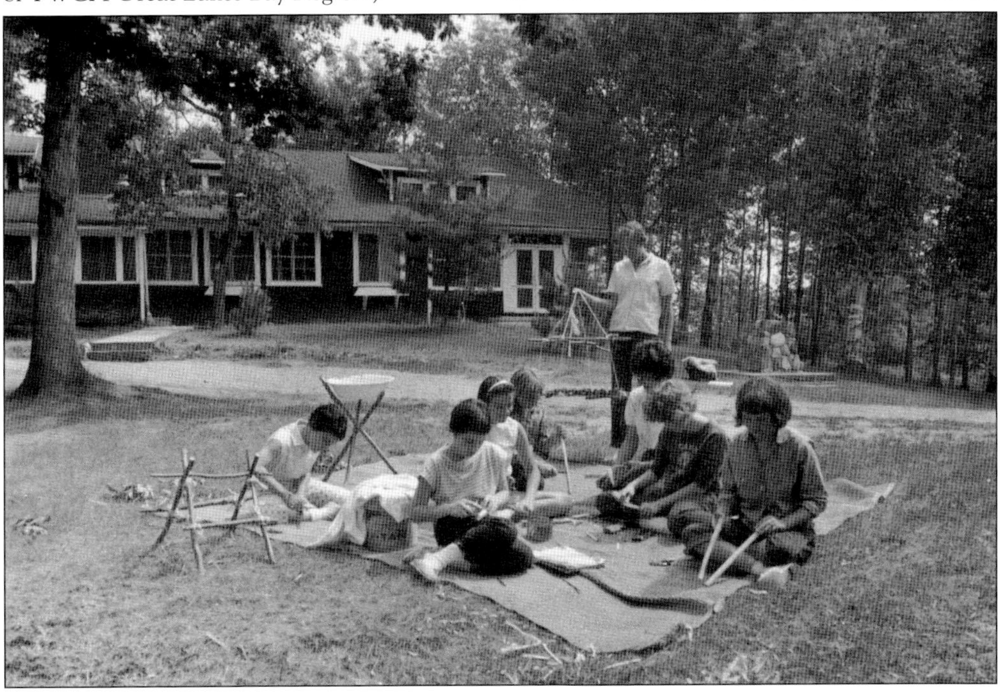

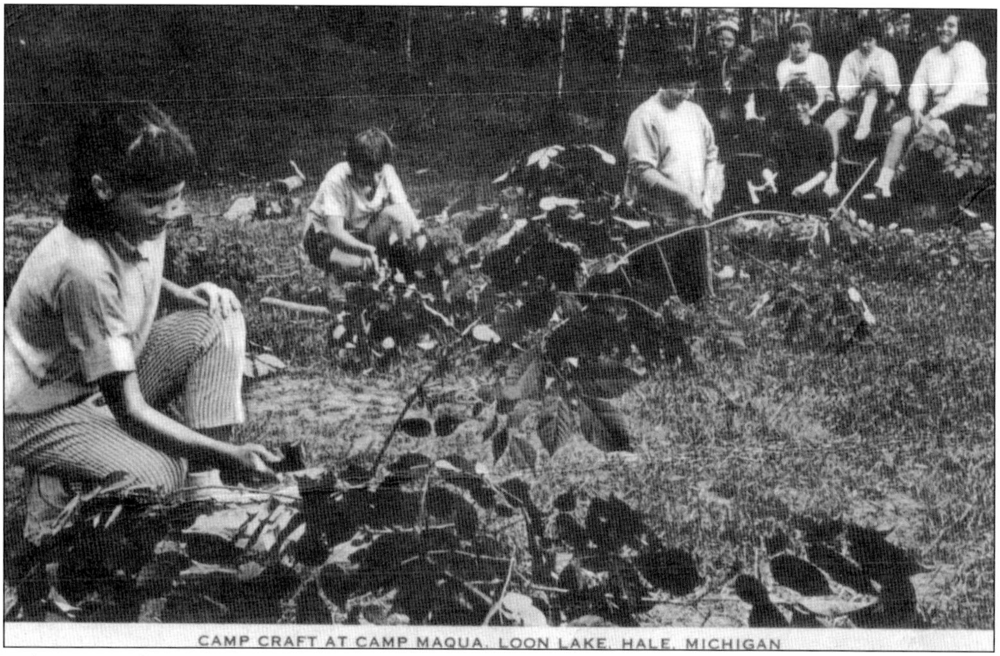

Valerie sent this postcard home to her parents in 1965 depicting a camp craft class. "I'm having a great time," she wrote, "it's been raining all the time we've been here." The girls learned to handle a hatchet and jackknife, pitch a rudimentary pup tent, start a fire, and read a compass. (Courtesy of Valerie Monto Richardson.)

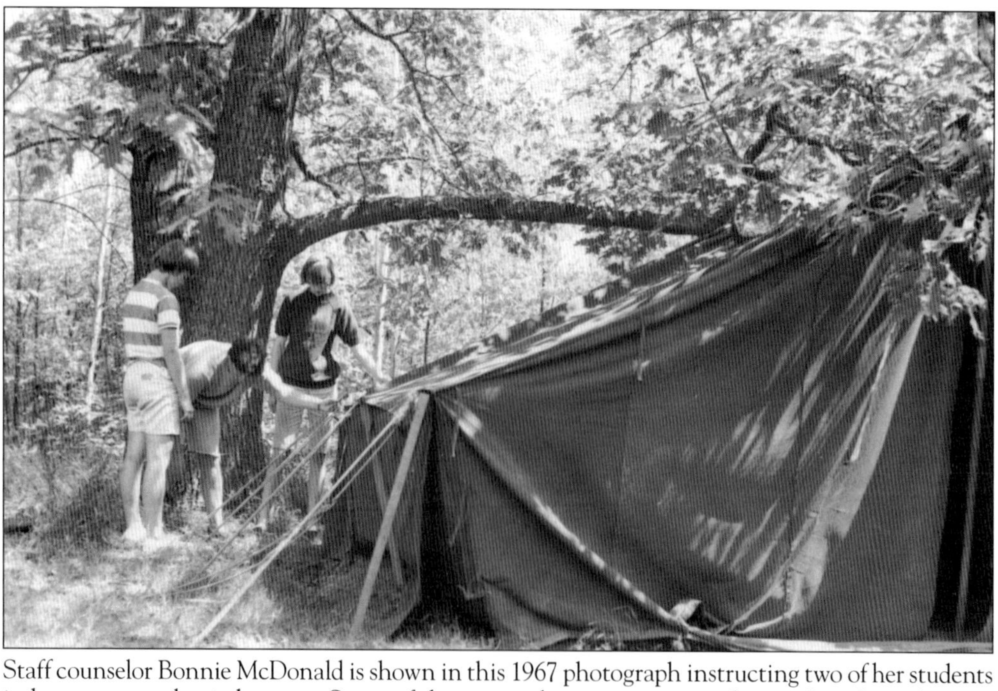

Staff counselor Bonnie McDonald is shown in this 1967 photograph instructing two of her students in how to properly pitch a tent. Some of the overnight canoe trips used tents, but the girls often slept under the stars. Paddling from Grayling to Luzerne for two days made for lasting memories of either soggy sleeping bags or great tans. (Courtesy of YWCA Great Lakes Bay Region.)

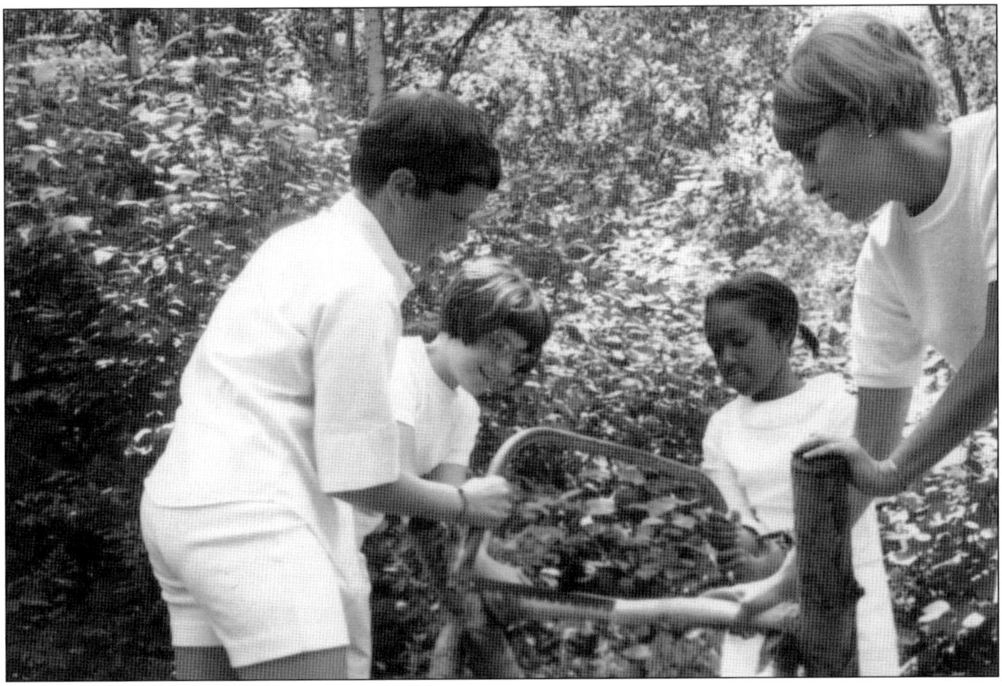

Anne Obey, the camp craft counselor in 1968, teaches campers safe cross-saw skills in this scene. Featured from left to right are Marcia Michelson, Jeri Smith, Rene Baker, and Anne. The girls also learned how to safely start fires and use conservation techniques. Girls used soft, fallen poplar but were never allowed to cut birch trees for their projects. (Courtesy of YWCA Great Lakes Bay Region.)

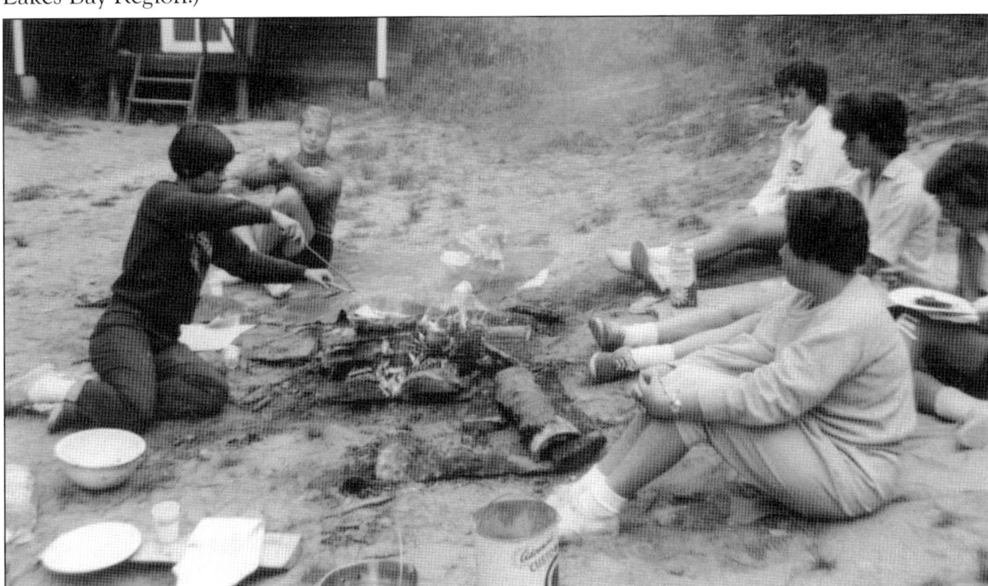

Counselor Lynn Whipple is shown cooking camp style near Senior Village in 1960 after managing to start a great fire. Often "fires were set, then simultaneously came the sound of striking matches, followed by low mutterings as the wind blew them out," according to a *Loon* staffer in an undated issue. (Courtesy of Ann Ward.)

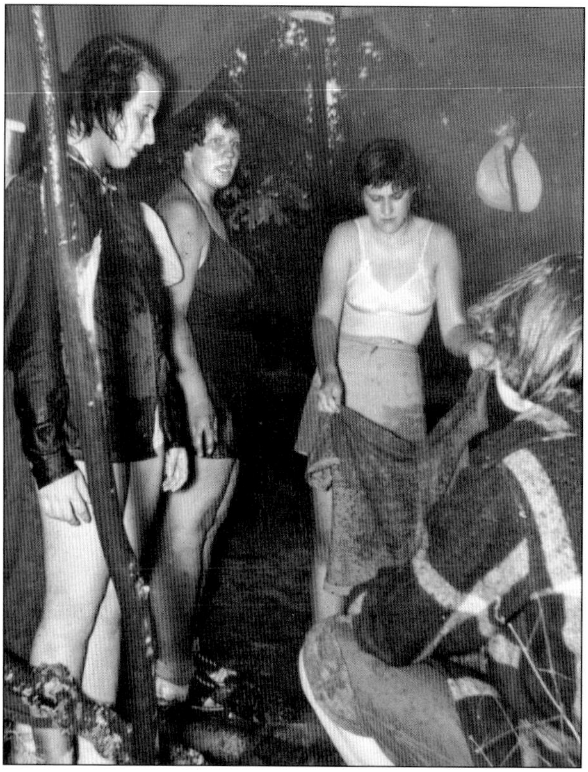

In 1951, there was a two-day adventure on the Au Sable River with counselor Irene Verbedian's hut and camp director Dorothy Dickie. After travelling upstream for miles, they found their ideal campsite after portaging at Loud Dam, near a small trout stream. The tents were pitched and the downpour began. Ann Gunn and Pat Parsons dried the clothing, while Judy Miller, Nancy O'Tool, and Marian Pope prepared dinner. Annette Brandt was the dishwasher, using the trout stream as a refrigerator and sand to wash dishes. Sleeping bags were unheard of, and instead blankets were rolled with newspaper for insulation. "Rain soaked canoe trip on Au Sable," was the caption on the photograph at left. Below, Nancy O'Tool, wearing her Camp Maqua *T*-shirt, prepares vegetables and meat in a can for camp stew, which was slowly cooked over the fire. (Courtesy of Pat O'Tool.)

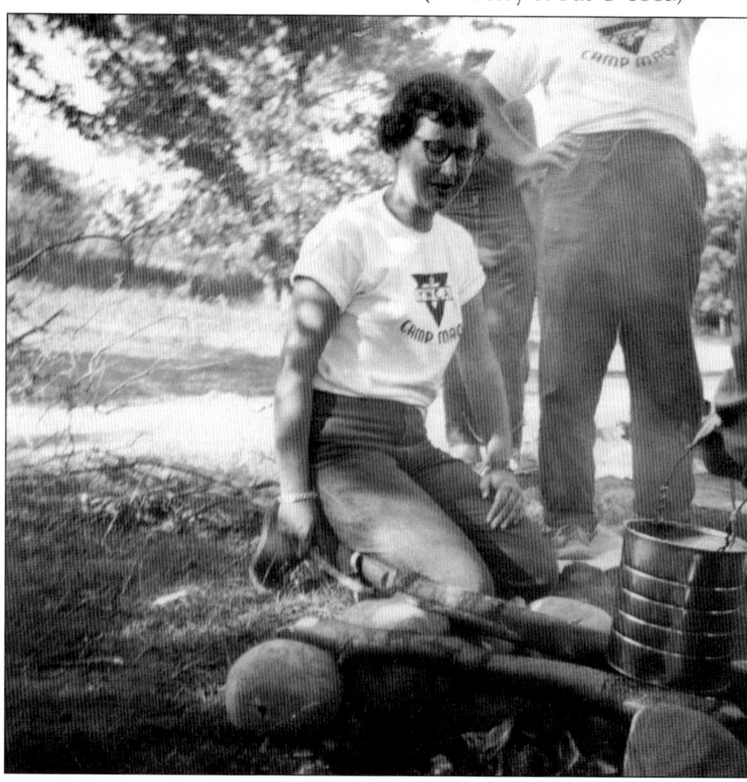

In the back left, Jane McKinley (left) and Barb Utter (right) await the truck that will pick them up, as friend Jody huddles under a blanket, fast asleep. These girls survived the heavy rains and tornado warnings on a three-day canoe trip, from Mio to Grayling, in 1957. Seeking shelter at lower ground on the banks of the Au Sable, they laughed as the container holding their "sanitary products" tipped and floated downriver. (Courtesy of Sue Utter Seelye.)

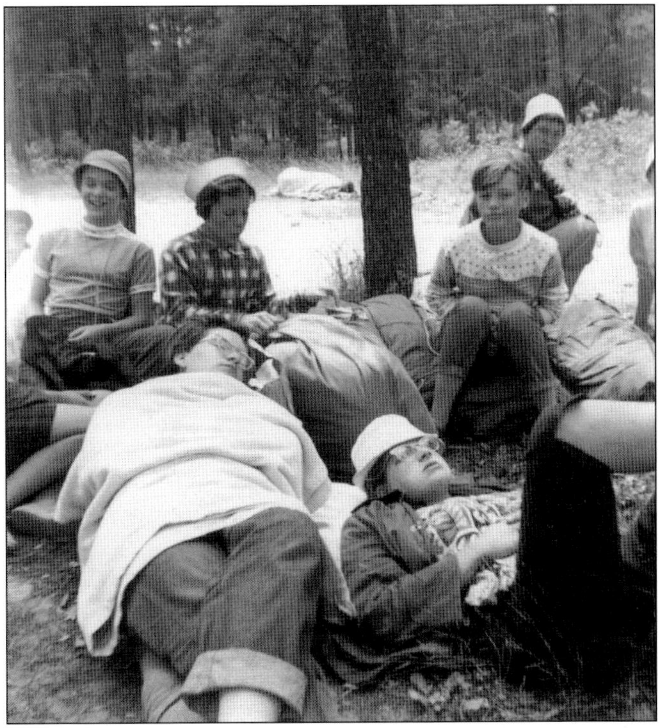

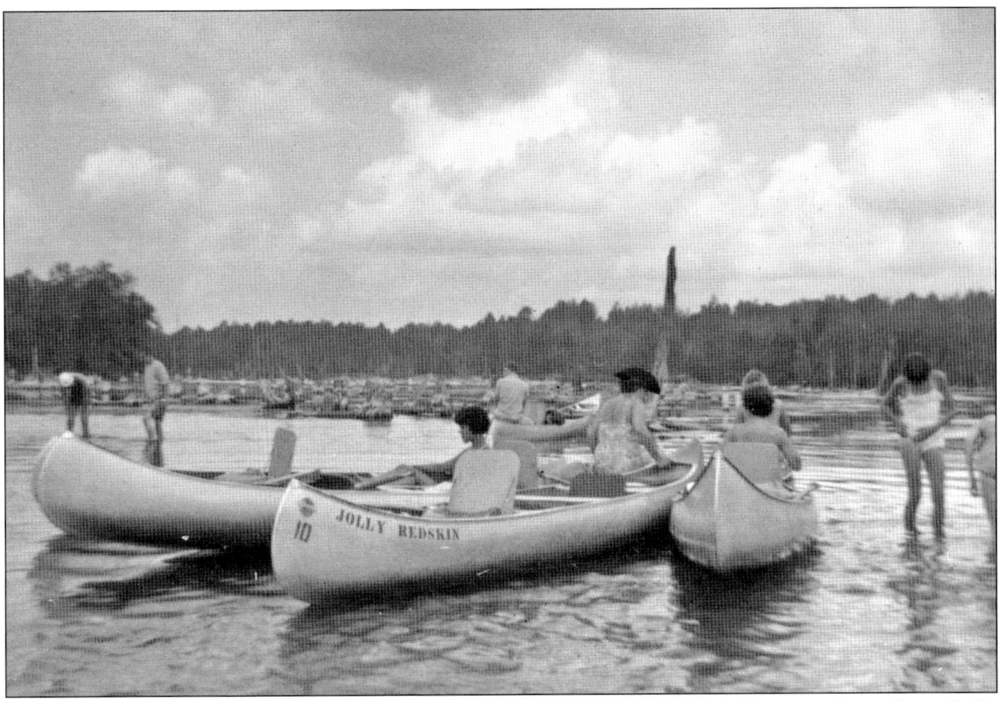

Qualified waterfront staff always accompanied the girls on their canoe trips up to Jewett's on Rifle River in Lupton, Rollways in Hale, and Jolly Redskins in Grayling. To keep track of one another, girls in one boat would chant, "High-low-eany-meany-i-ki-oo-chow-chow-pea-wa-wah," and the other boat would reply, "Eany-einy-ony-you-ho." (Courtesy of Ann Ward.)

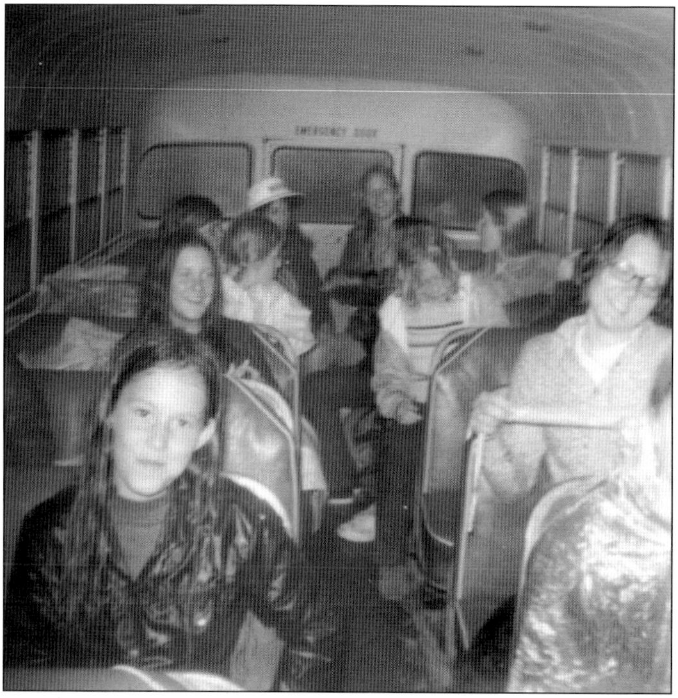

Sometimes, the ride to and from the canoe liveries was just as much fun as the overnight trips. The bus was loaded with grinning campers here in 1972, despite their wet clothing. Camper Andrea Gale (front left) has an un-dampened spirit as she poses for her friend's camera. (Courtesy of Shelley Harris.)

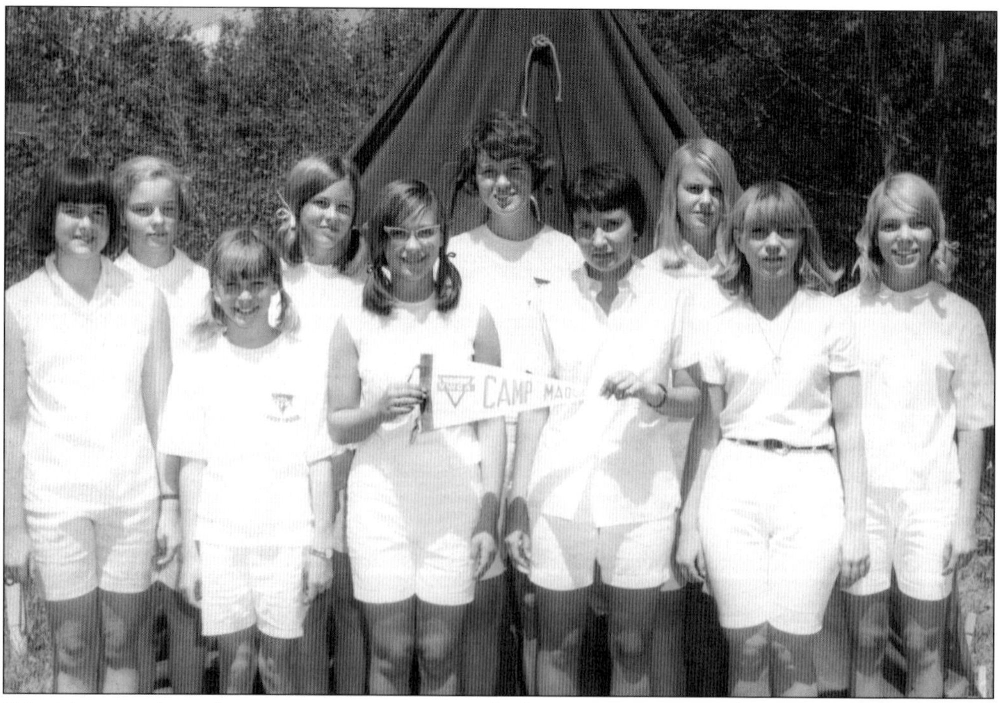

Primitive camping often meant eating soup made from greens or bits of Queen Anne's Lace and battling mosquitoes as the girls slept on the ground or in wooden platform tents. Seen here by their tent in the late 1960s are, from left to right, (front row) Jill Montbach, Jeanne Kiltie, unidentified, "Collie," and Kyle Higgs; and (back row) Barb Bozdech, Susan Kiltie, "Wendy," Debbie DeBoard, and Nancy Stark. (Courtesy of Susan Kiltie.)

An article appeared in the July 12, 1975, issue of the *Loon* about the "Primyland" or "Primy" primitive camping and the girls who backpacked to Alcona Dam Pond. M. Foss, A. Falvey, M. Moore, J. Bernard, S. Vater, and Beth Hickner (pictured) had good intentions of going to bed early the night before but stayed up until 1:00 a.m. trying to remember the lyrics to Beth's favorite song. (Courtesy of Amy Johns-Ikler.)

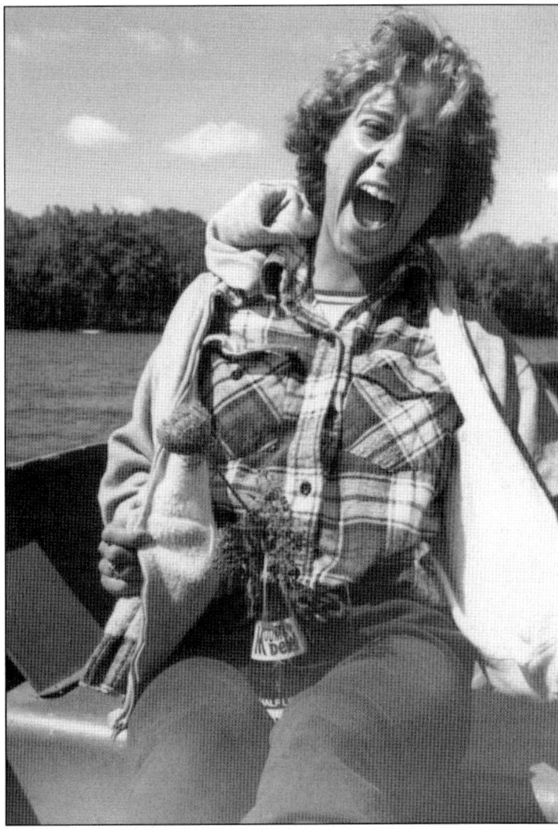

In 1972, Priscilla Johns had an idea to paint a racing stripe on the new outhouse in primitive, which the girls cleaned daily and kept "fly-tight" with rocks and sand. Pictured from left to right are, (first row) Kim Peck, Karen Magidsohn, Marti Myman, Sue Prieskorn, and Diane Miller; and (second row) Pam Hartz, Annette Prankienas, Maggie Ward, B.J. Falvey, and Cindy Smith. (Courtesy of YWCA Great Lakes Bay Region.)

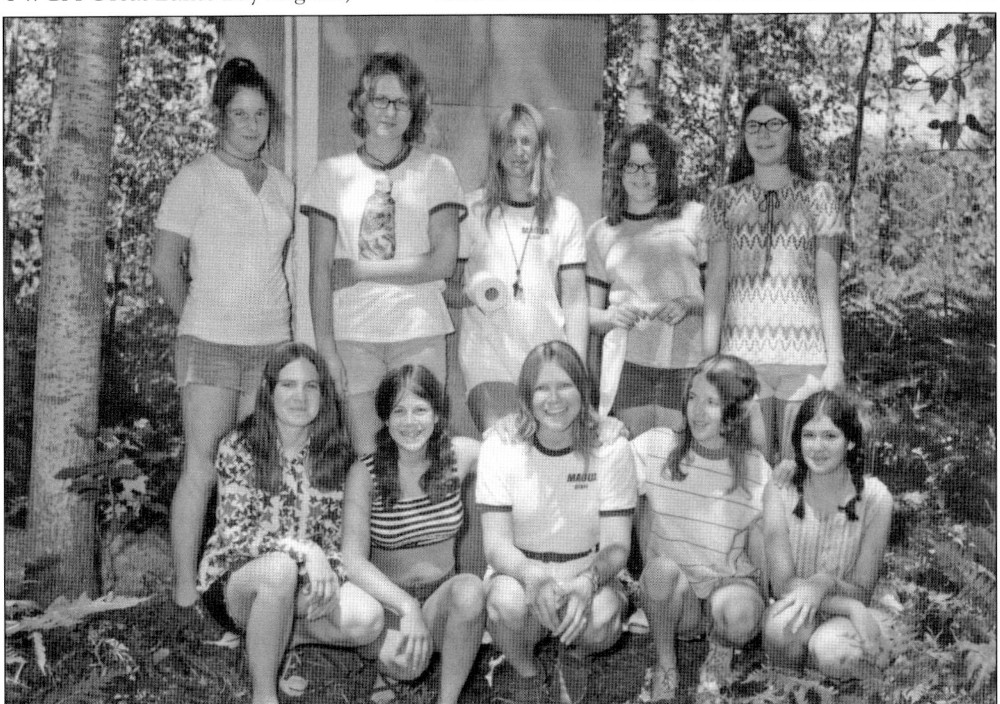

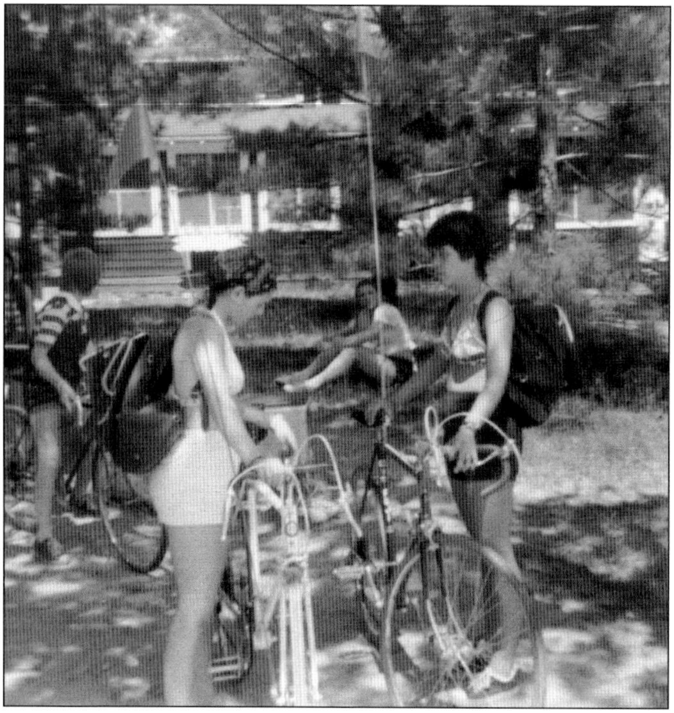

Carol Hulett, camp health director in 1974, snapped this photograph as Pam Hartz (front left), Mary Bent (front right), and "Jr." left with three more girls on a 40-mile circular bike tour. Spending the night in pup tents, they cooked over an open fire, ate pack lunches, and rode the Rifle River campground trails before returning on the third day with only scraped knees, sunburns, and memories. (Courtesy of Carol Hulett.)

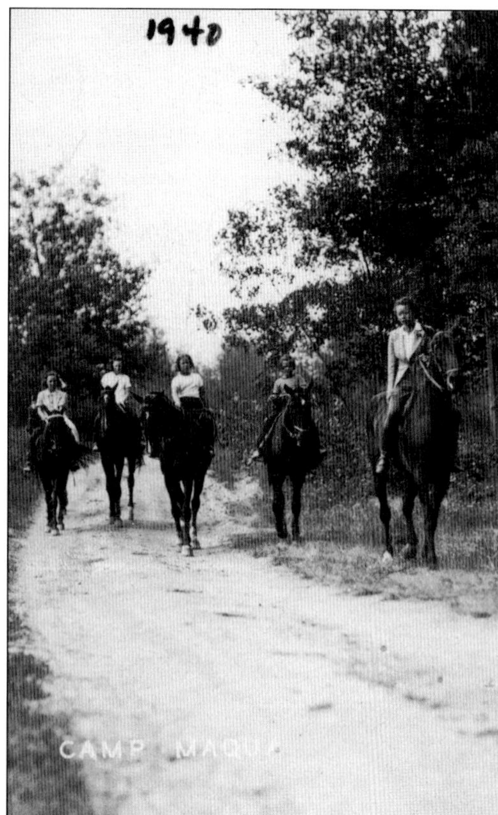

Equitation, or the practice of horsemanship, was first offered in 1934. In the 1940s, the girls would tie a towel at the end of their bunk beds so the counselors would wake them early to ride. Five girls are seen here trail riding in 1940. They would pluck at the wild raspberry and thimbleberry bushes as they rode and pop the berries into their mouths. (Courtesy of YWCA Great Lakes Bay Region.)

From 1947 to 1970, the Webb family rented horses to the camp and were involved in the instruction and caretaking programs. Kay's scrapbooks were filled with letters from "horse crazy" girls, and her family later developed such lasting friendships with campers that they received invitations for college visits and weddings. Mert Webb is shown here with Peanuts, Gyp, Salt, and Gay. (Courtesy of Sascha Immerman.)

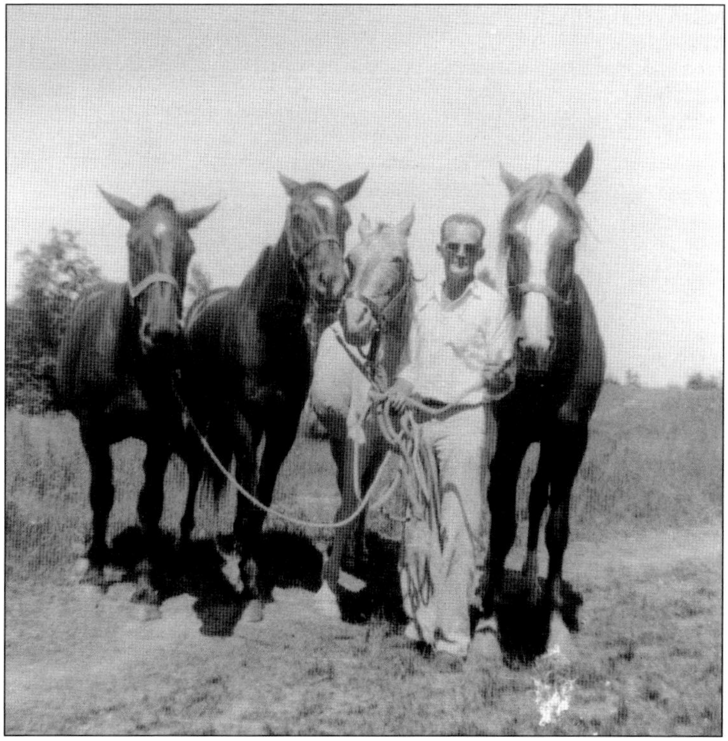

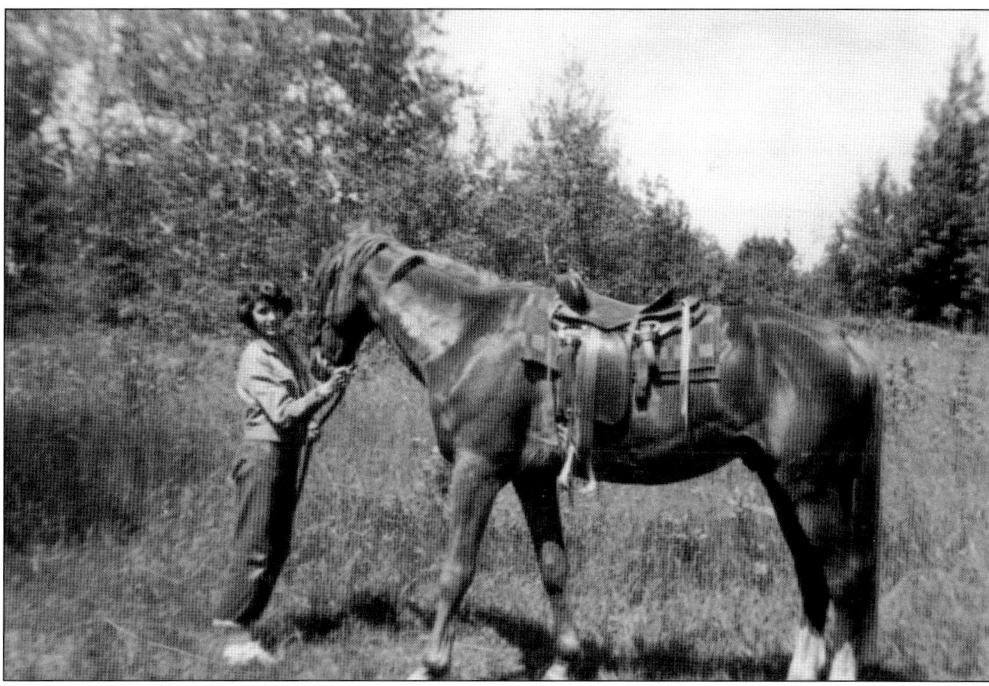

Marsha, like so many campers, began riding as a young girl. Her first riding experience at camp was frightening, as her horse took off with her into a meadow. She developed a passion for riding and stowed some horse manure in her suitcase to hide in her dresser drawer at home until her mother discovered it. Marsha is shown here with Gay in the 1950s. (Courtesy of Sascha Immerman.)

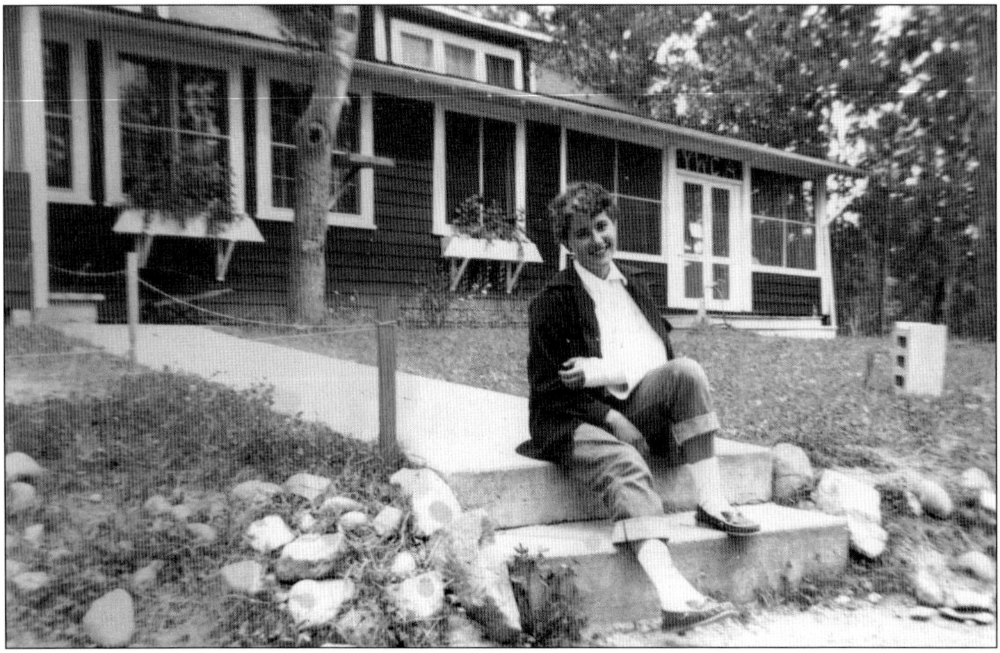

While racing with one of the stable boys in 1952, Marsha's cinch and saddle broke. "One horse plus one cantor equals one broken arm," stated an article in the *Loon*. Refusing to go home, she continued to instruct with a broken arm, teaching "giddy-up-and-go horseback skills." With a smile and her arm in a sling, Marsha poses on the lodge steps. (Courtesy of Sascha Immerman.)

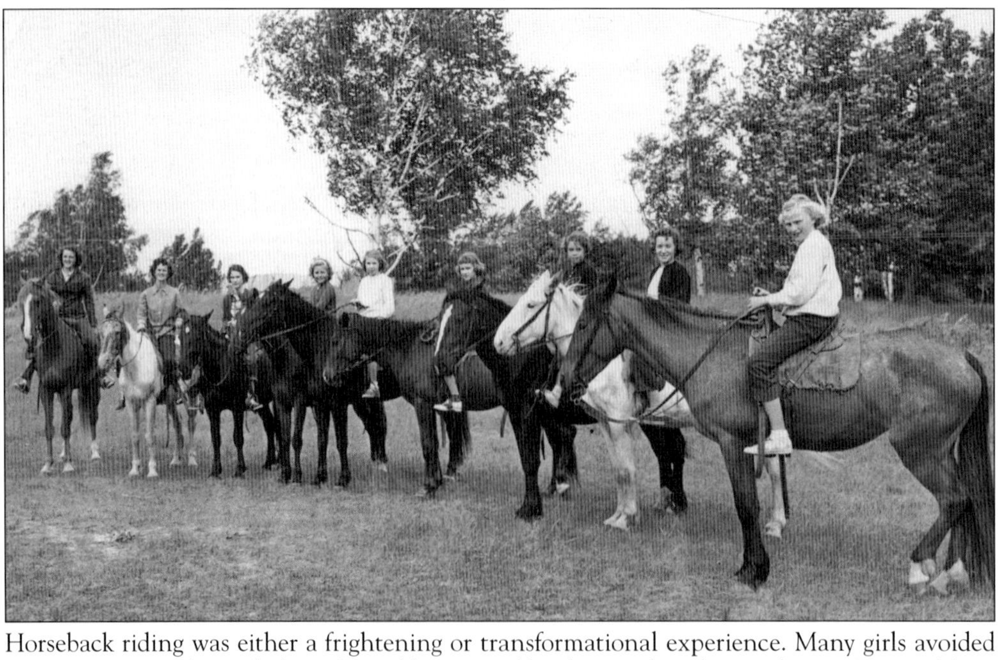

Horseback riding was either a frightening or transformational experience. Many girls avoided other activities to better hide in the stable area and be close to their favorite horses. Pictured from left to right, riding instructors Bea Pursell and Kay Webb accompany Mary Ann Michaels, Janet Fischer, Karen Writh, Carolyn Hartz, Susie Ruterbusch, Margo Horowitz, and Alice Atages on a ride in 1950. (Courtesy of YWCA Great Lakes Bay Region.)

Camp registration declined in the years with no riding instruction. Ex-camper Mary Lou Goggin returned as the riding director in 1959. Seen here in her riding ring, giving instruction on fundamentals, Mary Lou (second from left) joked that with five classes and eight girls in each class, the horses' names were easier to recall. (Courtesy of YWCA Great Lakes Bay Region.)

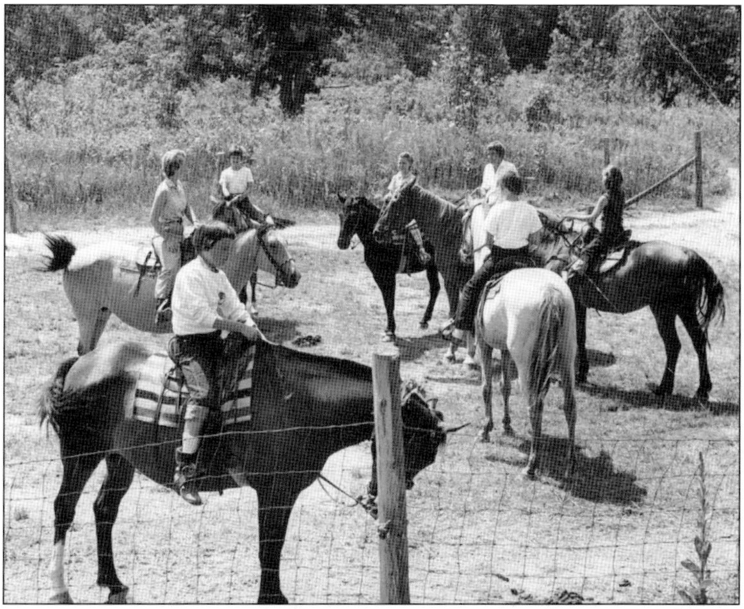

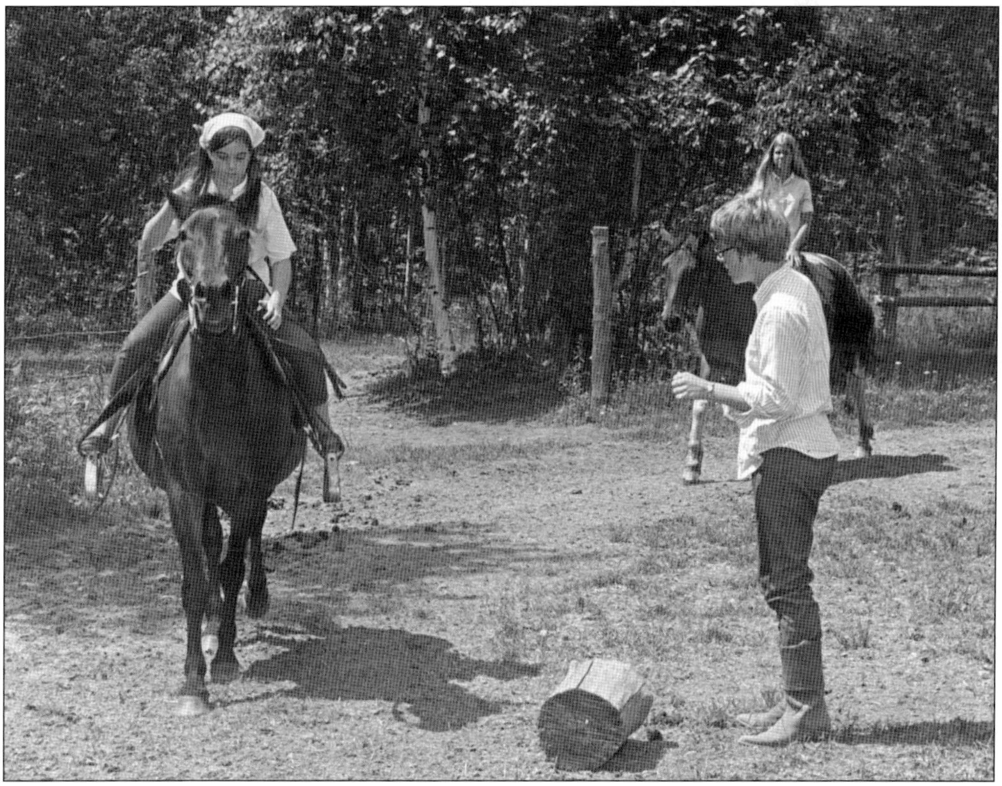

Brooke Harland, director of riding in 1969, liked to develop a rider's confidence and lessen her fears in an introductory class that did not feature a horse. Beginners had morning classes when the horses were more cooperative, intermediate riders moved quickly through lessons to trotting, and advanced classes rode the trails and steeper paths near Explorer's Hill. (Courtesy of YWCA Great Lakes Bay Region.)

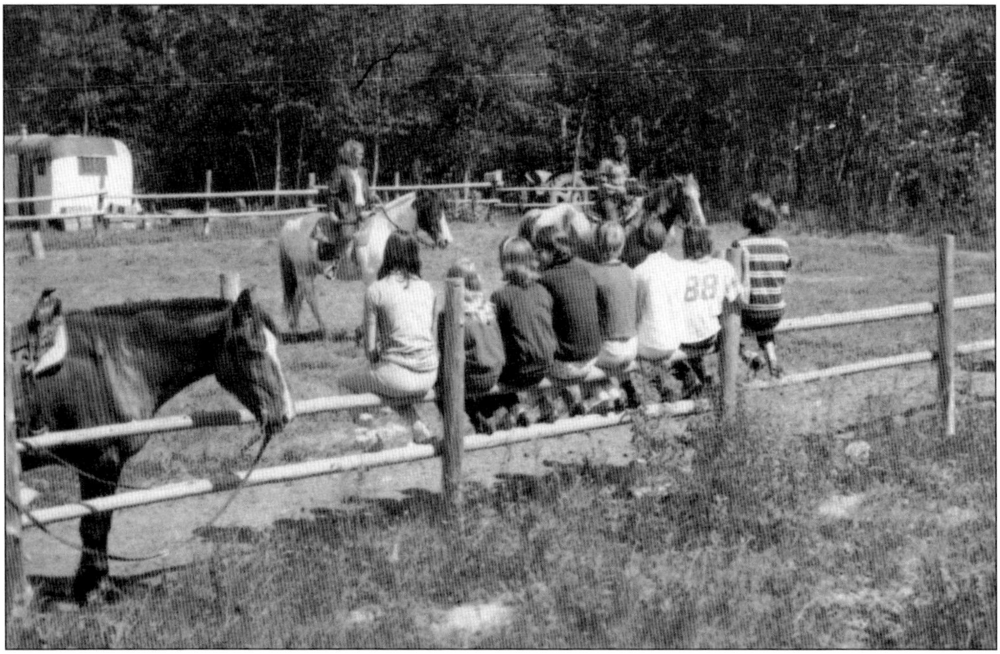

"We had among this year's string: 2 biters, 4 kickers, 3 rearers, 1 bucker, 2 fence pullers, 2 fence climbers—each horse had at least one of these faults, some more than one," wrote Carol Wahl in the 1974 riding report about her "four rank horses with sore feet, hard mouths and ill tempers." Two tame horses are shown in the corral in this undated photograph. (Courtesy of YWCA Great Lakes Bay Region.)

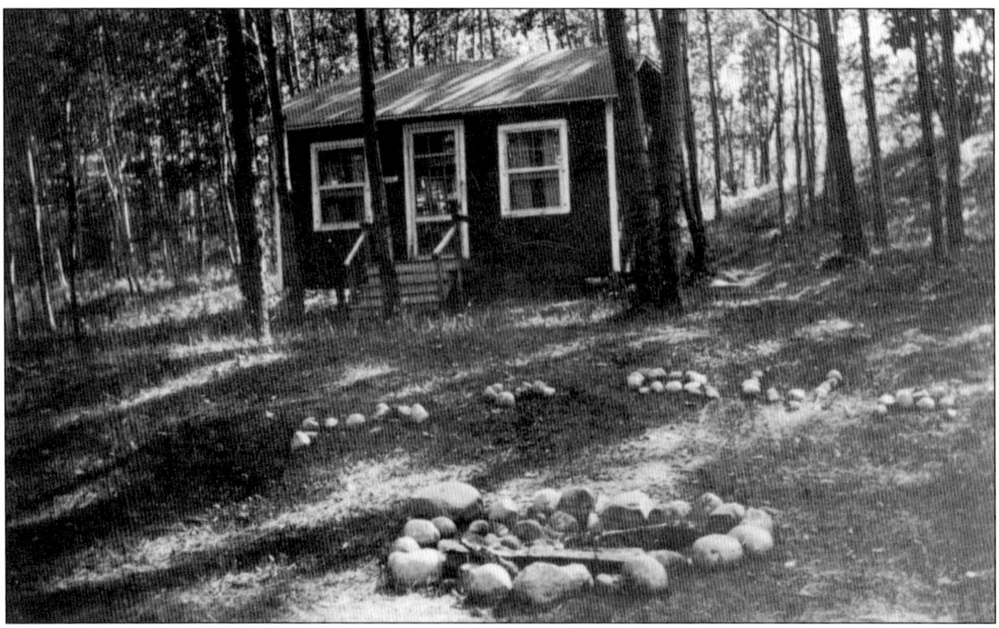

Situated behind the boathouse, near the campfire pit, the "handicraft" hut was built in 1927. A front-entry door with six screened windows allowed great ventilation for the girl's projects. A stone fireplace on the back wall was great for keeping warm on cooler days and added coziness to this small hut. (Courtesy of YWCA Great Lakes Bay Region.)

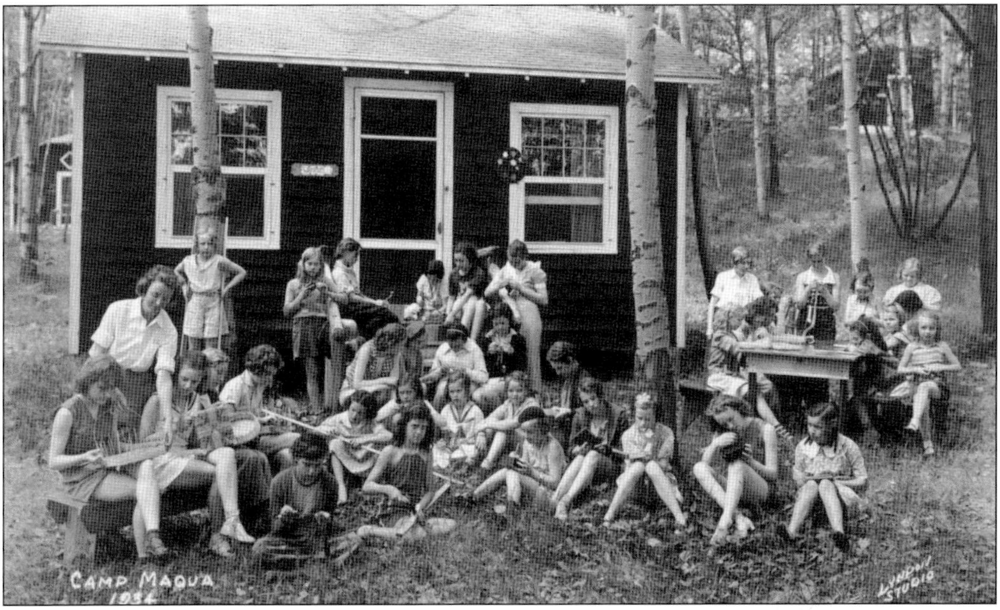

The photograph above, from 1934, shows the front of the craft hut and a few signs on the exterior, including "Wampum" by the door and an artist's palette by the window. The instructor on the left poses with several classes involved in their basket weaving, whittling, and craft boxes. Sleep huts can be seen in the background on both sides of the building. The photograph below, from 1936, shows the girls engaged in puppet making, burlap embroidery, weaving, and the construction of small stools. A 1936 article by Alice Knepper names a number of the girls: Donna Olson, Patricia Young, Natalie Seaholm, Glenna Asher, Nancy Walker, Romaine Schmidt, Alice Domle, Sister Convery, Peggy Chamberlain, Dorothy Land, Barbara Thurber, Nancy Olfs, Dorothy Johnson, Virginia Fellowes, Celia Pollard, Marion Jerome, and Catherine Williams. (Courtesy of YWCA Great Lakes Bay Region.)

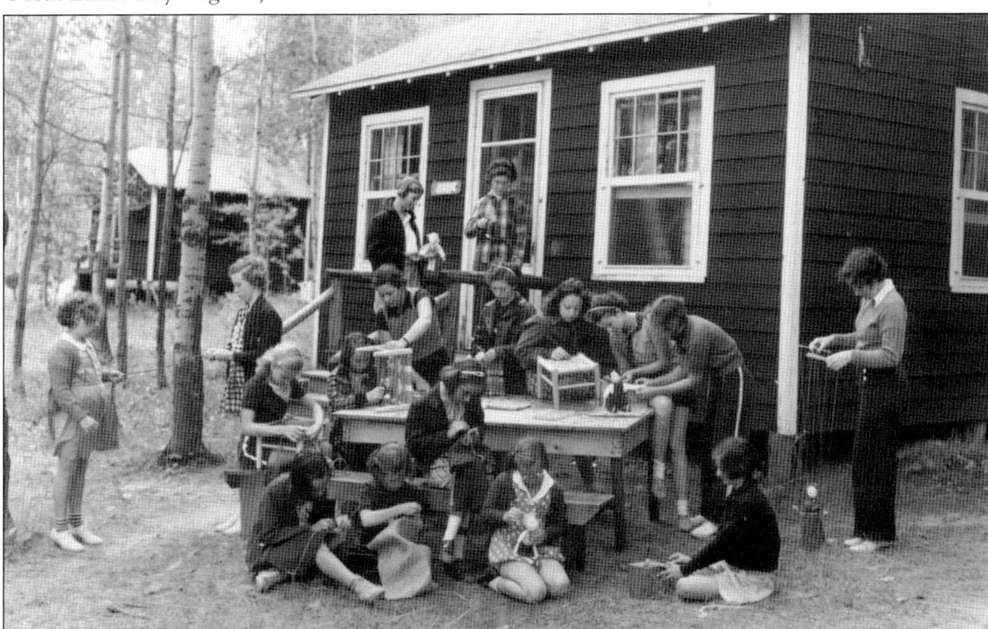

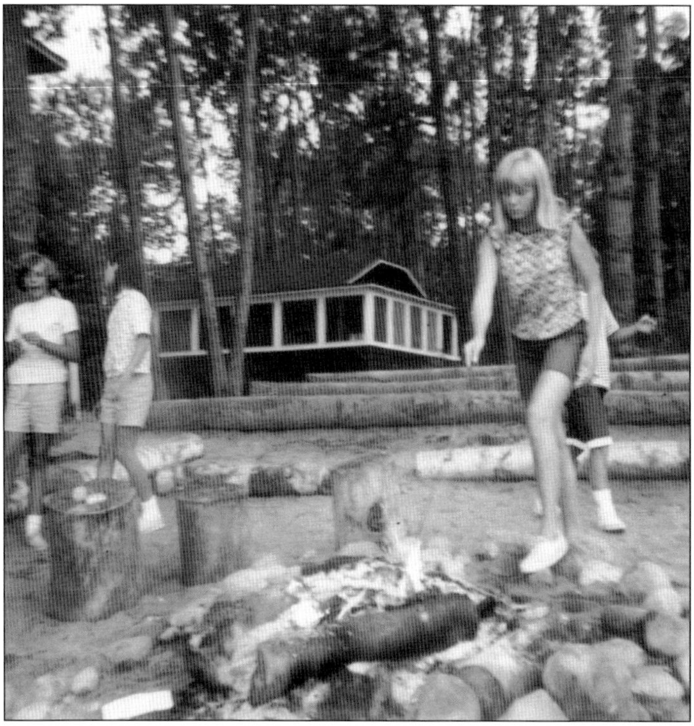

Camp committee notes from October 1936 mentioned the need for a screened porch on the arts and crafts hut, as its activities had become so popular that more room was needed. This image from 1966, with junior counselor "Squirt," shows the wraparound porch on two sides, with the new entrance on the left. (Courtesy of Valerie Monto Richardson.)

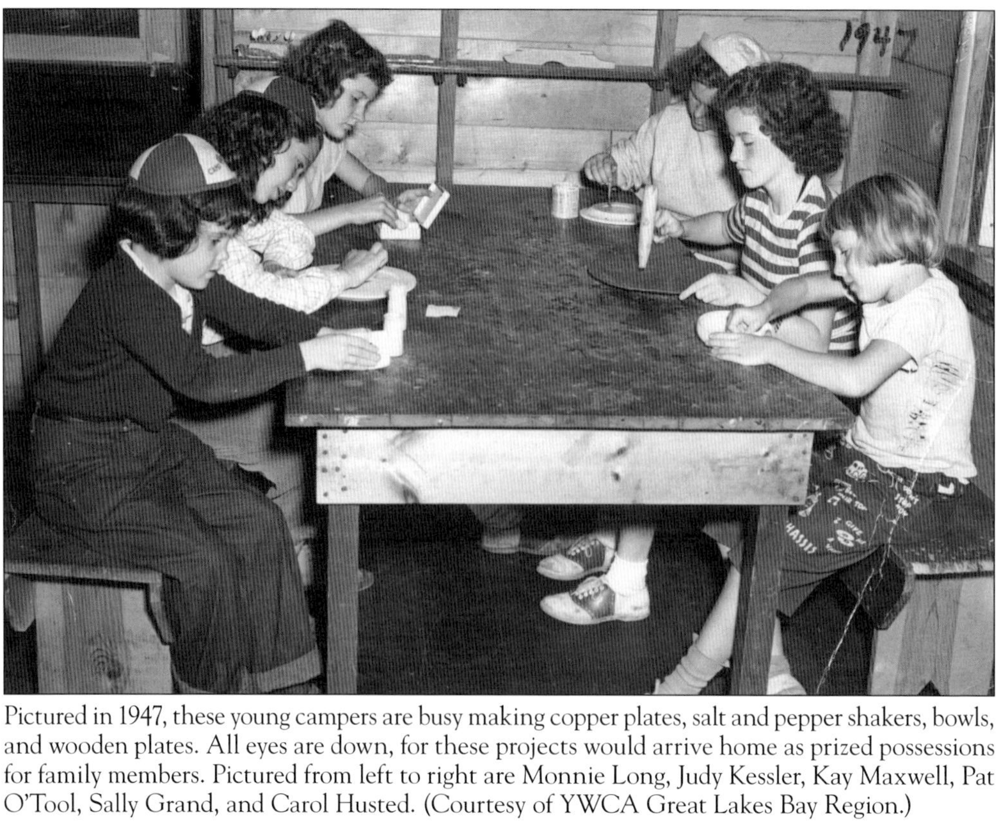

Pictured in 1947, these young campers are busy making copper plates, salt and pepper shakers, bowls, and wooden plates. All eyes are down, for these projects would arrive home as prized possessions for family members. Pictured from left to right are Monnie Long, Judy Kessler, Kay Maxwell, Pat O'Tool, Sally Grand, and Carol Husted. (Courtesy of YWCA Great Lakes Bay Region.)

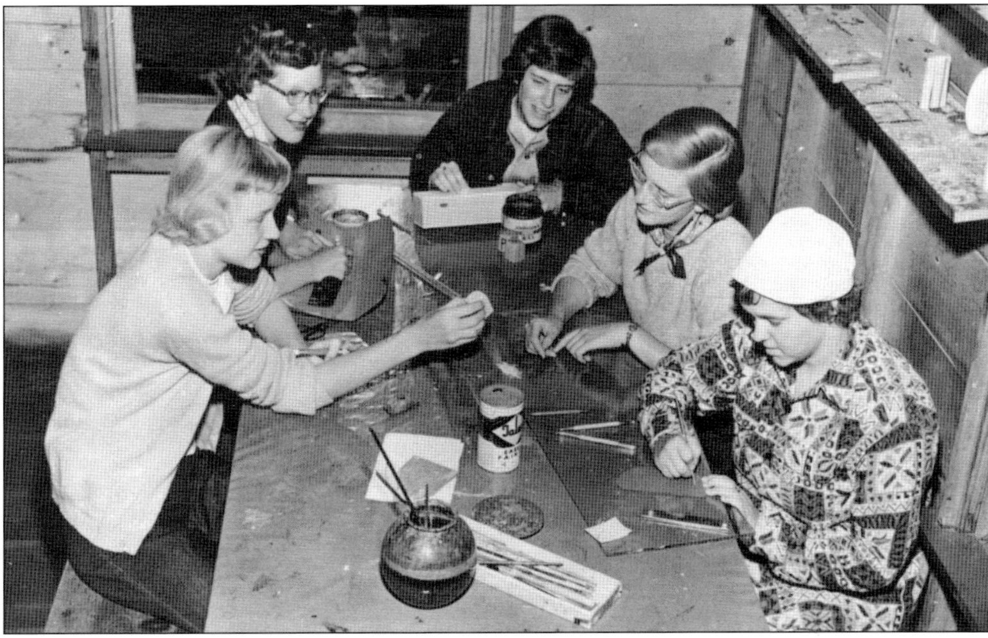

Pat O'Tool was the oldest of the four girls in her family. She sent this postcard home in July 1951, with her sister Nancy and herself in the scene. Pat loved arts and crafts, which influenced her decision to become an art teacher. Working diligently on their projects are, from left to right, Pat Parsons, Nancy O'Tool, Mary Jane Keschmer, Vicki Smukal, and Pat O'Tool. (Courtesy of Pat O'Tool Smith.)

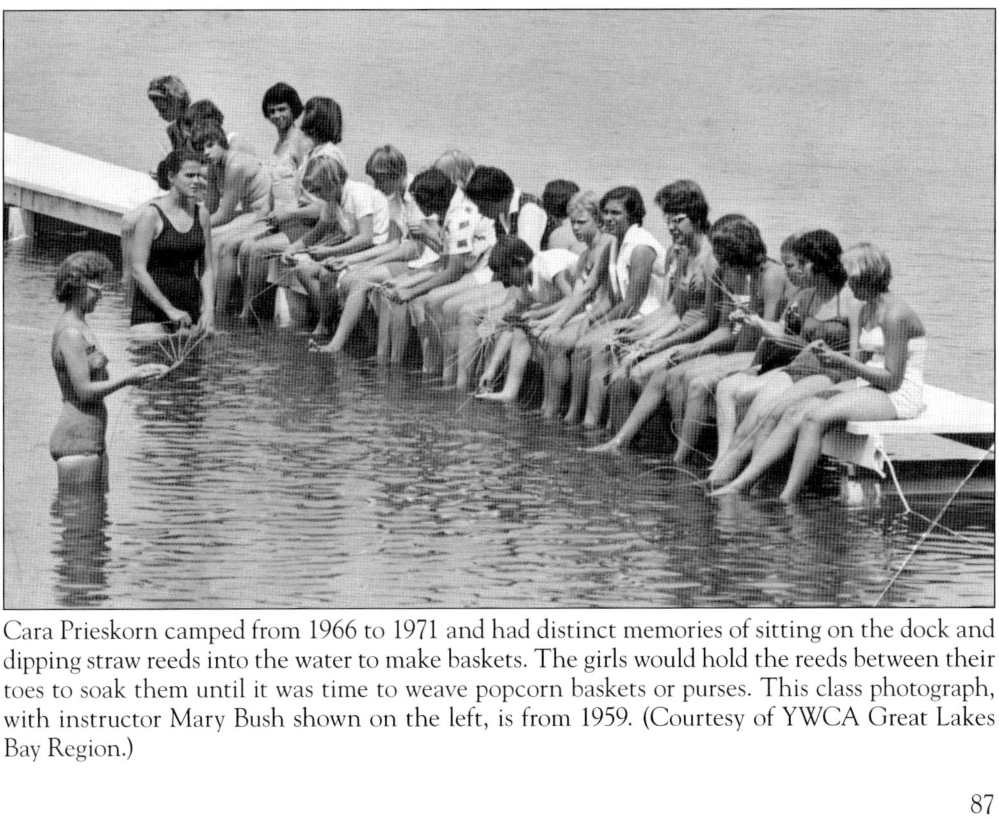

Cara Prieskorn camped from 1966 to 1971 and had distinct memories of sitting on the dock and dipping straw reeds into the water to make baskets. The girls would hold the reeds between their toes to soak them until it was time to weave popcorn baskets or purses. This class photograph, with instructor Mary Bush shown on the left, is from 1959. (Courtesy of YWCA Great Lakes Bay Region.)

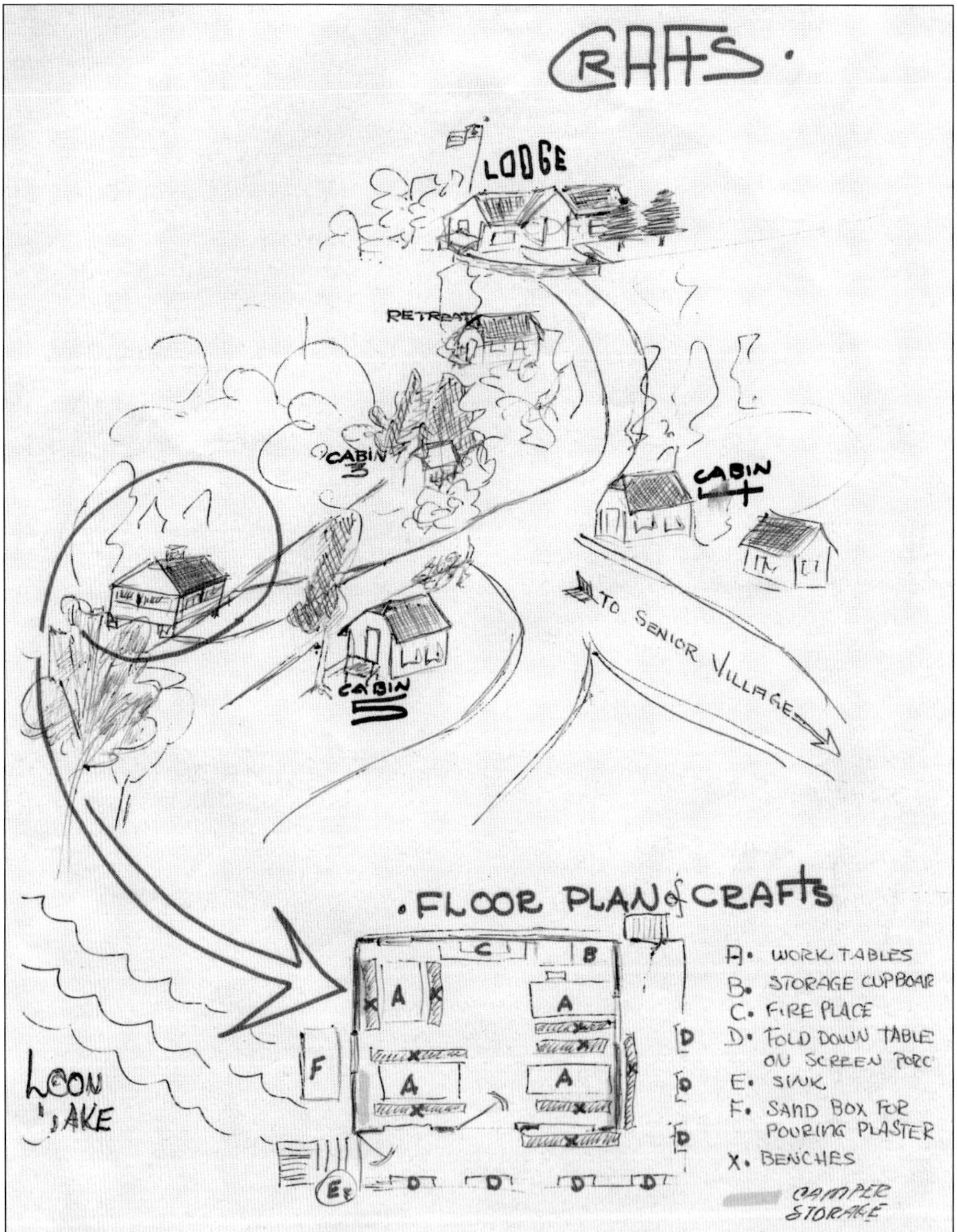

Emogene Host was the crafts director in 1969 and illustrated a diagram of the craft hut. She loved that it had a fireplace, and on cool days she removed the kindling and firewood from beneath the hut and built a fire. A sand box sat outside for pouring plaster, and her "Keep Maqua Clean" barrel held all craft scraps and broken pieces. Incorporating nature into her projects, she scheduled her groups by age and met with them two to three times a week. The older girls, who loved to make items for themselves as opposed to their families, were allowed to fire their projects and utilize tools for soldering and lacquer applications. Decoupage, copper enameling, and leather friendship bracelets were all popular that summer. (Courtesy of YWCA Great Lakes Bay Region.)

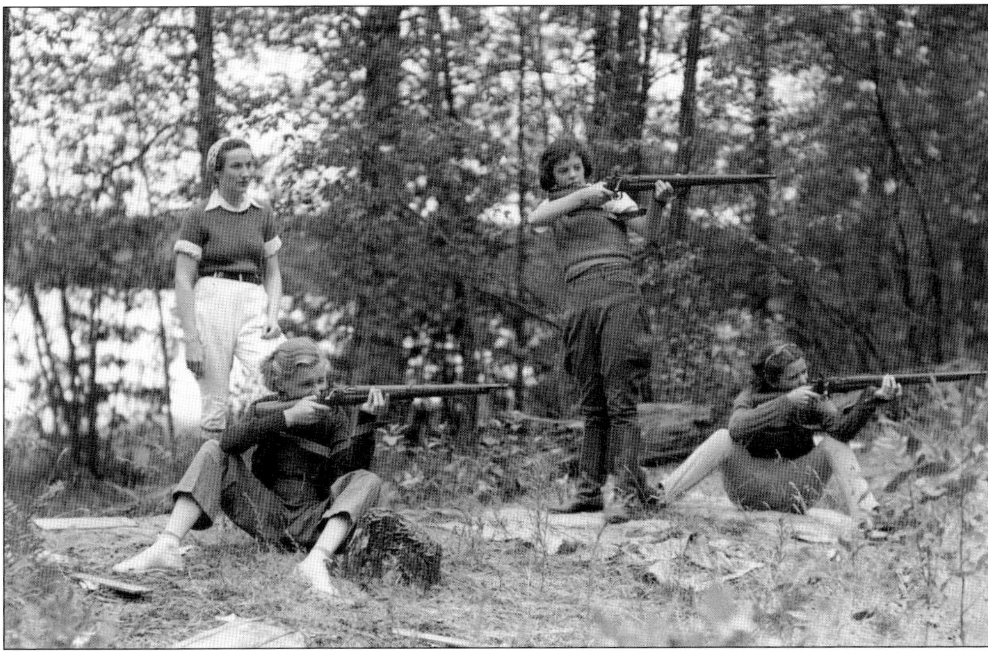

Riflery instructor Helen Koth stands at left with three students who appear to be quite close to the lake during their practice in this c. 1938 postcard. Camp notes do not indicate when riflery was offered as an activity, but many girls developed a lifelong passion for shooting after their first classes at camp. (Courtesy of YWCA Great Lakes Bay Region.)

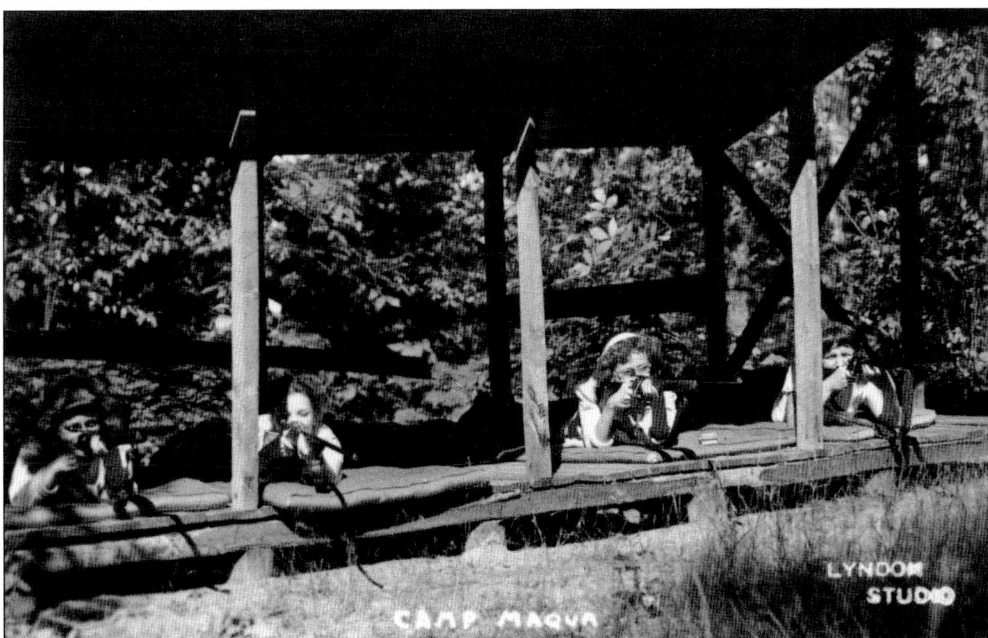

Girls 12 and older were able to take riflery, and many returned home to surprise parents with awards and marksmanship certificates. Tally Cone, a 1960s camper, never knew she could shoot a rifle until camp. This postcard from 1946 illustrates one of the shooting positions, as four girls take aim from mattresses in the lean-to. (Courtesy of Pat O'Tool Smith.)

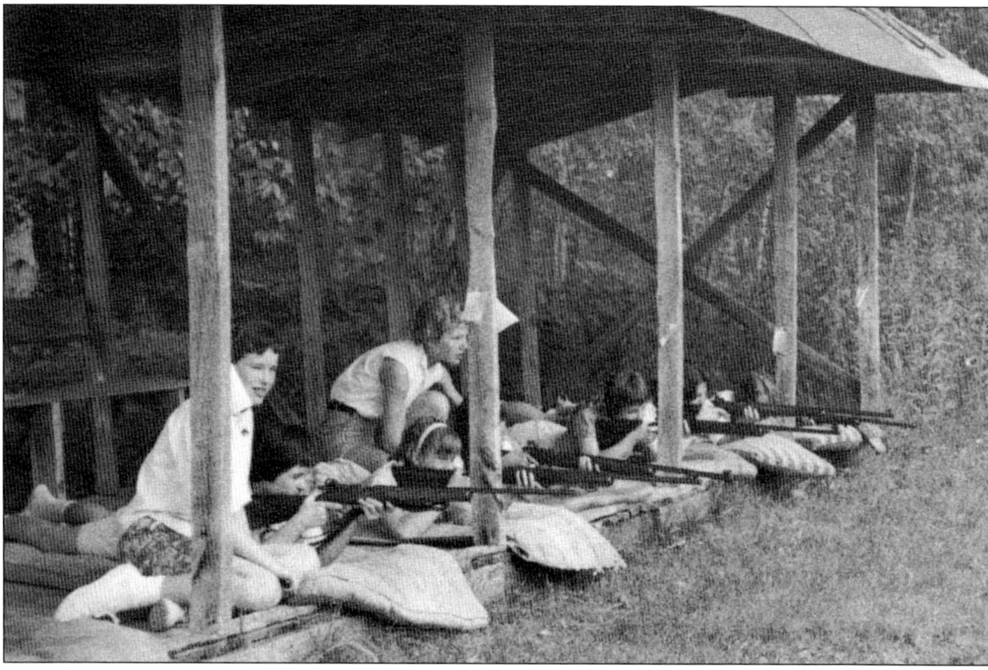

In 1950, the lean-to, made from car parts, was enlarged and moved to a new location away from the living quarters. The guns were stored in a locked cabinet, and the cost of rounds was charged to girls' accounts. The first day was spent on safety, and since the range was close to the horse trails, a red flag was installed to acknowledge shooting was in progress. Firing ceased as riders passed. This image dates from 1960. (Courtesy of YWCA Great Lakes Bay Region.)

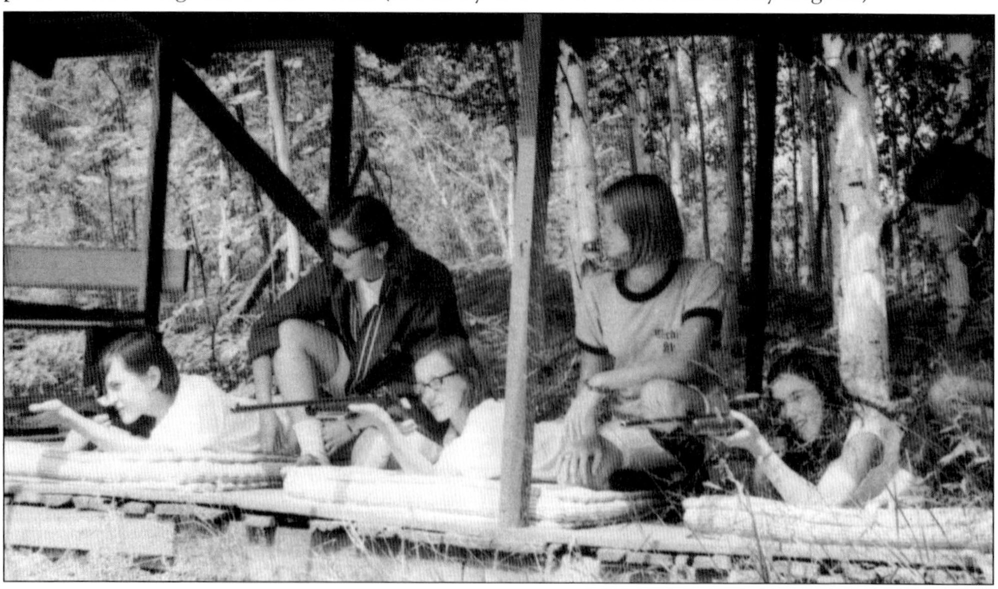

The Kiltie sisters were fond of bird hunting with their father, but Susan credited camp for her continued interest in riflery. Despite the mosquitoes, she earned her badges and now runs tournaments for the Boy Scouts in Detroit. Pictured on the range in 1968 are, from left to right, unknown, instructor Sue Wiegand, unknown, Jeanne Kiltie, and her friend Julie Richardson. (Courtesy of YWCA Great Lakes Bay Region.)

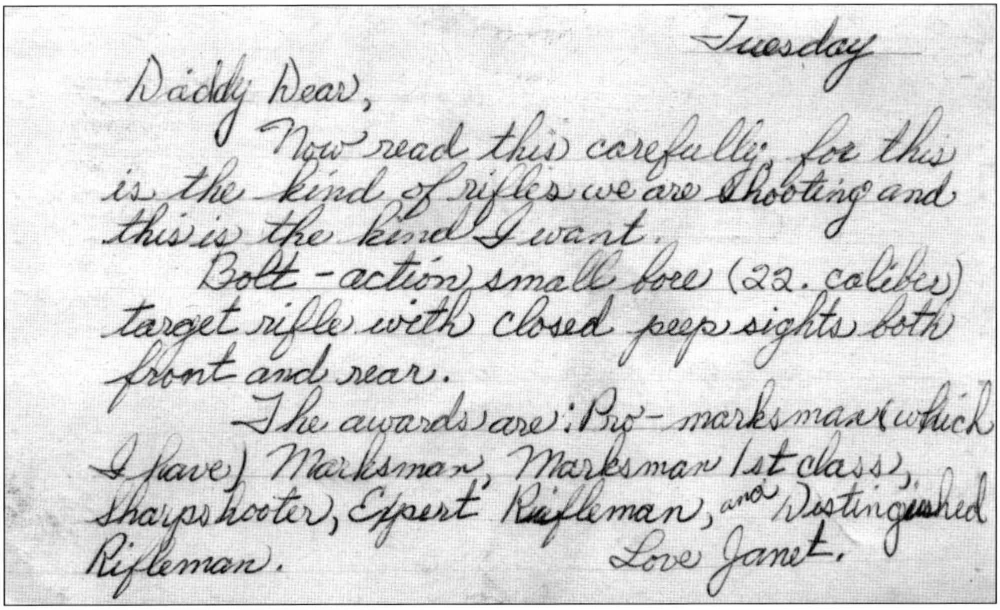

Tuesday

Daddy Dear,

Now read this carefully for this is the kind of rifles we are shooting and this is the kind I want.

Bolt-action small bore (22. caliber) target rifle with closed peep sights both front and rear.

The awards are: Pro-marksman (which I have) Marksman, Marksman 1st class, Sharpshooter, Expert Rifleman, and Distinguished Rifleman.

Love Janet.

Much to her father's delight, Janet Dixon took riflery at camp and excelled. The class was connected to the National Rifle Association, which was highly respected for gun safety and responsibility. Janet was an only child, with a father who was a hunter and believed she should learn everything about firearms. She admitted that she took the class to please him and out of curiosity, but she earned three marksman badges her second year at camp and gained the highest score of the summer of 1952. For the girl who loved riflery, the score of 44 was better than any bull's-eye! Her delightful postcard, with a request for a specific gun, convinced her dad to buy her the gun for her 13th birthday, which did not please her mom. Janet saved all of her badges. (Courtesy of Janet Dixon.)

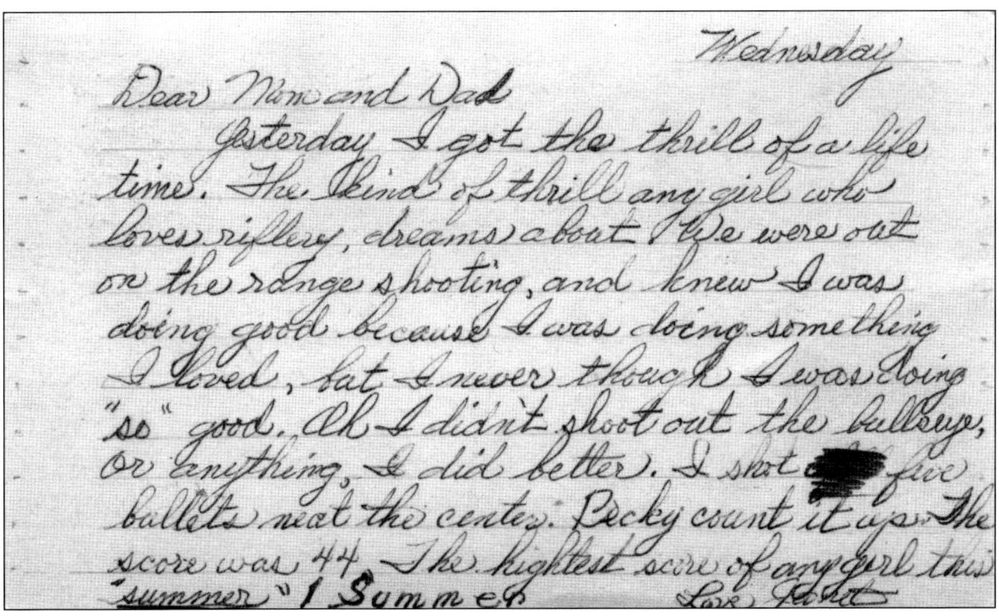

Wednesday

Dear Mom and Dad

Yesterday I got the thrill of a life time. The kind of thrill any girl who loves riflery, dreams about. We were out on the range shooting, and knew I was doing good because I was doing something I loved, but I never though I was doing "so" good. Oh I didn't shoot out the bullseye, or anything, I did better. I shot [illegible] five bullets near the center. Becky count it up. The score was 44. The highest score of any girl this "summer" 1 Summer.

Love Janet

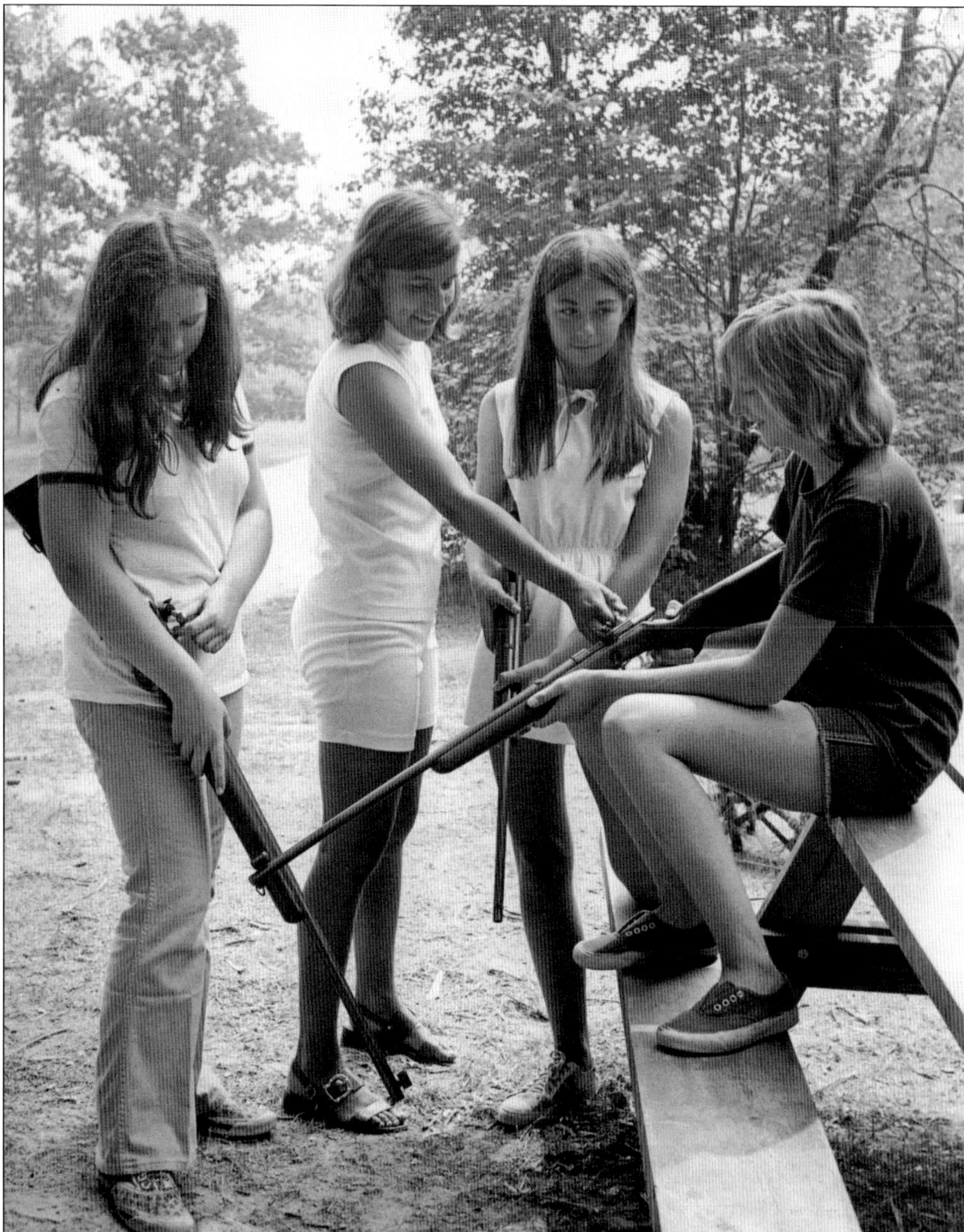

Sharon Williams, second from left, was the best in her coed riflery instruction class when the "Y" sent her to learn the basics—despite her inexperience with a gun. A counselor for one year and sports director for two, she is seen here with fellow instructor Chris "Chops" Lambert (seated) in the late 1960s offering a riflery tip. "Ready on the left, ready on the right, fire, lay your guns down and go see your target," was her drill. "Chops" loved riflery and had learned on an old single-shot .22 rifle from her grandfather when she was fairly young. At college, she took a hunting safety class and enjoyed learning to shoot standing, sitting, and lying down. In her last year at camp, after a stint as the tennis and riflery instructor, she became the sports director. (Courtesy of YWCA Great Lakes Bay Region.)

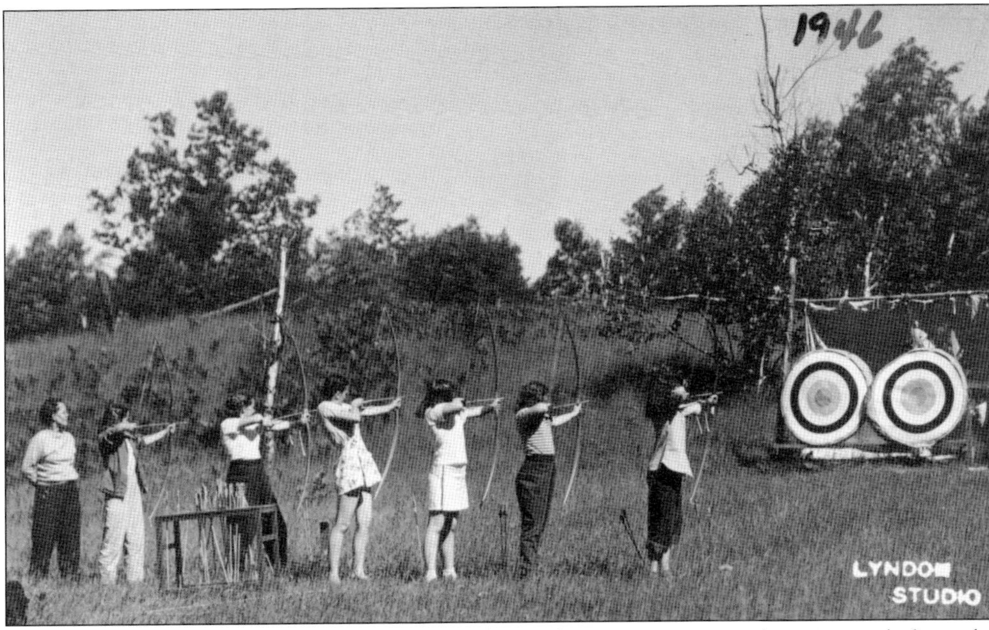

Early camp brochures from the 1920s did not list archery as an activity, but postcards from the 1940s show such classes in session. The rules were always explained on the first day, and girls had to be at least 12 in order to participate. The archery range was east of the lodge, and in later years a larger hill was constructed behind the targets for safety. Diplomas were awarded through the Camp Archery Association. (Courtesy of YWCA Great Lakes Nay Region.)

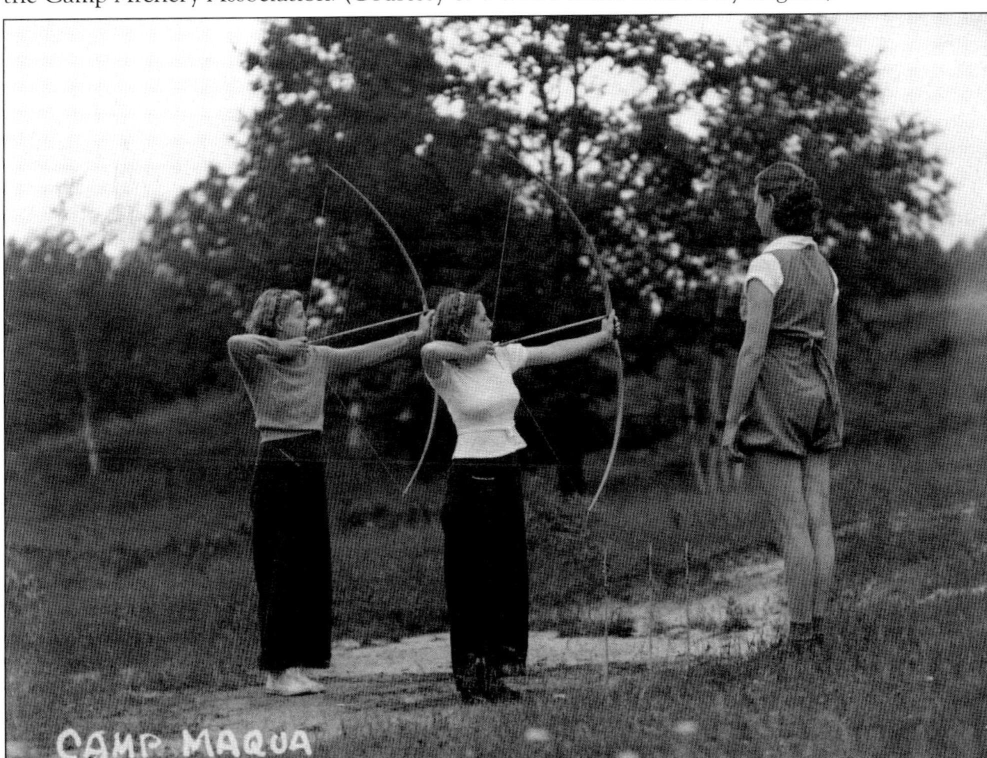

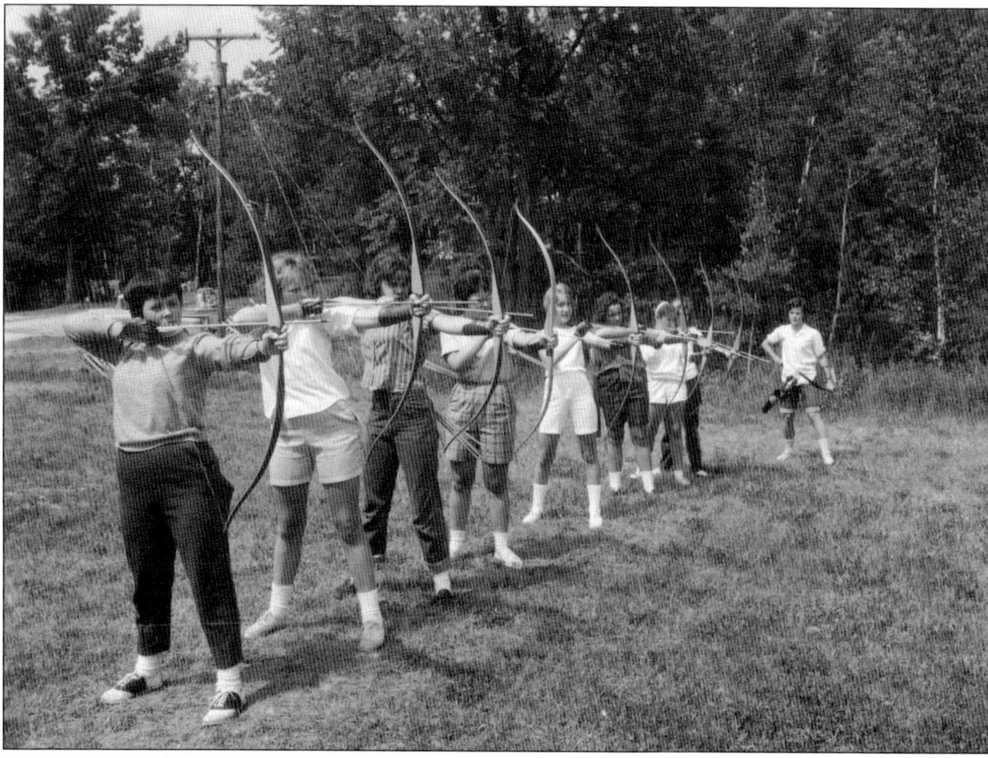

One edition of the *Loon* mentions archery as a "nationwide popular sport" and encourages campers to practice to become Robin Hood. Many of the girls had the desire but discovered that bruised forearms from improper form, poor vision or depth perception, and other issues kept them from hitting their targets. Others took their newfound skills and continued after camp. Two classes are featured in these images from 1961. (Courtesy of YWCA Great Lakes Bay Region.)

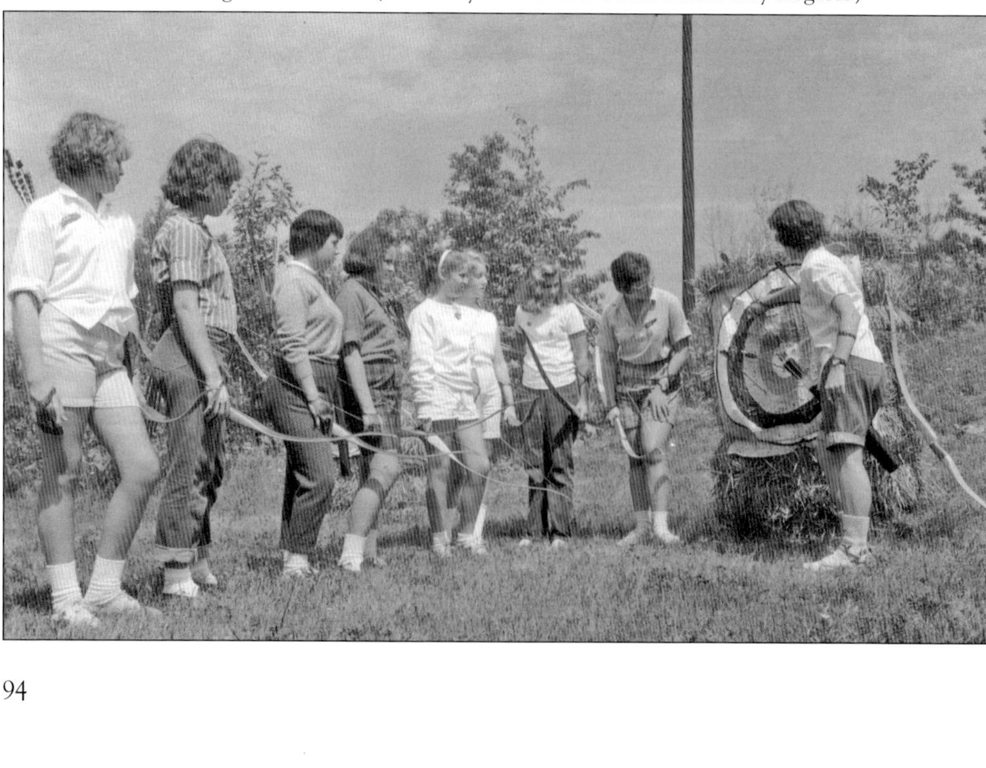

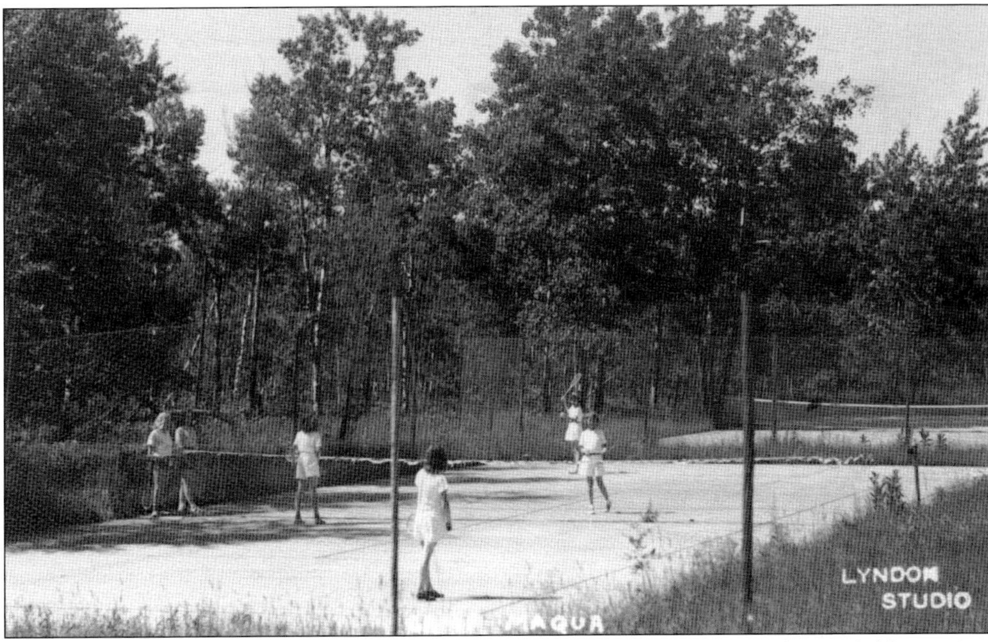

"The first ball was served over the new tennis court at Maqua by Miss Gertrude Wenfield, president of the Camp Maqua club, whose members financed the construction of the court, to Miss Marie Lemberger the Camp Director," states an article from the 1930s. The courts were "tilled, leveled off and grass was planted in black swamp dirt, which was used as a special covering." Dances had been scheduled every two weeks at the YMCA gym to raise the money to fund the court. It was later converted to an athletic field when the new cement courts were built in 1940. The tennis courts were also used for basketball, with backboards installed on each end. The postcard above is from 1946. The photograph below features Kikki Sekles, the tennis instructor in 1960, with her class. (Above, courtesy of Pat O'Tool Smith; below, YWCA Great Lakes Bay Region.)

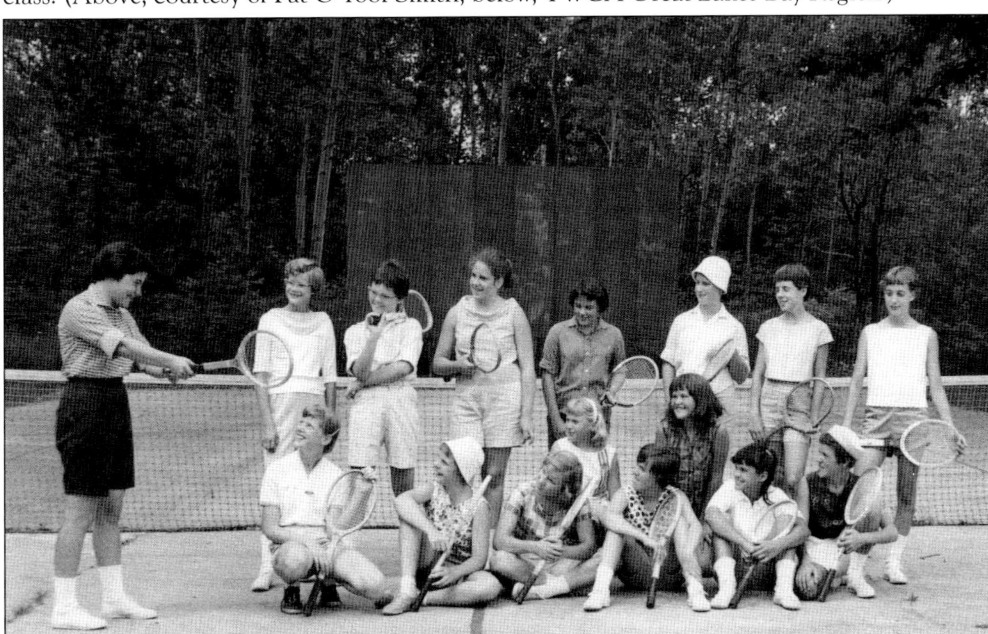

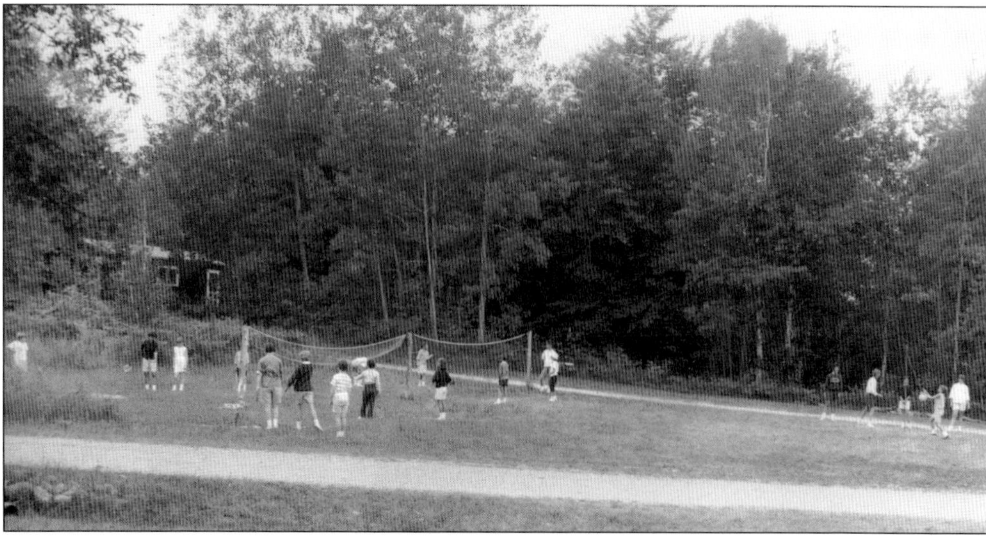

The tetherball and badminton activity areas were separated by the road, which led to the infirmary (seen in the background) in 1962. This area also served as a great spot for baseball. On the screened porch of the lodge, facing the lake, shuffleboard and ping-pong tournaments often took place—which were perfect for rainy days. (Courtesy of YWCA Great Lakes Bay Region.)

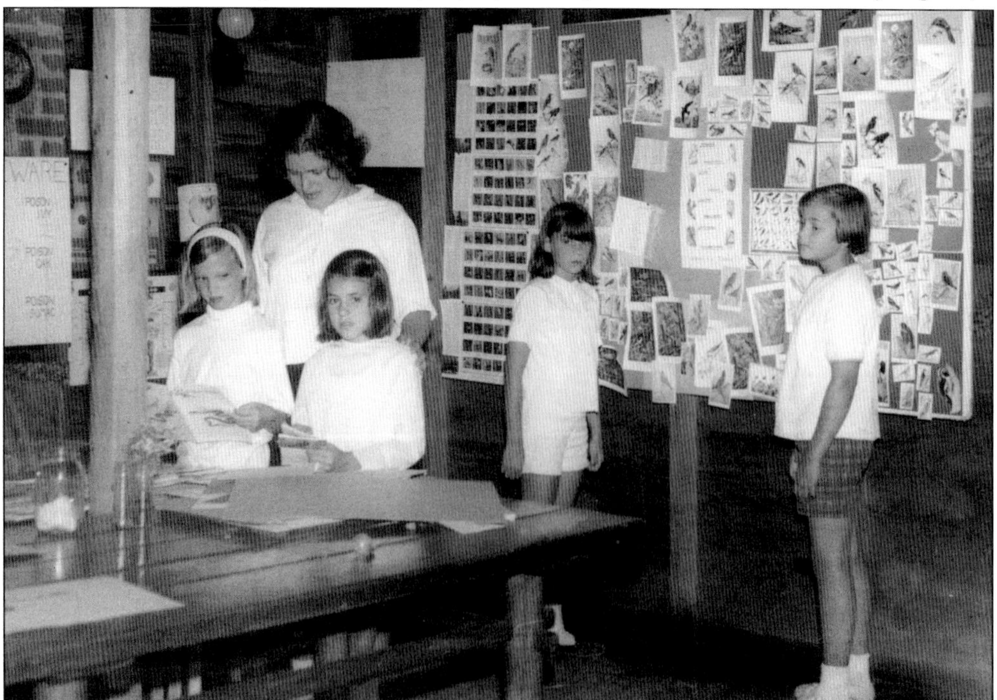

Dutton was home to the nature center for many years. This interior photograph of one of the workrooms was taken in 1965, with a nature class in session. Large cabinets and workrooms were home to nature books, butterfly collections, snakes, turtles, frogs, and snails. It was not uncommon to see bird's nests, pressed leaves, and charts for insect, bird, flower, animal, tree, and leaf identification. The upper room had extra sleeping quarters. (Courtesy of YWCA Great Lakes Bay Region.)

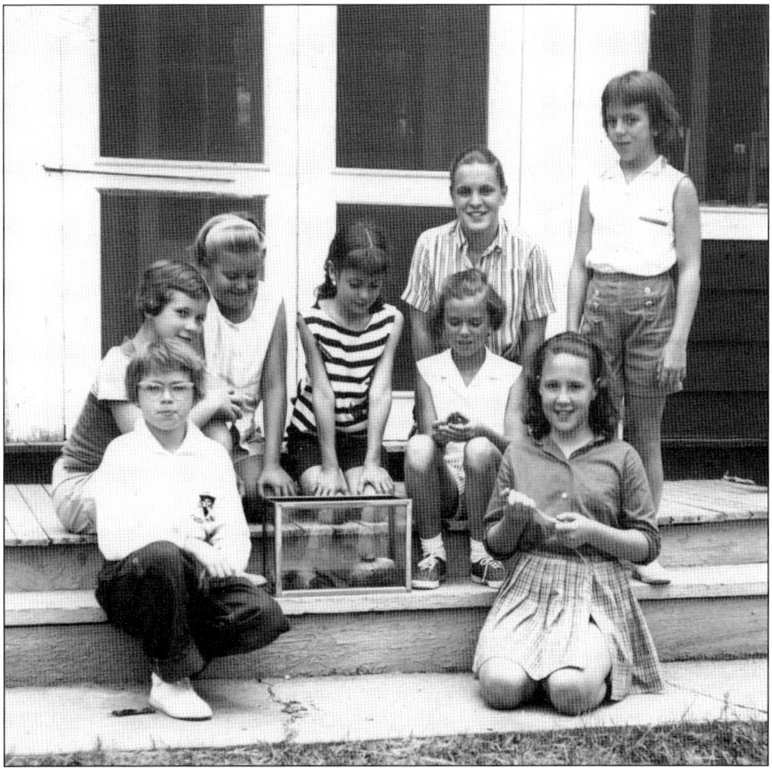

Karen Kaiser, known as "Billie," applied to become the nature director in 1959. With her interest in biology, the programs were of great interest to her students. She and her father worked together to develop the nature center with new cages and charts for the walls. Seen in 1960, her class poses with turtles and garden snakes on the lodge steps. (Courtesy of YWCA Great Lakes Bay Region.)

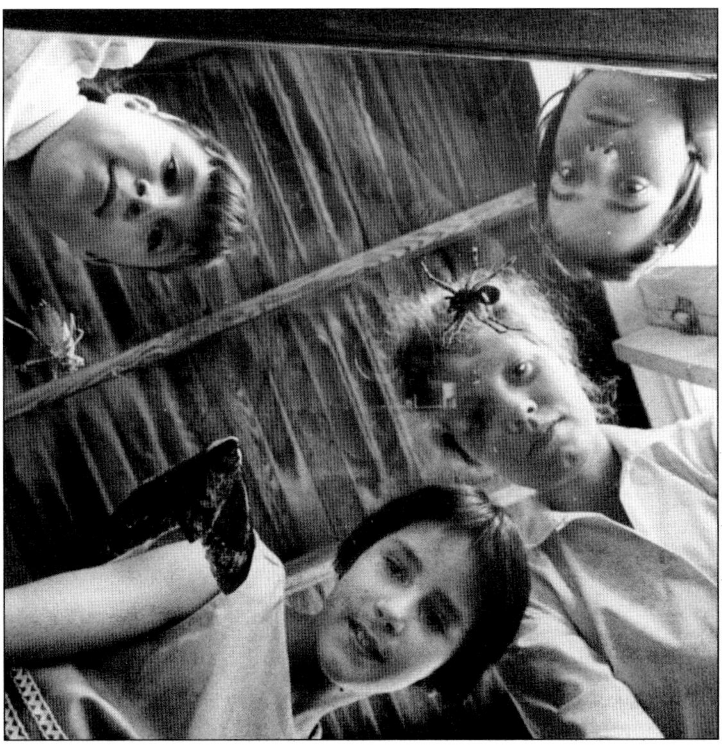

Younger and older campers alike enjoyed the nature class, which often included dissection, trips to Turtle's Cove to catch minnows, turtles, and frogs, and the observation of plant life and oxygen cycles. Identifying plants, which included poison ivy and sumac, were especially important, and there were often contests between cabins. Seen here identifying insects in 1961 are, from left to right, Joan McKinney, Phyllis Finn, Sheryl White, and Jane Simmons. (Courtesy of YWCA Great Lakes Bay Region.)

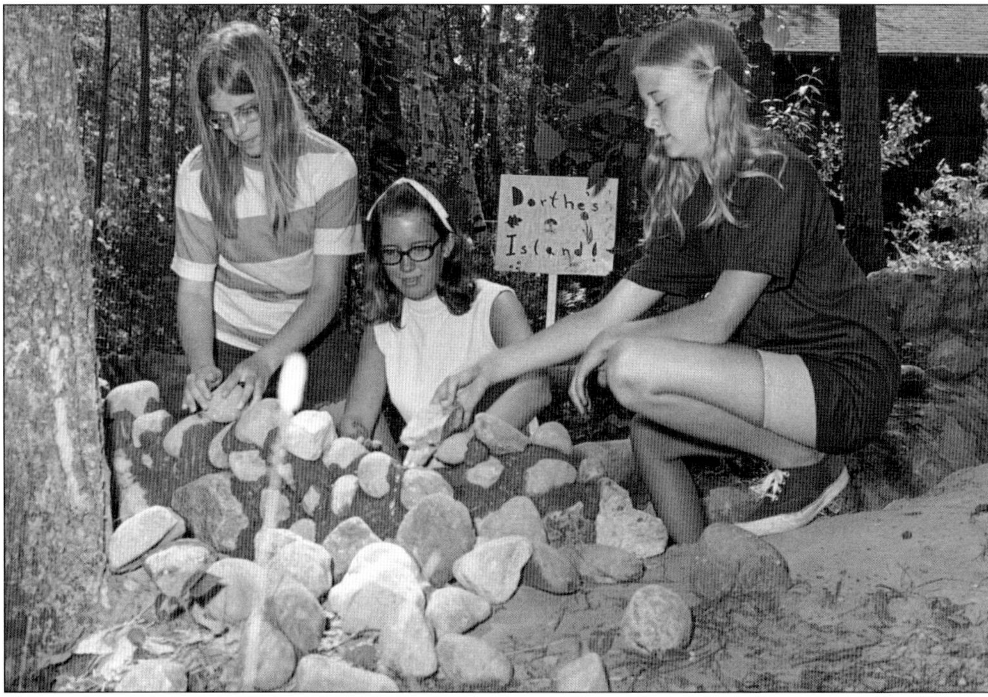

Dorthe's Island was an outdoor *ferrineus*, which is Latin for "made from earth." In 1967, campers dug a trench near Dutton to make an island with a cement moat. Flowers, moss, and stones lay on the island. Joan McKinney, the nature director in 1970, had her class repair the cracks made by tree roots. Above, three girls add rocks to the moat in 1969. Pictured below is Audrey Delcourt (left), who in 1968 was a freshman at Albion College majoring in Biology. As nature director, she loved arranging scavenger hunts and dissection projects—which included a cow's head for an anatomy lesson. She utilized her own interests and knowledge to develop her program, as seen in this photograph of her pressing plants with students. (Courtesy of YWCA Great Lakes Bay Region.)

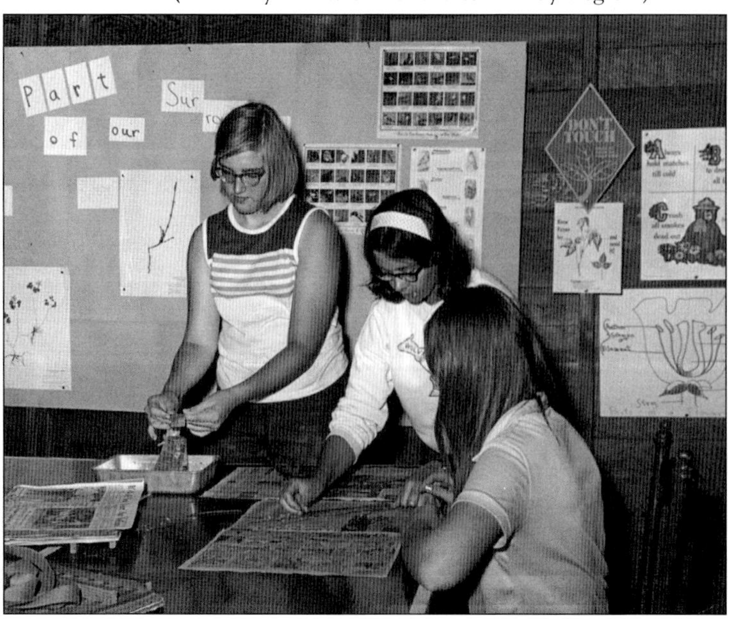

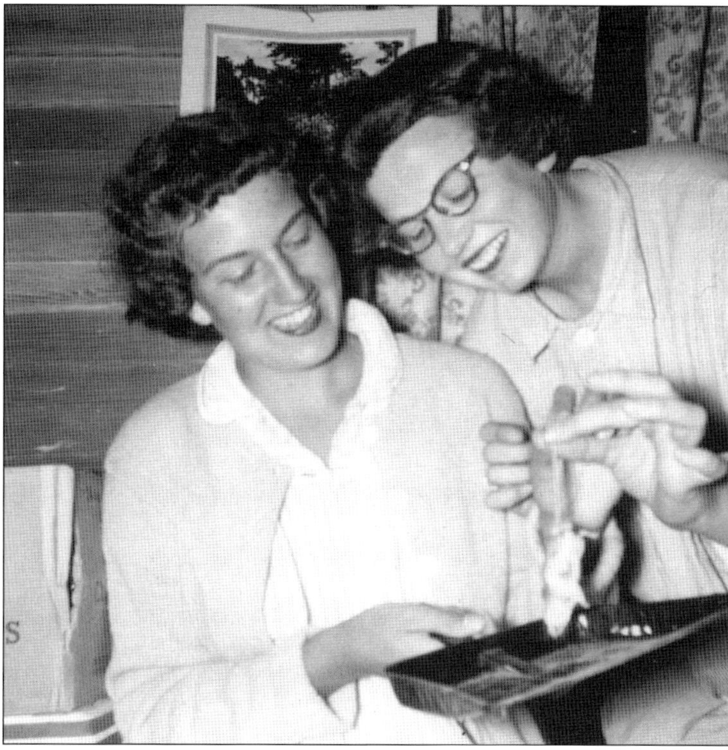

Nature could also be found inside, as chipmunks, mosquitoes, and bats found crevices, and Daddy Long Legs lurked in the camp brownies. Raccoons, squirrels, skunks, and deer roamed at night, rustling in the bushes. Mice also found their way into sleeping quarters, giving birth in unexpected spots. Over the years, pet snakes, dogs, and even a goat named Daisy all joined campers at Maqua. (Courtesy of Pat O'Tool Smith.)

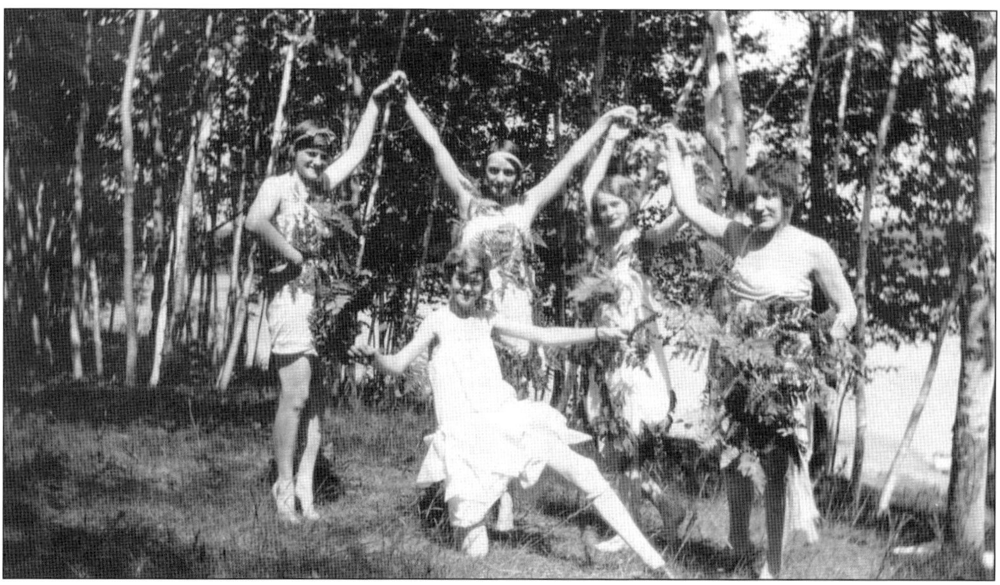

Outdoor Pageantry was listed as an activity in 1925. Dance and dramatics were a vital part of the camping experience in the early 1920s, as seen in this "Woodland Fantasy" tableau. Scarves, costumes, and fern bouquets spurred on the imagination of the fairies and nymphs for their routines. (Courtesy of YWCA Great Lakes Bay Region.)

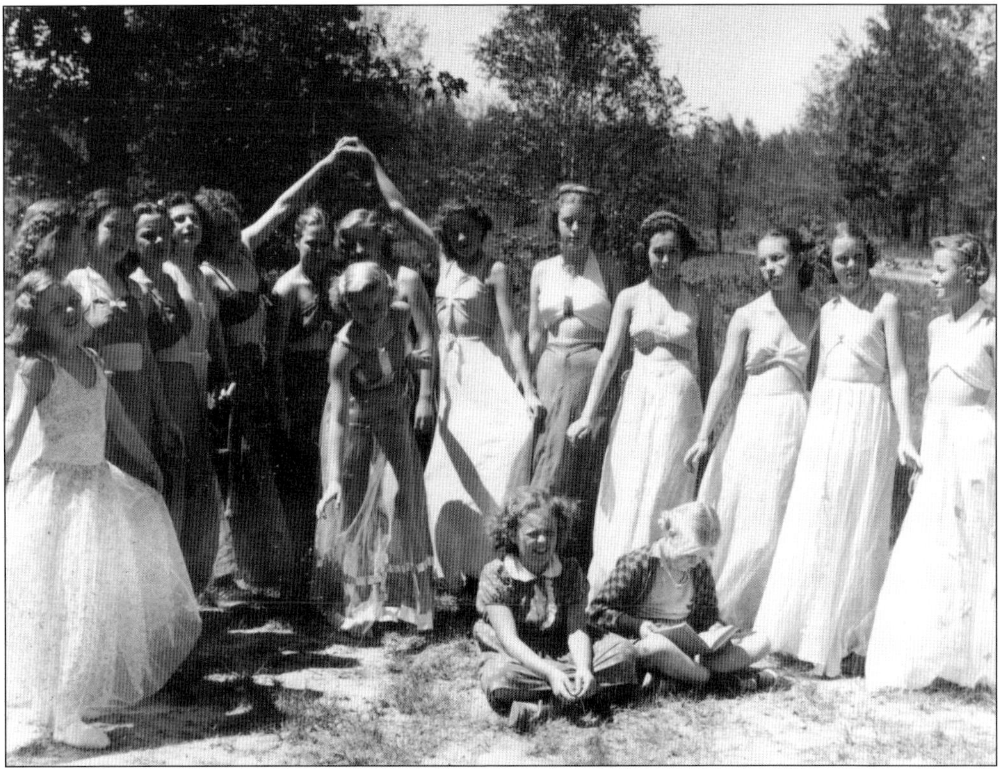

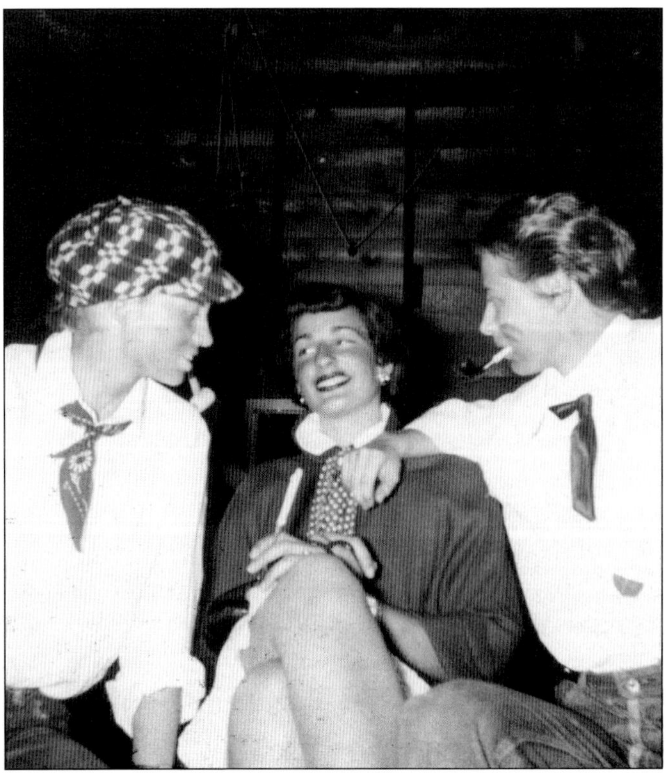

According to various articles and scrapbooks, Lee Merkel taught Natural Dancing in the 1930s, with "rhythmic expression and analysis, following the Martha Graham School of Terpsichore." Dressed in flowing, gauzy costumes, the girls pose in dance mode. (Courtesy of YWCA Great Lakes Bay Region.)

When the counselors came to camp, they knew to fill their footlockers with dress-up items, especially if they had been to camp in previous years. Although there was usually a trunk on the premises with additional items for skits, "Nan, Thora and Corky" appear to be ready for their parts. (Courtesy of Pat O'Tool Smith.)

With the absence of boys, the girls often dressed as young men for skits and dances. "Sharon and Pat [right] on a date," was the caption on this image of one of the dances held at the lodge. Corsages were fashioned from nature, dance cards were designed, and themed tables added to the fun. (Courtesy of Pat O'Tool Smith.)

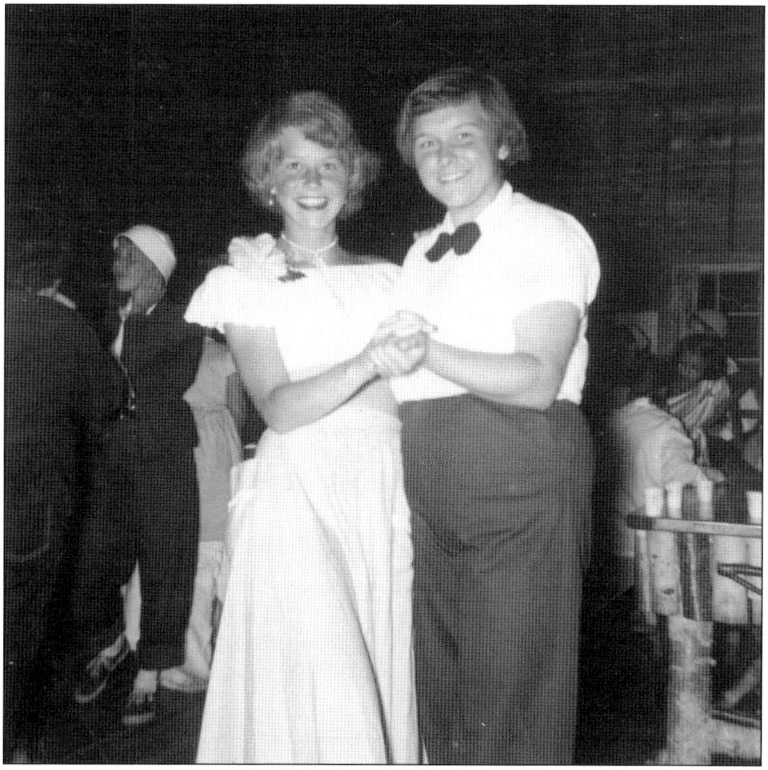

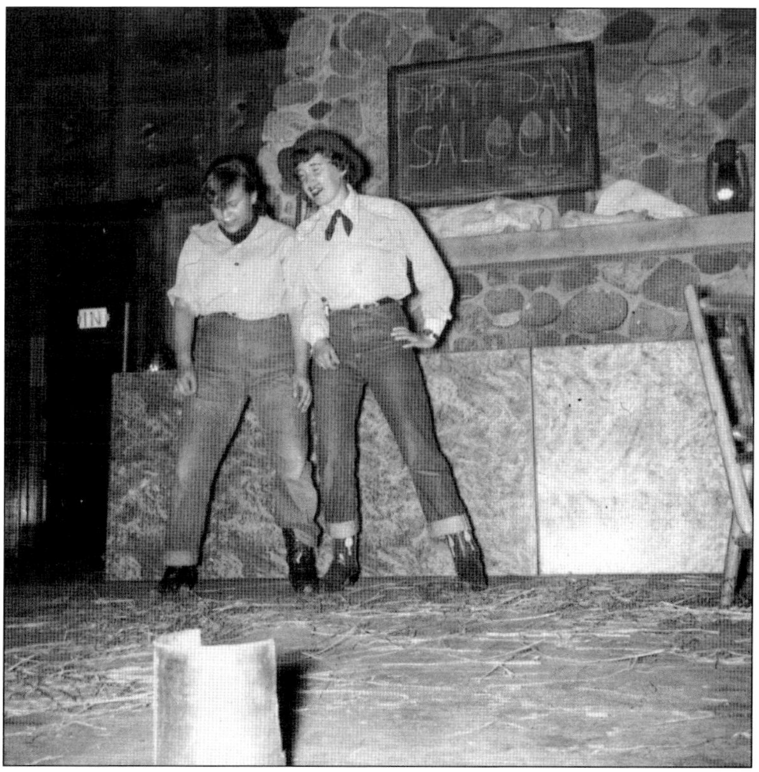

"Now our story takes place in a lawless town. They've called in Hiccup to calm things down," was a line from the O'Tool sisters' skit, which they practiced relentlessly. "Poison Pete" (Pat), on the left, doubled as "Ugg the Indian," and "Wild Bill Hiccup" (Nan) had her second role as "Diamond Lil" in this skit from the early 1950s. (Courtesy of Pat O'Tool Smith.)

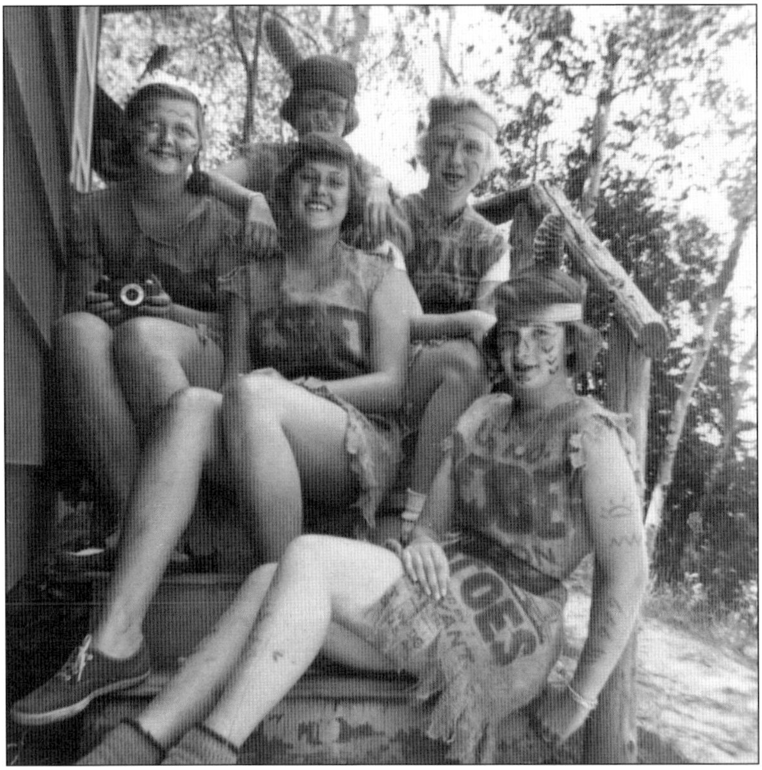

Indian powwows were popular at camp, and costumes were often fashioned from burlap sacks purchased from the grainery. The girls ironed crayons to make patterns on their costumes and wore feathered headbands and war paint. This group of young Indian maidens poses in 1951. (Courtesy of Pat O'Tool Smith.)

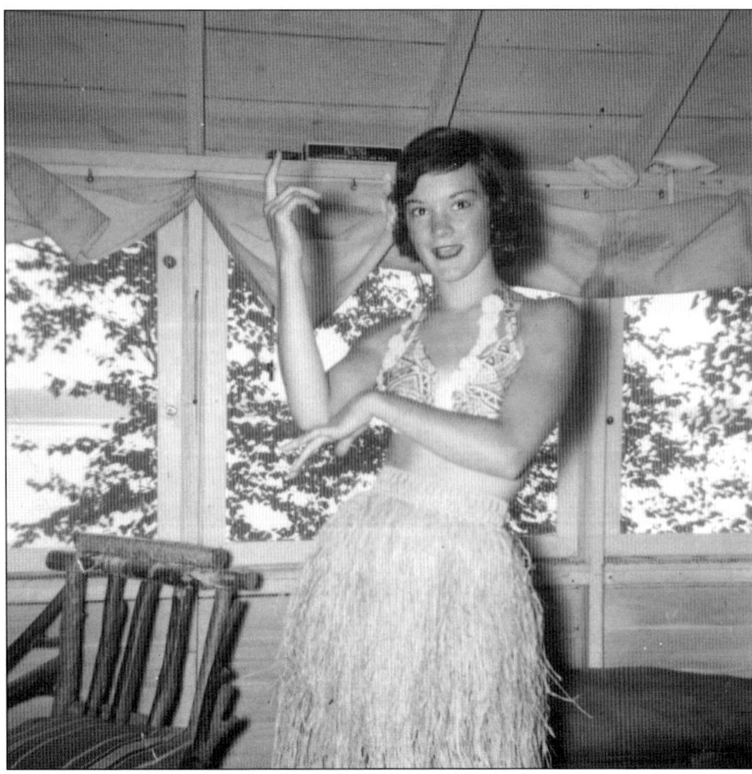

Pictured in 1953, Pam Farley is ready to dance the hula for one of the camp skits. She had taken lessons on a family trip to Hawaii and was dressed for the part. This photograph was taken on the second story of Dutton, overlooking Loon Lake. One of the rustic log chairs can be seen at the lower left. (Courtesy of Pat O'Tool Smith.)

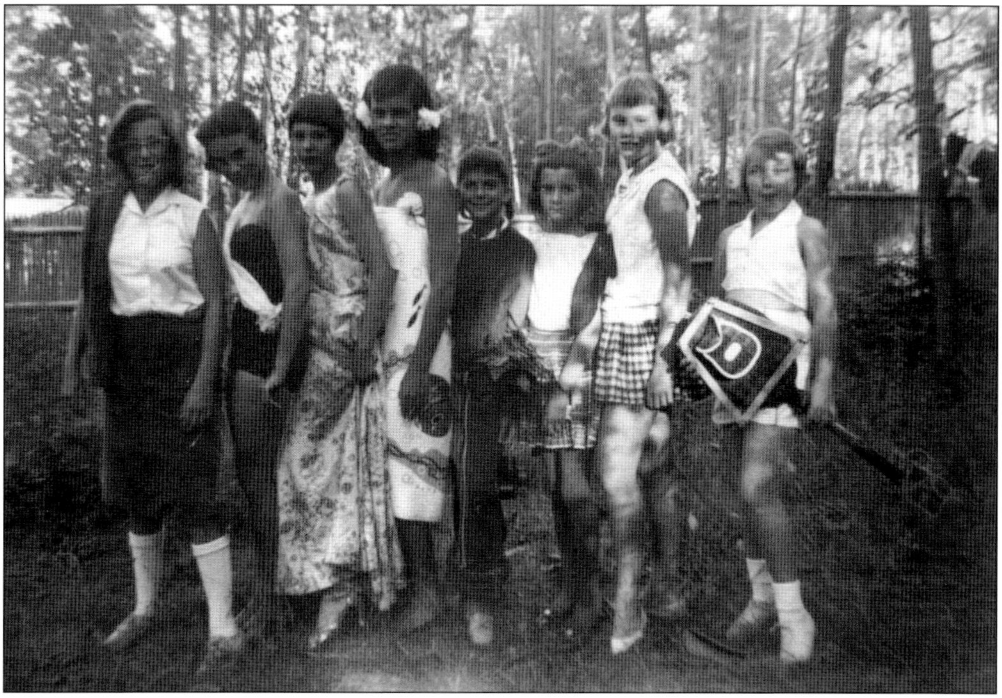

Holidays were celebrated each session, including Christmas in July, Independence Day, and Halloween. Creative costumes were made with items brought to camp and lots of imagination. Here, Ann Ward (sixth from left) stands in a lineup with friends Rosemary Orgren (fifth from left) and Linda Stanton (fourth from left) for the 1958 camp Halloween party. (Courtesy of Ann Ward.)

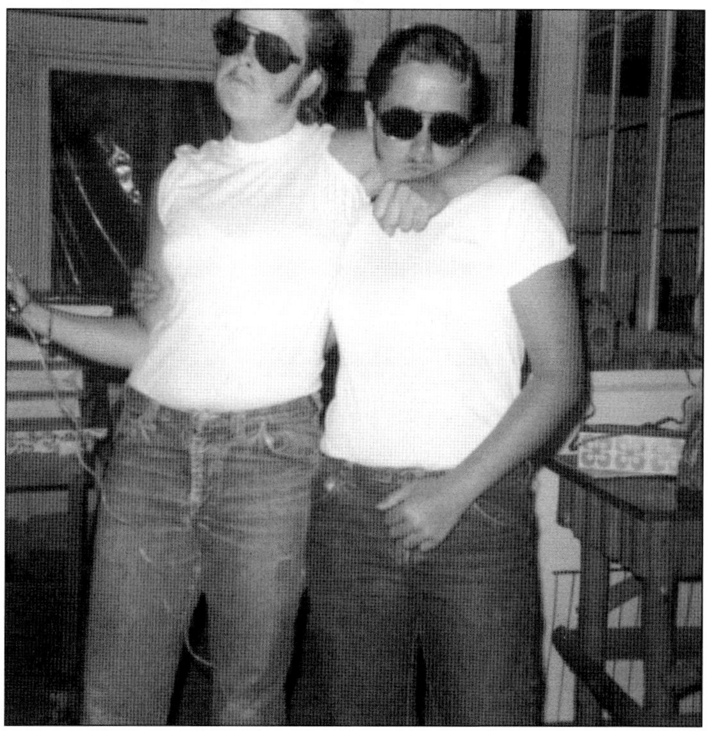

The original "Daddy Cool" skit was performed by Jennifer McLogan and Laurie Cullen, but Doris Engibous and Priscilla Johns inherited the roles. Based on a 1957 song by The Rays, campers encouraged the girls to get into their cool roles after meals. Doris is shown strong-arming "Greaser Cilla" in 1973. (Courtesy of Priscilla Johns Bond.)

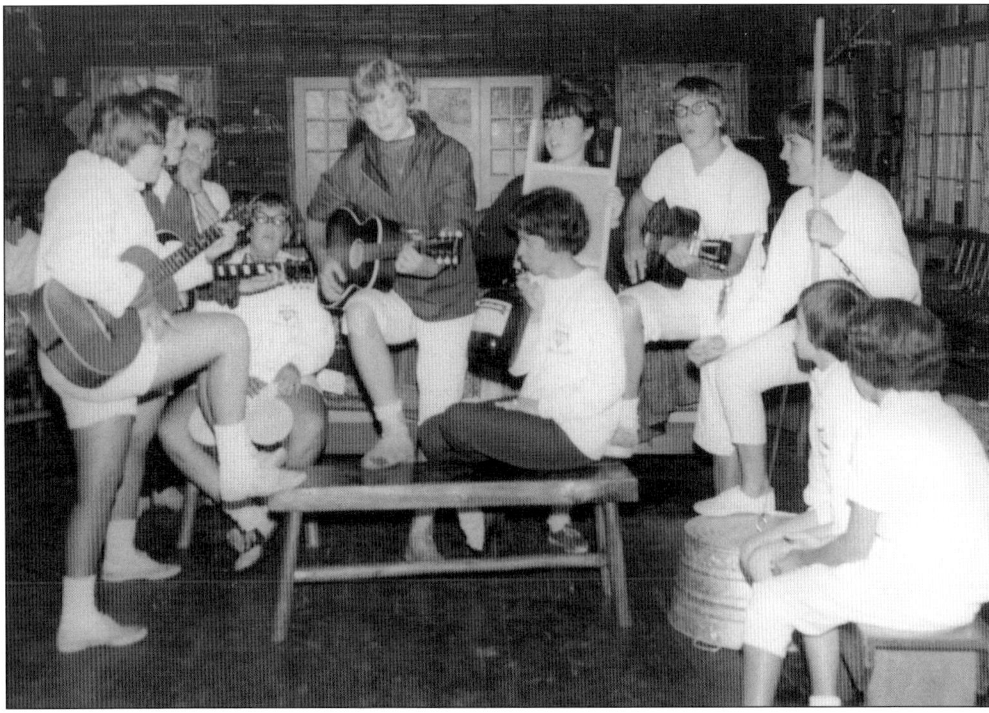

Music wove the thread of camaraderie through the camp. In the 1960s, folk songs were sung alongside all of the favorite camp songs at campfires. Pictured in the lodge in 1963, "Moochie, Dizzy, Mel, Sunni, Frenchie, Chip and Smokey" were part of this band. Chip is on bongos, Kerry is in the center on guitar, and Kitty is on the washboard. (Courtesy of YWCA Great Lakes Bay Region.)

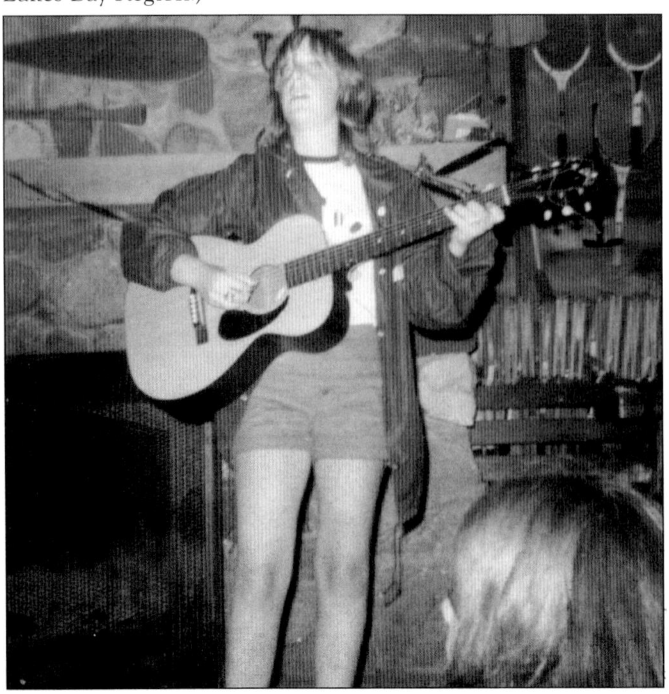

Debi "Strings" Gotlieb was 13 when her mom taught her to play the guitar. She and her sisters Lori and Marci were inspired by folk singers. Debi continued to play coffee houses and bars at college in the 1970s once camp sessions were over. (Courtesy of Karen Magidsohn.)

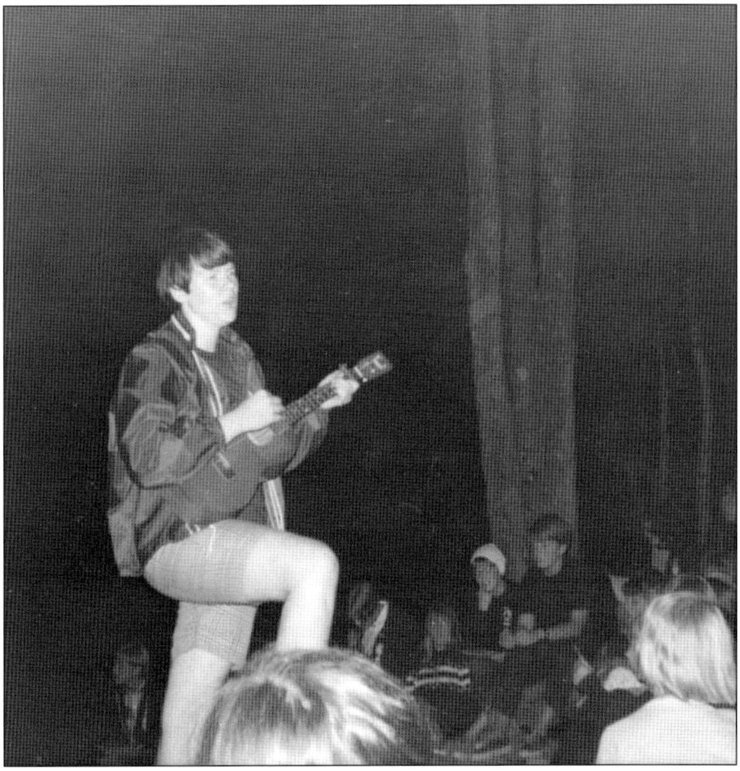

Barbara "Beanie" Haggart rose in the ranks from sports director to program director to camp director, a position she held for three years in the early 1970s. The girls she mentored remember a baritone ukulele or 12-string guitar in her hands while she sang, as well as the large song sheets (seen below) posted on the lodge walls. (Courtesy of Barbara Haggart.)

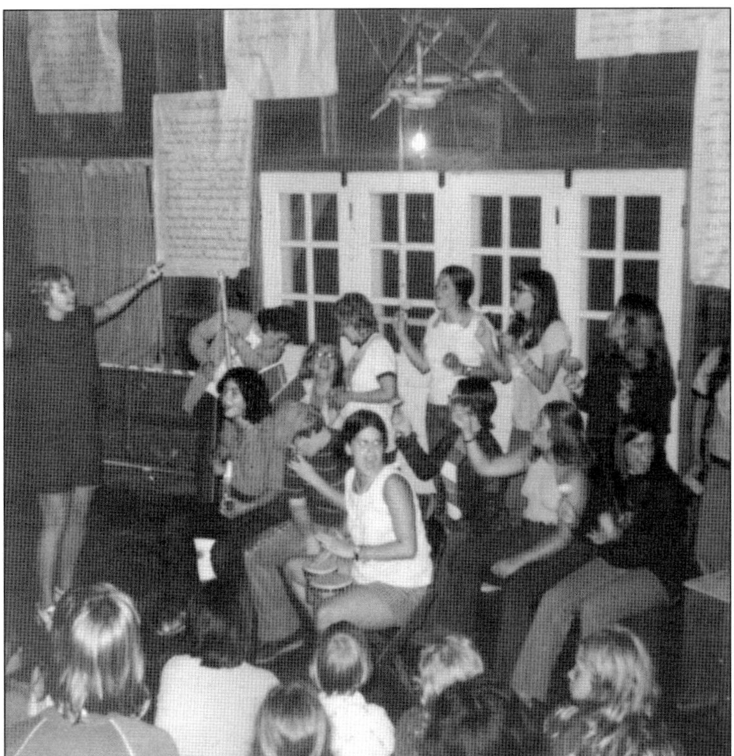

An enthusiastic staff jug band, complete with bongos, noisemakers, kazoos, and real and make-shift instruments, entertain campers in 1974. Carol "Hypo" Hulett was the health director and bandleader. Mary Toburen, Pam Moore, Denise Roman, Kim Wood, Val Unger, Joanne Smith, Carol Morely, Dedde Watton, Ann Rogalski, Sarah Smith, and Becky Hahn were all band members. (Courtesy of Carol Hulett.)

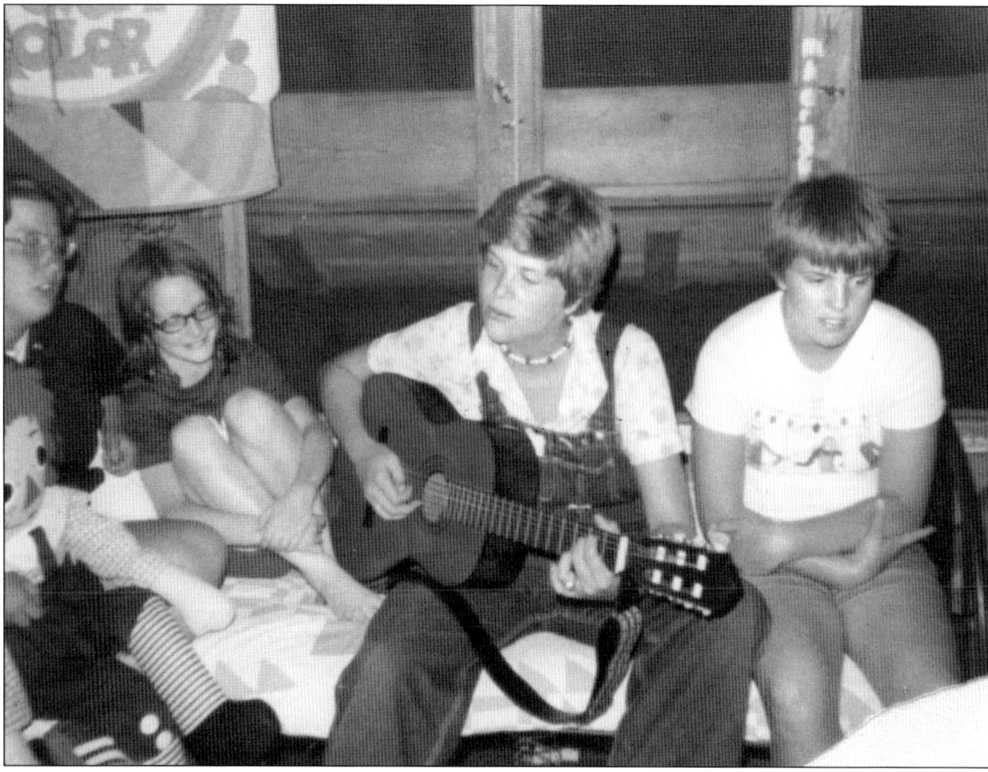

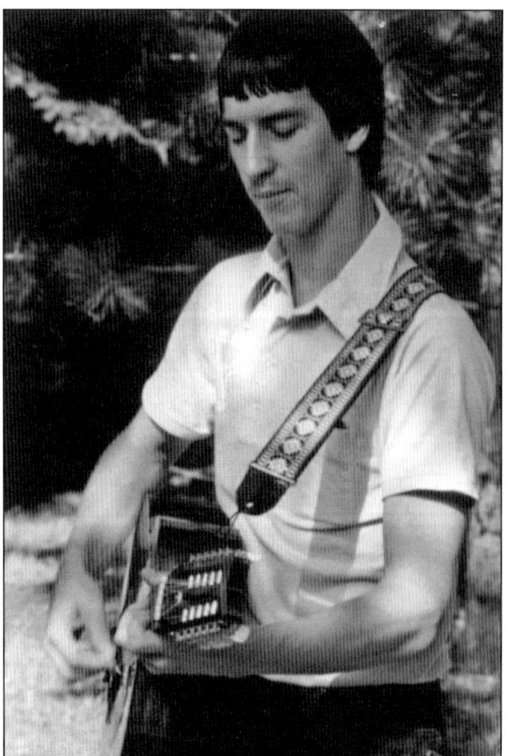

The 1960s were a time of beads, Dr. Scholl's sandals, bandanas, overalls, and folk singing. Cindy "Spaz" Knapp is seen here with her guitar in 1976 inside one of the huts playing for Mary, Mary Gumbleton, and Suzy "Squirt," who worked as a junior counselor. (Courtesy of Kellie Moore Thelen.)

Ken Dike, who was the director Camp Maquois when the two camps merged, is seen here in 1977 with his Yamaha 12-string guitar at an opening-day campfire. Self-taught in 1973 by listening to his fraternity brothers, he picked up enough to strum his way through the camp and folk songs of the day. (Courtesy of Amy Johns-Ikler.)

Four

Traditions, Friendships, Photographs, and Farewells

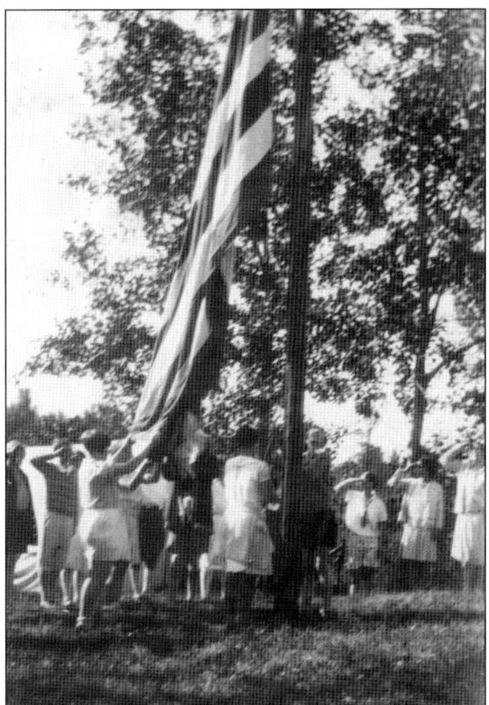

Pictured in 1928 are campers and staff gathering around for the very important tradition of raising the flag. Rain or shine, girls formed a circle around the flag and recited the Pledge of Allegiance. It was an honor to be chosen for the color guard, and the girls practiced their walk with dignity and pride. (Courtesy of YWCA Great Lakes Bay Region.)

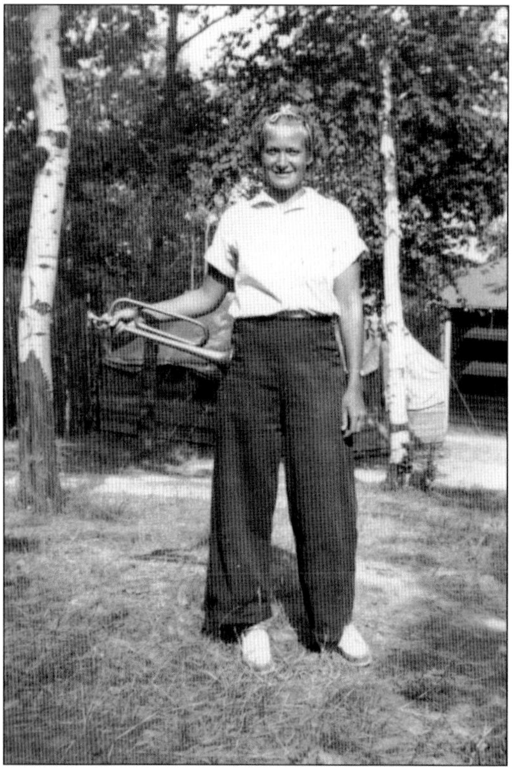

At left, a bugler stands in front of a tent in the 1930s, poised to blow taps. Reveille was taken very seriously, and it was an added bonus to have a bugler at camp, especially in the 1940s, when a bugler summoned the girls to their meals. Below, dressed in their whites and proud of their country, the staff of summer 1962 gathers around the flagpole with their campers. Some mornings were so hot that girls fainted. In 1961, "The Bells of Freedom" were rung all over the country for justice, rights, and peace, and the campers participated. Sharon Williams recalled only two years, 1972 and 1973, when the flag was not raised, in opposition to the Vietnam War. (Courtesy of YWCA Great Lakes Bay Region.)

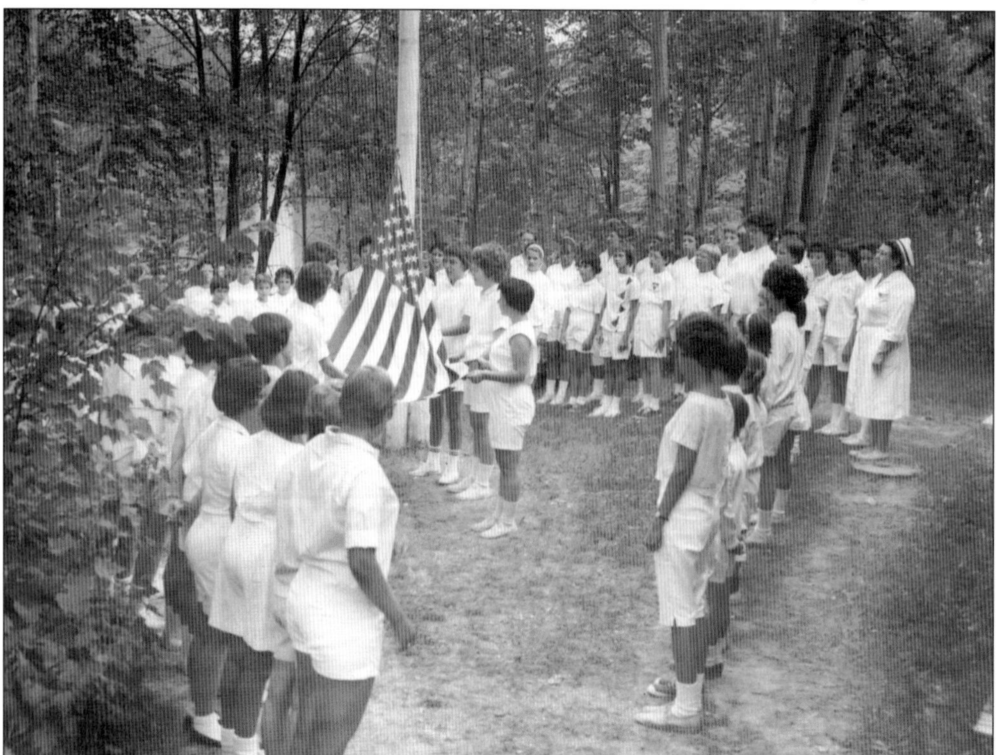

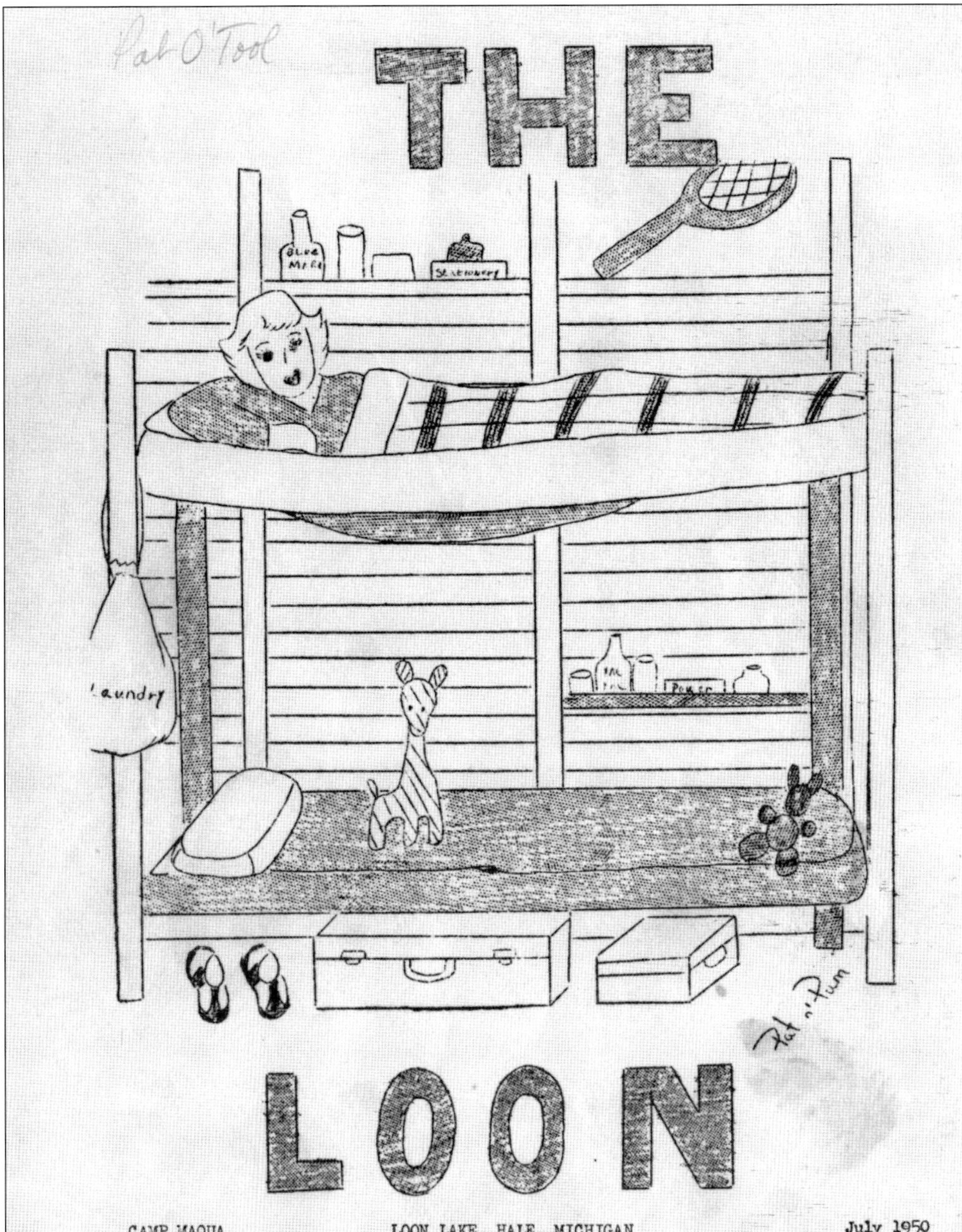

Friendship circles, candle ceremonies, and the friendship wall were all Maqua traditions. Harriet Crumb, who camped in 1925, recalled a candle ceremony representing faith, love, courage, and purity. Each girl would write her biggest fault on a piece of paper and burn it. Services were beside the shoreline, and each camper brought a stone forward for the six-foot-long friendship wall. This tradition continued for decades, with names and dates going back to the beginning of the camp inscribed on the rocks. Songs such as "Follow the Gleam" were sung, and many of the traditions were recorded in the camp newsletter, the *Loon*, which began in the early 1920s. Its staff consisted of campers and counselors who featured poems, artwork, fads of the day, addresses of staff, and vignettes of daily happenings. (Courtesy of Pat O'Tool Smith.)

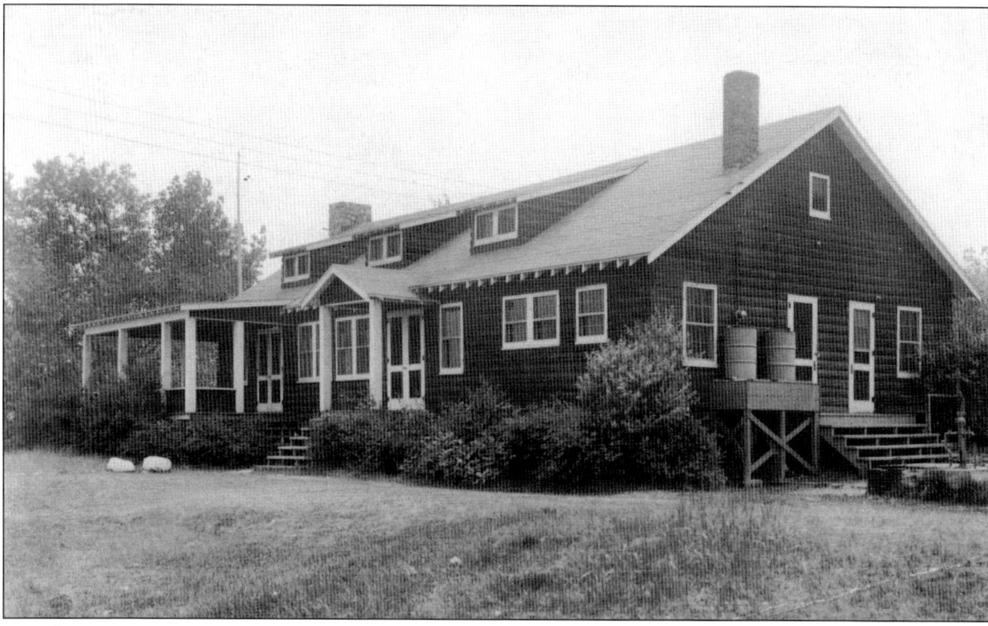

Two boys' camps were part of Camp Maqua's rich history. Camp Mahn-go-tah-see (above) was the YMCA camp on the north side of Loon Lake. It was a two-mile swim or a quick boat ride away and the source of endless myths and legends for the girls since 1924. Numerous pranks between the staff of both camps, as well as arranged activities and secretive trysts, were common. Sightings of the boys often brought squeals as they boated past. Camp Iroquois (postcard below) was a YMCA camp on Sand Lake, within 10 miles of Maqua. It operated as a camp from 1915 until 1977, when financial issues forced a decision to merge it with Maqua. Camp Maquois was the new coed camp on Loon Lake, but in 1978 the camp closed its doors. (Courtesy of YWCA Great Lakes Bay Region.)

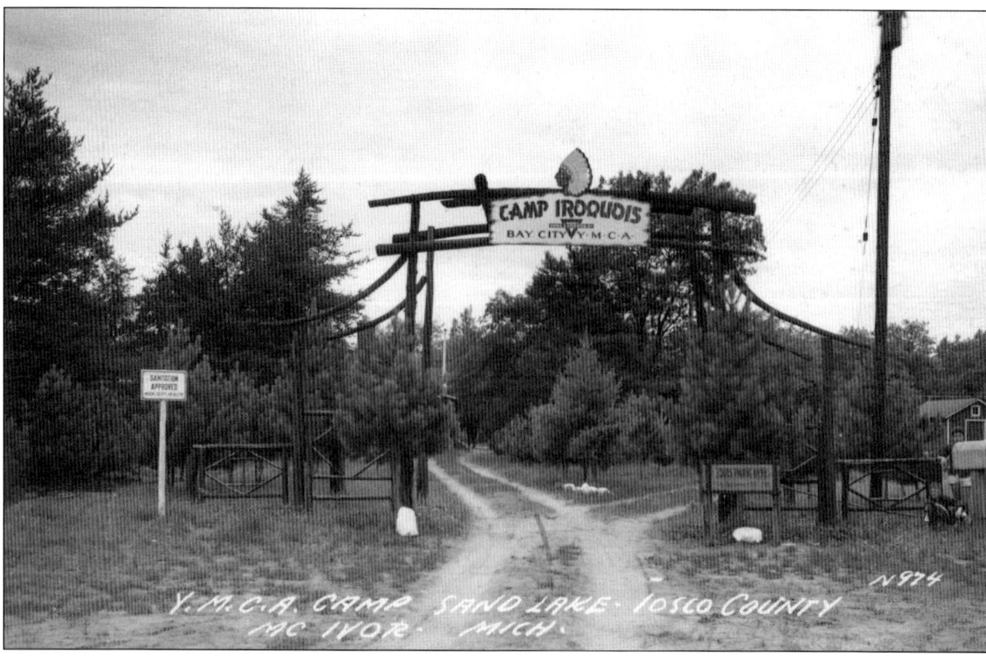

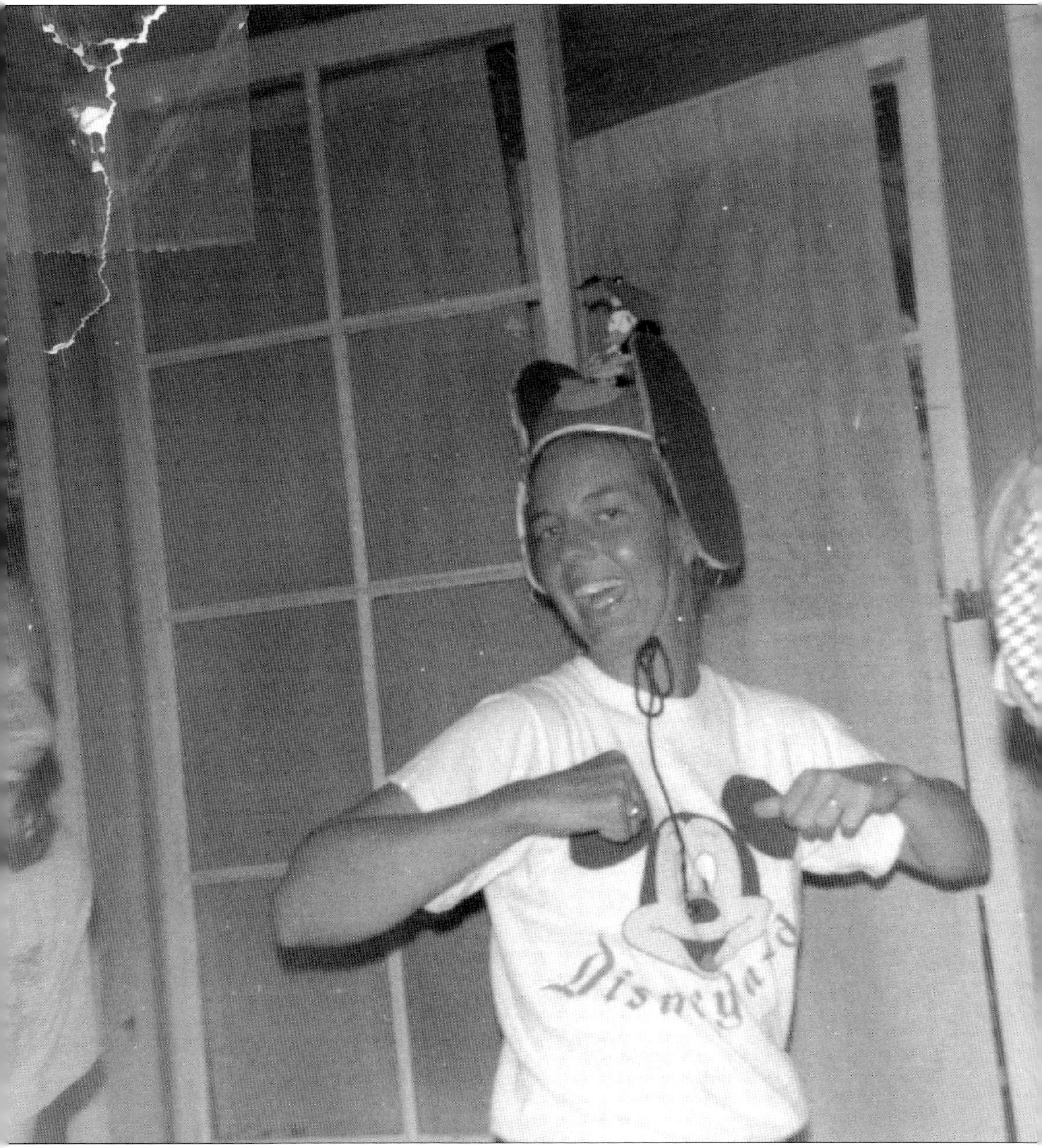

Nicknames were common at camp, but none could have been cooler than "Super-doo," which fit Sue Purdue perfectly. An extrovert who camped at Maqua before her first job as a kitchen aide, Sue later became the tennis instructor. Described as an asset to the staff, the activity director took note of Sue's great teaching techniques, which increased enrollment the summer of 1968. (Courtesy of Karen Magidsohn.)

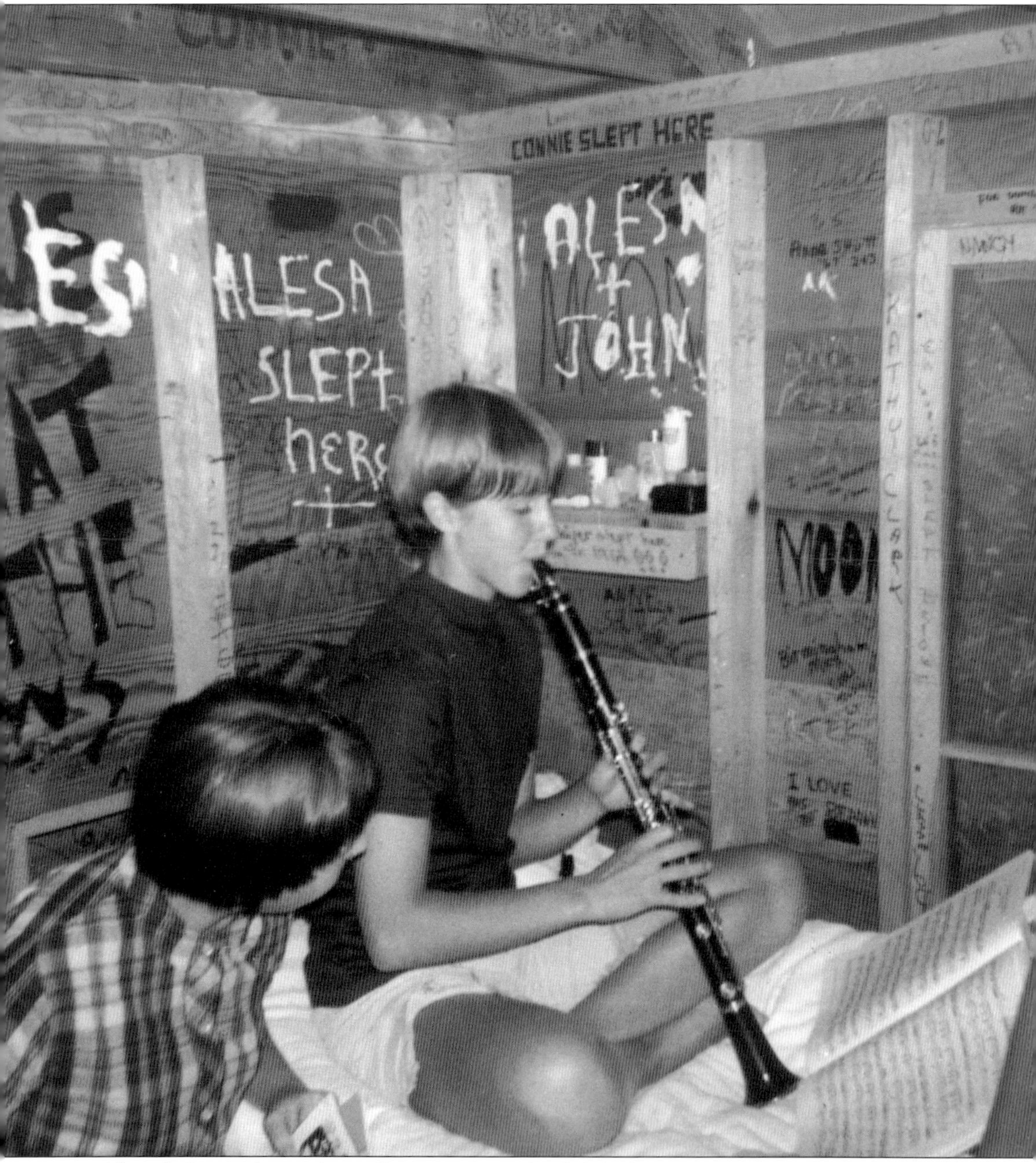

Although frowned upon by staff, generations of girls left their names on the walls of their huts. Campers often brought extra toothpaste or lipstick to make sure they had enough to leave their mark. Here, a young unidentified musician sits in her hut, surrounded by walls of names. (Courtesy of Valerie Monto Richardson.)

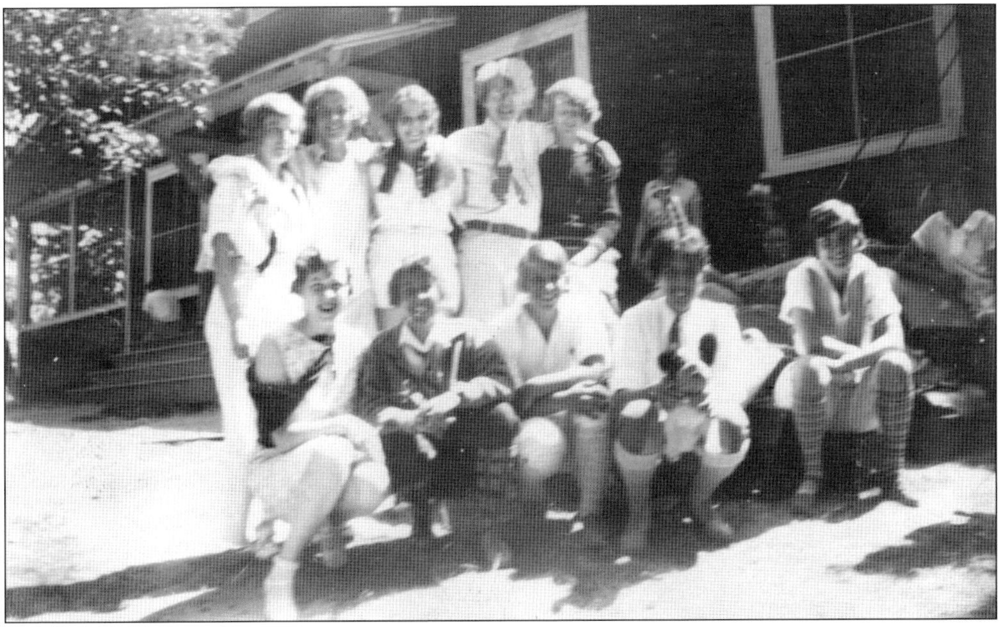

Many organizations connected to the YWCA utilized Maqua for camping, including this group of Girl Reserves from Central High School in 1929. They camped for three days and were accompanied by Mrs. F. Hewitt, Rebecca Ann Perry, and Mrs. Robert Barnett. Other organizations, including civic and church groups, used the camp for work weekends, volunteering to perform maintenance on the buildings and grounds. (Courtesy of YWCA Great Lakes Bay Region.)

Seven friends pose in front of Hut Eight in 1947, including, from left to right, (first row) Shirley Colbert, Pat Kula, and Dorothy Niedzielski; (second row) Carolyn Abbott, Mary Lou Winn, Ethel Feldman, and Betty Miller. Living in a hut with no running water was an experience for these girls! (Courtesy of Pat Kula Reinlein.)

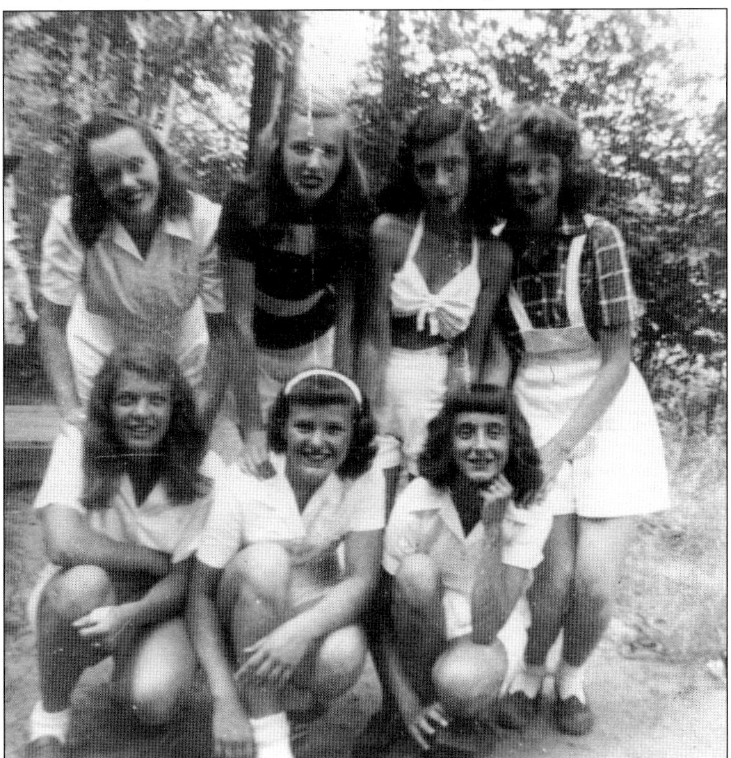

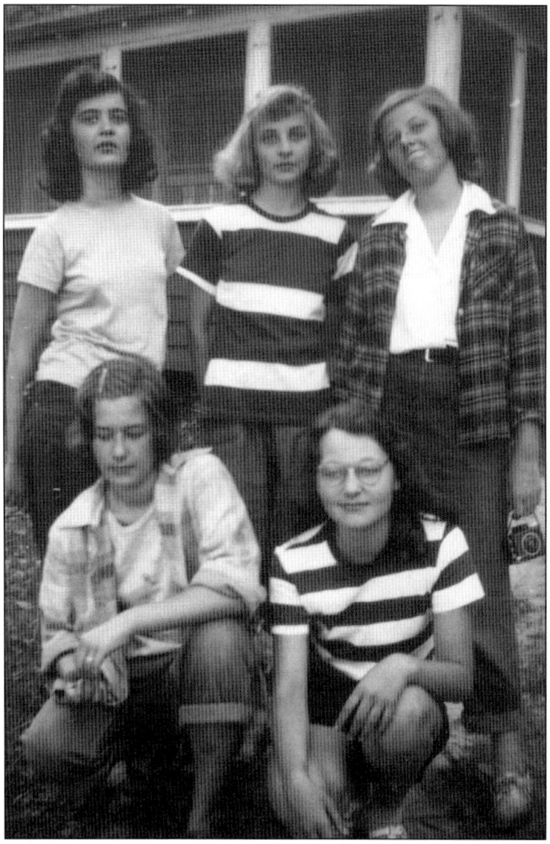

The four girls in this photograph from the 1940s were part of the "Bay City Gang" and ended up in Hut Nine on the water. From left to right are (first row) an unidentified girl and Judy Rowden; (second row) sisters Jane and Jean McDonald and Susan Harris. Many friends liked to be in the same cabin, but concerned counselors often made sure that the new girls did not feel left out. (Courtesy of Judy Rowden Sauve.)

The "Handy Drive Bunch" were all good friends from Bay City who camped in Hut Three in 1958. They are, from left to right, (first row) Ashley Campau, Linda Birch, counselor Ruth Ann Kaufman, Dianne Hale, and Kayleen Jacques; (second row) Barbara Warner, Peggy Samson, and an unidentified girl. Barbara and Peggy treated the newcomer as an honorary member. (Courtesy of Minette Jacques Lefkiades.)

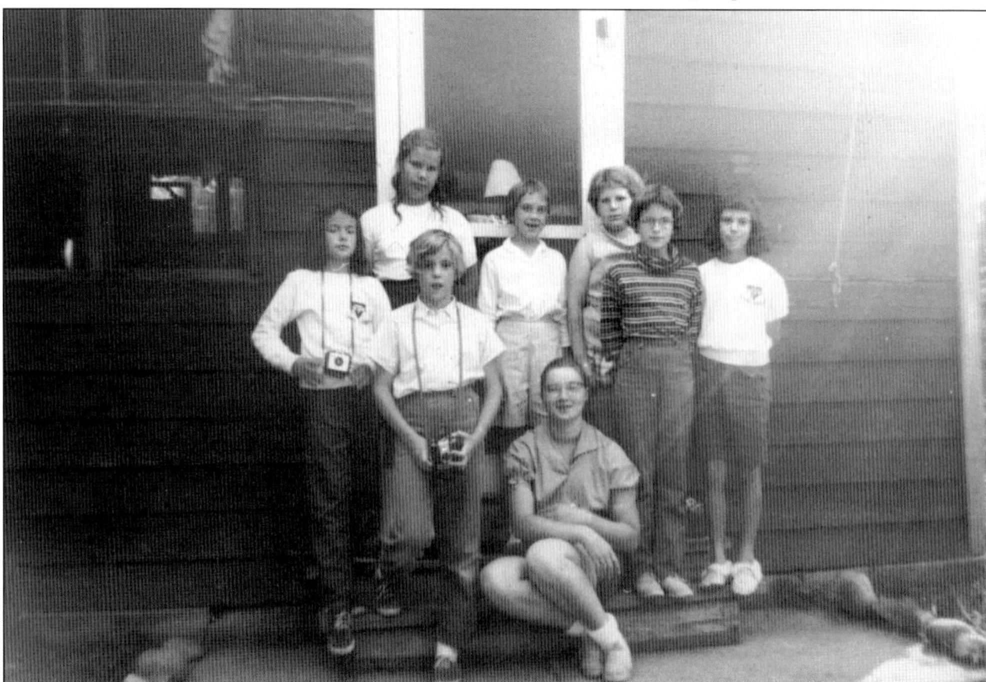

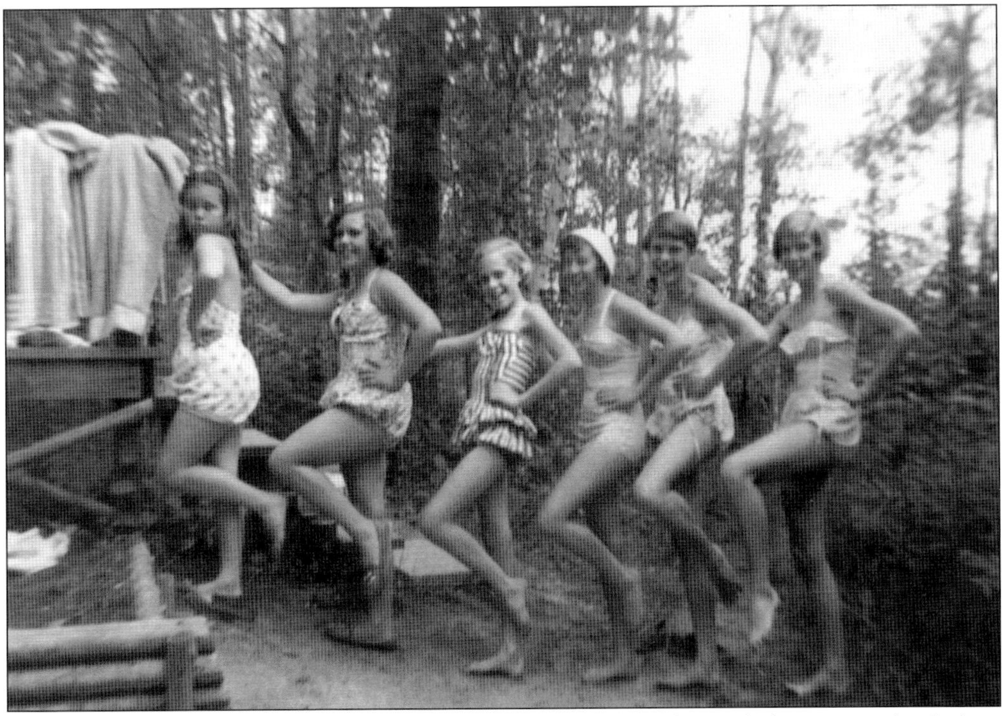

Four of these Bay City girls, known as the "Fifth Street Gang," had attended camp together before, while the fifth friend had a mother and two daughters who attended. This 1956 photograph features, from left to right, Kerry Weber, Carolyn Parke, Ellen Hydorn, Fran Jobe, Ellen Sue McGillivray, and Kay Mary Young. (Courtesy of Ellen Hydorn Campbell.)

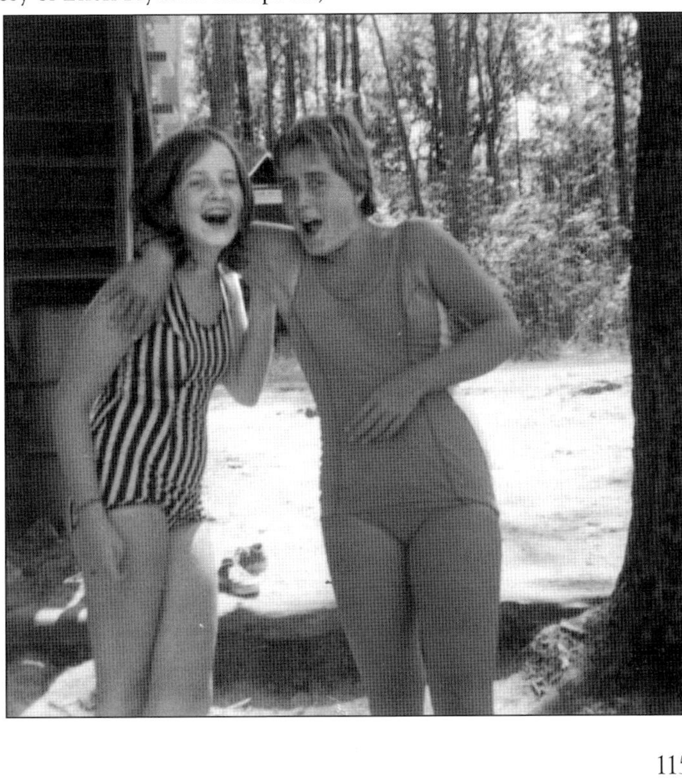

The camping experience was a great way for sisters Amy (left) and Cilla Johns to acclimate to the family move from New York to Michigan in the late 1960s. The girls, pictured in their Speedos in 1973, were competitive swimmers and worked the waterfront after serving as camp kitchen aides. (Courtesy of Priscilla Johns Bond.)

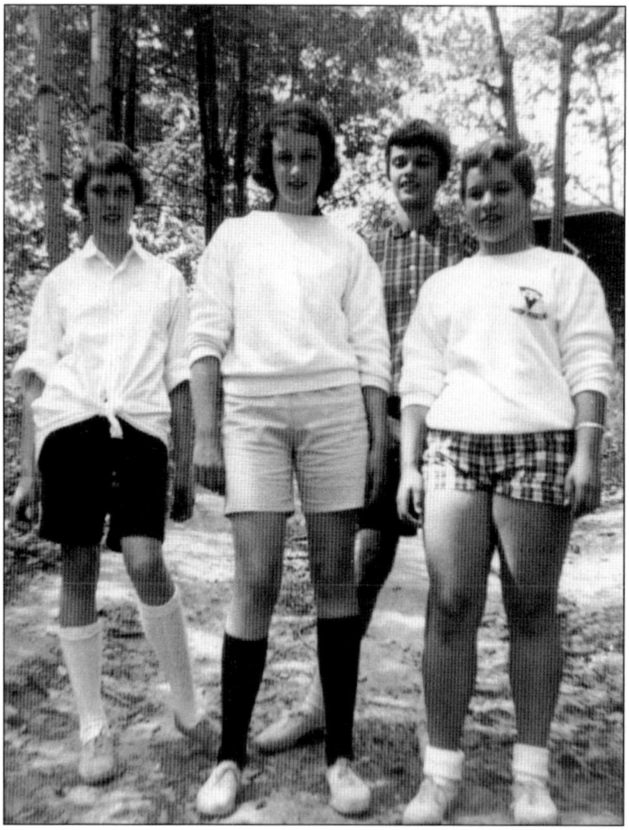

Camp was a place to make new friends while working. Junior counselors Susie Utter (left), "Seedy," Sandy, and Ellen Sue pause for a photograph in 1958. Assisting in the kitchen, cabins, or with other activities, CITs (counselors in training) were in the wings to become full-fledged counselors. (Courtesy of Sue Utter Seelye.)

"Counselors and Committee Members to Attend Affair Planned Saturday" was the headline of a June 6, 1937, article describing a rally planned by camp director Ruth Buckwalter. Presumably the camp mother or hostess was at the front of the line in this photograph from the same year with all staff members dressed in their nautical uniforms. (Courtesy of YWCA Great Lakes Bay Region.)

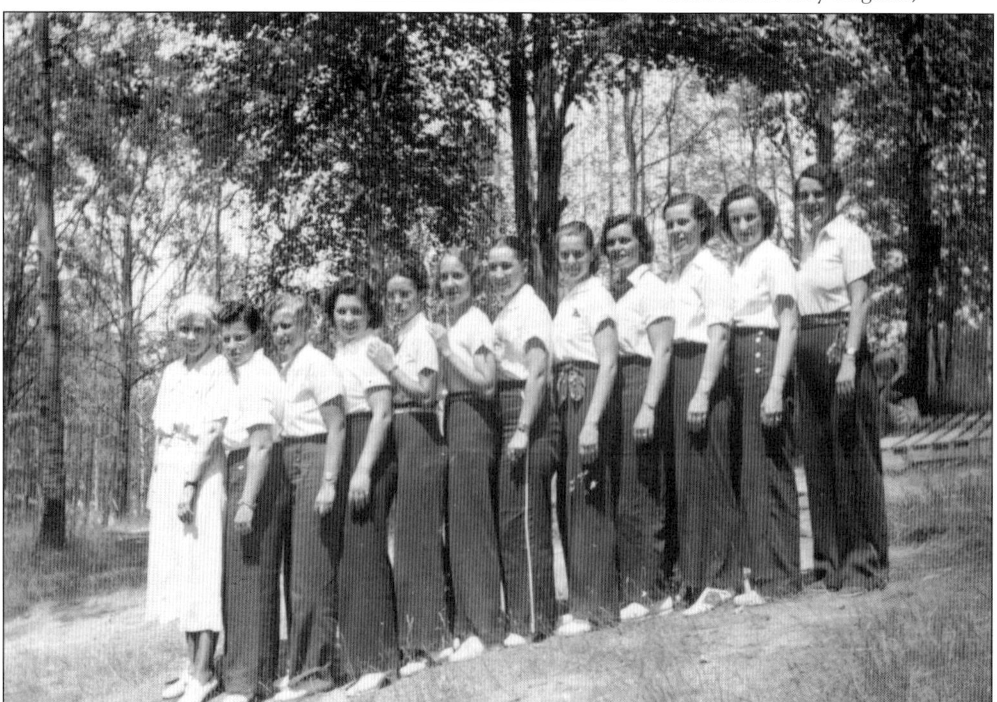

In later years, tradition dictated wearing whites for photographs and Chapel Hill services. Kathy Sullivan's cabin mates autographed this photograph from 1961. Posing in front of the granite lodge fireplace are, from left to right, (first row) Jeannie Vanderberg, Jane Van Hamlin, Kathy Sullivan, and Ruth Wiesen; (second row) Jan Zawalski (counselor), Linda Potts, Mary McKee, Anne Brett, and Sandy Robins. (Courtesy of Kathy Sullivan Kuerbitz.)

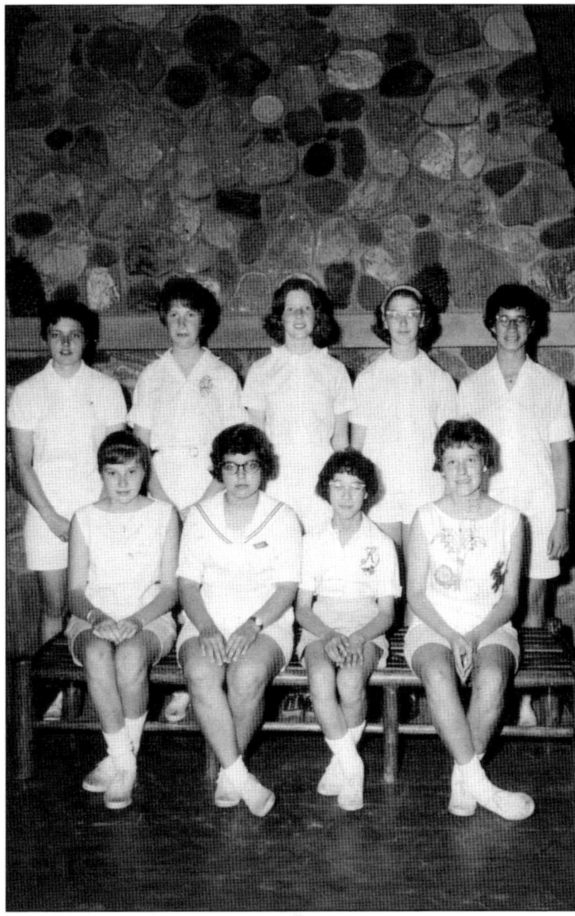

Autographs on the back of this photograph from 1940 include the names of Ann Thomas, Lila Drummond, Shirley Anderson, Marian Clift, Nancy Simons, Pat Murphy, Eva Gulick, Joan Herbst, Mary Virginia Miller, Marie Ouilette, Dotty Taylor, Lucie Derby, Pat MacAulay, Georgia Suliburk, Margaret Fletcher, Alberta Williams, Nancy Foss, Elizabeth Payne, June Harris, Gloria Moore, Nadine Bell, Phyllis Blanchard, Barbara Rhoads, Bette Wilson, Dorothy Lemanski, and Marie Brugger. (Courtesy of Dorthea Kelton O'Laughlin.)

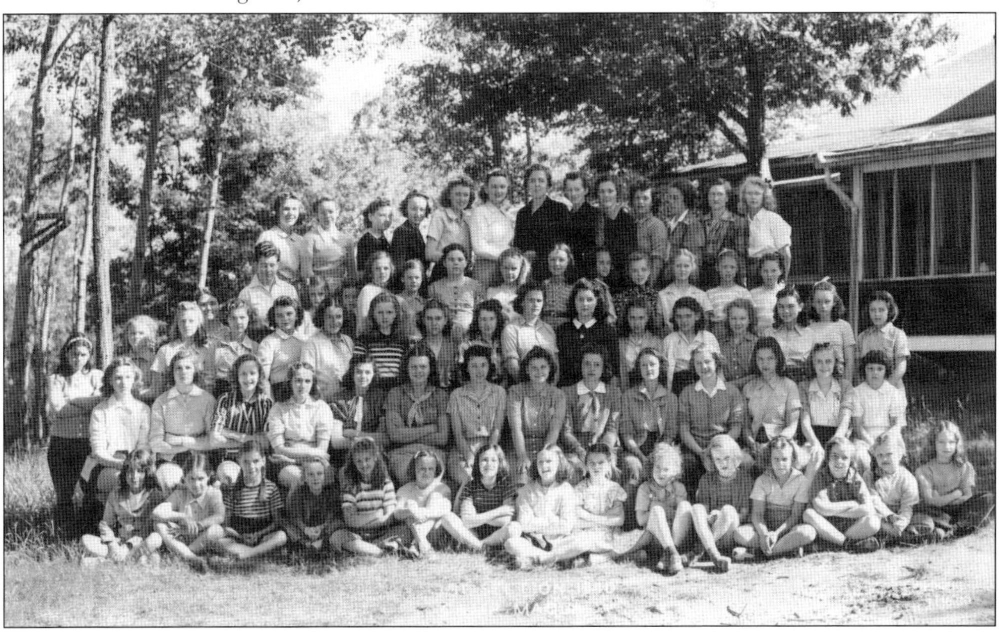

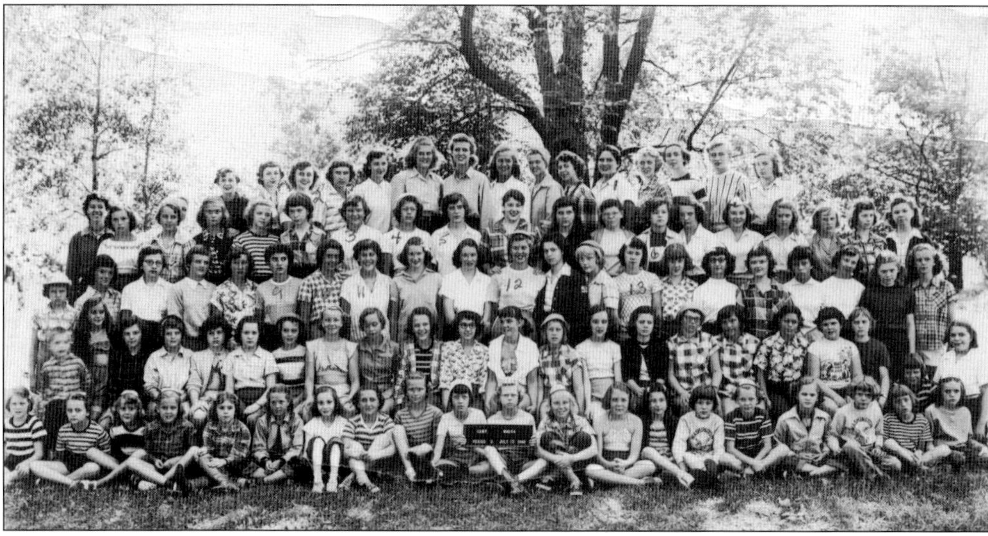

Pat saved numerous photographs of her days at Maqua. This lineup was typical of the 1940s group photographs, which were taken by the lodge. Lucy Harding, Judy Asline, sisters Sue and Jean Vaupre, Judy Miller, Pam Farley, Muriel Levinson, Judy Rowden, Ann Gunn, Yolanda Erickson, Gail Willet, Betty Ganser, and sisters Pat and Nancy O'Tool all attended this 1949 session. (Courtesy of Pat O'Tool Smith.)

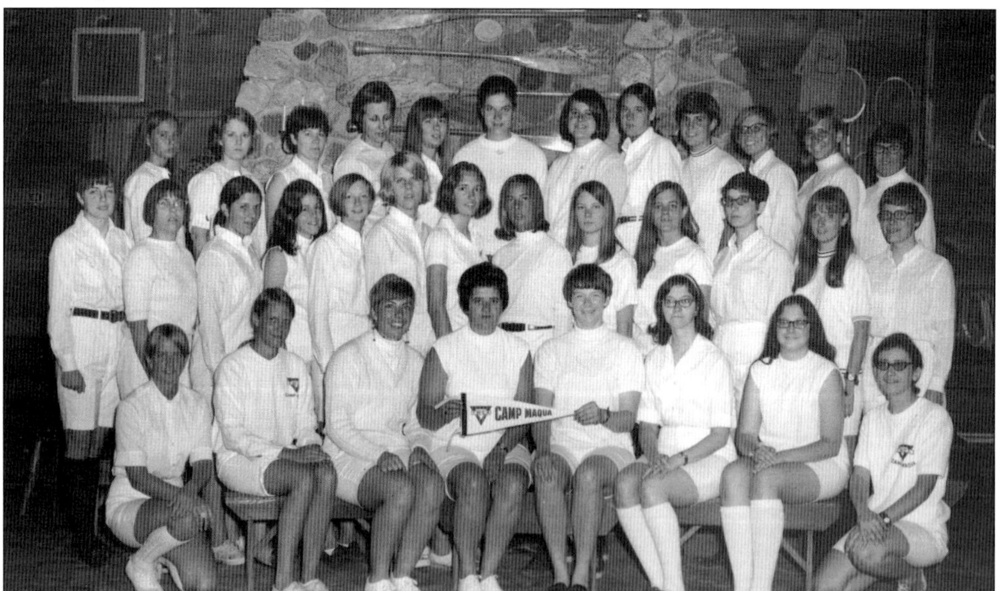

Dorthe Balaskas, seen here holding the Maqua banner in 1969, ran a tight ship during her reign as camp director and mentored many of these girls in leadership. Pictured from left to right are (seated in the front row) Laurie Burch, Jennifer McLogan, Nancy Sautter, Dorthe Balaskas, Barbara Haggart, Audrey Delcourt, Stephanie, and Sue Wiegand; (middle row) Linda Doering, Kitty Braham, Karen, Robin, Chris Lambert, Anne Obey, Gail, Sue Purdue, Jeanne Kiltie, Ann Pennington, Barb, Marge, and Brooke Charland; (back row) Monica, Chris Varney, Bette, Emmy Host, unidentified, Nadine Ackley, Jill, Ann Carney, "Smokey," Trish Sautter, Laurie Borgeson, and Linda Harp. (Courtesy of Shelley Harris.)

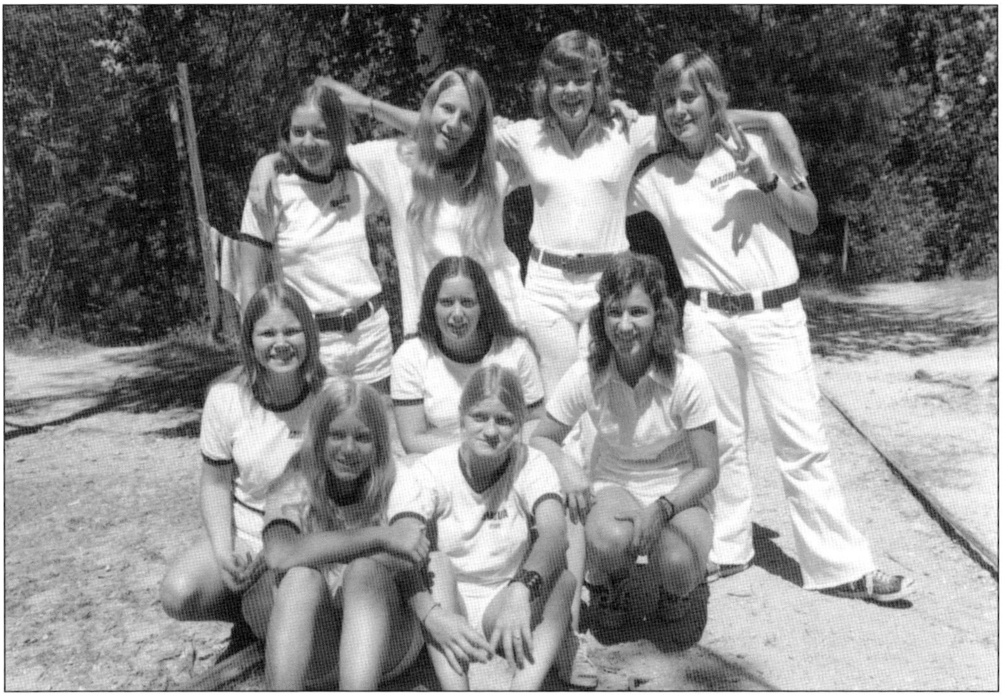

Besides flashing the peace sign, traditions in the 1970s included girls wearing Maqua tee shirts as part of their whites. Shown from left to right in this 1972 staff photograph are (first row) Barb Remus and an unidentified girl; (second row) Marty Wyman, Marcia Michelson, and Sharon Williams; (third row) Susan Carney, Debbie Osher, Doris Engibous, and Priscilla Johns. (Courtesy of Priscilla Johns Bond.)

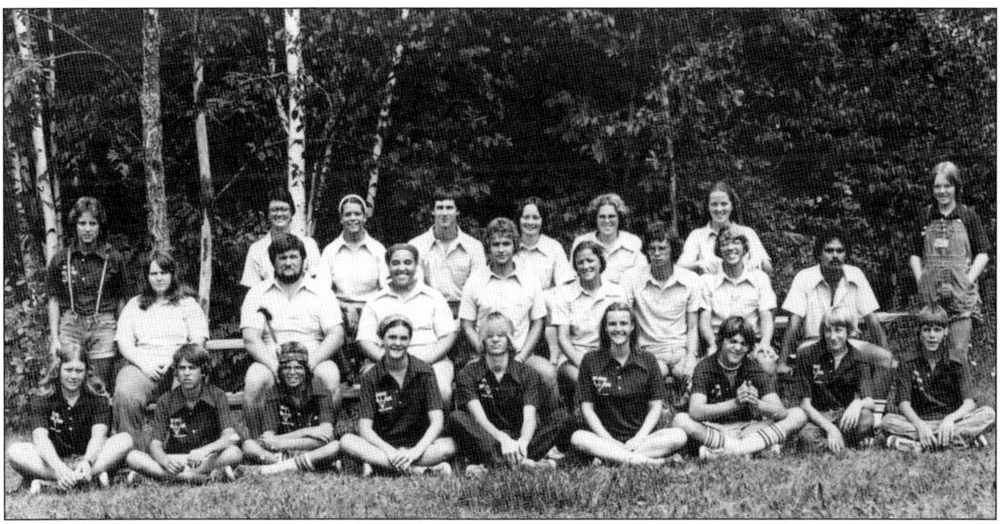

This photograph shows the 1977 staff for the newly formed, coed Camp Maquois. From left to right are CITs (first row) Sandy Shepard, Chris Grobbil, Brad Funk, Mardi Link, Bob Davis, Mary Randy, Jerry Akers, Jeff Funk, and unidentified; (second row) Beth Hickner (standing), Rhonda Thayer, Joe Liberati, Karen Selby, Bernie Moore, Mary the nurse, Hans de Jong, Dave Hayward, Mel Hurst, and Patty Shepard (standing); (third row) Marla Bolzman, Mary Weber, Ken Dike, Mary Stack, Lea McDill, and Amy Johns. (Courtesy of Kellie Moore Thelen.)

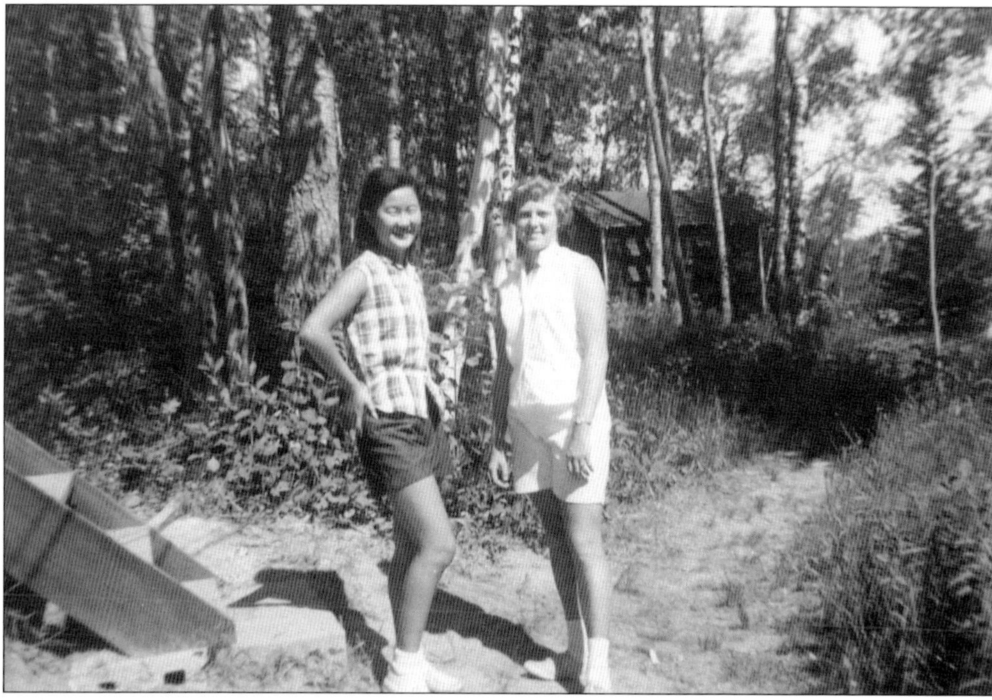

Girls from China, Finland, and Japan served on the staff as early as 1934. They served in many different capacities at camp, including the doctor in residence. Noriko Asano, nicknamed "Nikki," was described as fun-loving, sweet, and shy. Here, she is pictured in front of Hut Six in 1959 with "Buzz." When the camp went coed, Hans de Jong travelled all of the way from Holland to join the staff. (Courtesy of Minette Jacques Lefkiades.)

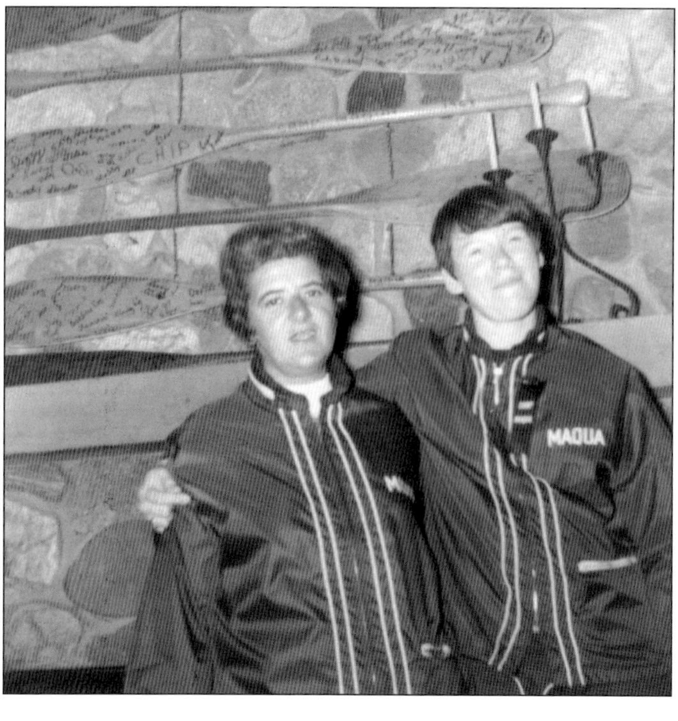

Here, Dorthe Balaskas (left) and Barbara Haggart pose in their green Maqua wind shirts. Dorthe was camp director for eight years, until 1969, and assisted Barbara as she rose through the ranks to become director from 1970 to 1971. Both educators enjoyed a reputation for compassion and leadership, and they mentored many future leaders within their tight-knit staff. (Courtesy of Barbara Haggart.)

Counselors were carefully selected since they were responsible for eight campers per cabin and led numerous activities that required strict safety procedures. This candid shot from 1971 shows, from the left, (first row) Barbara Haggart, Ann Carney, and Sue Michelson; and (second row) Sue Carney and Sue Patenge. (Courtesy of Karen Magidsohn.)

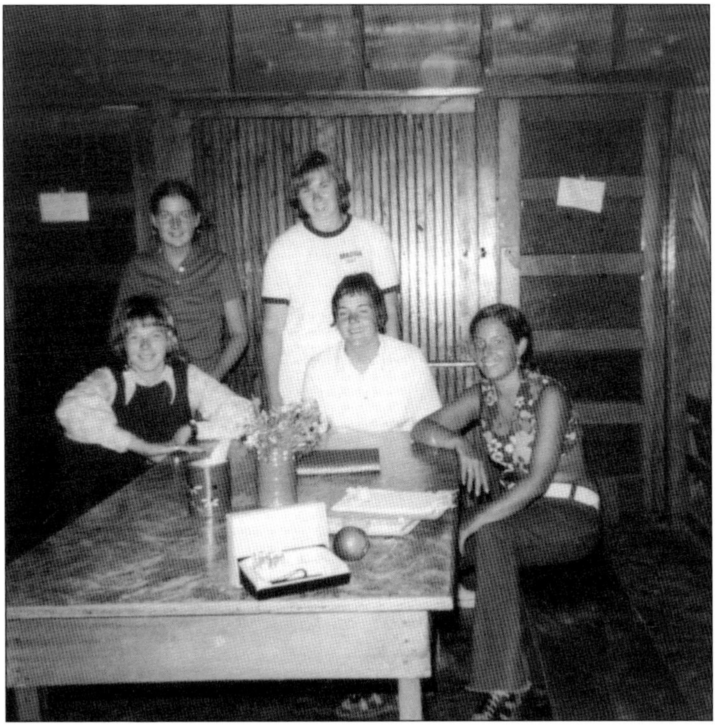

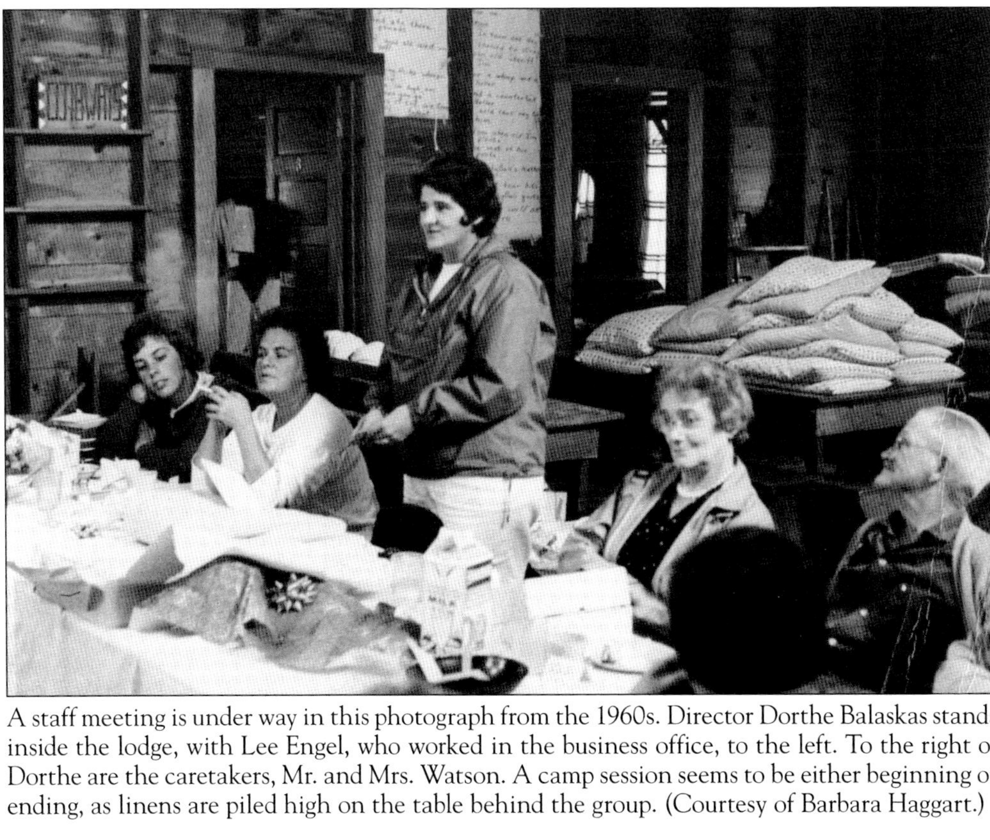

A staff meeting is under way in this photograph from the 1960s. Director Dorthe Balaskas stands inside the lodge, with Lee Engel, who worked in the business office, to the left. To the right of Dorthe are the caretakers, Mr. and Mrs. Watson. A camp session seems to be either beginning or ending, as linens are piled high on the table behind the group. (Courtesy of Barbara Haggart.)

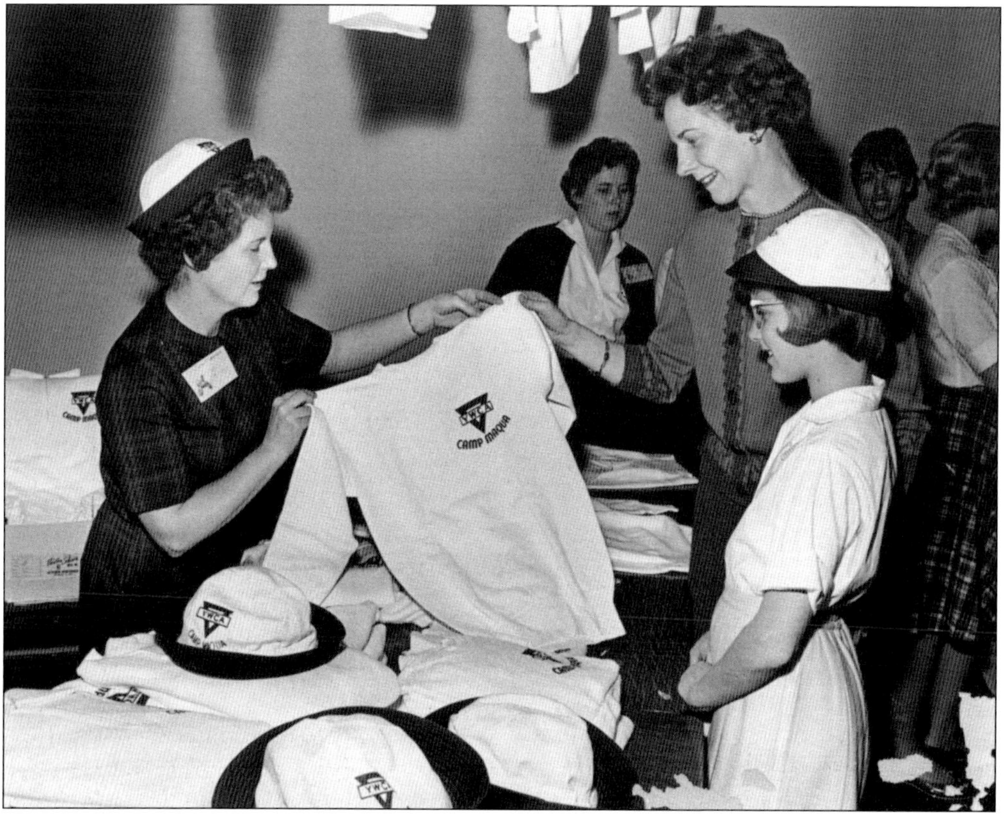

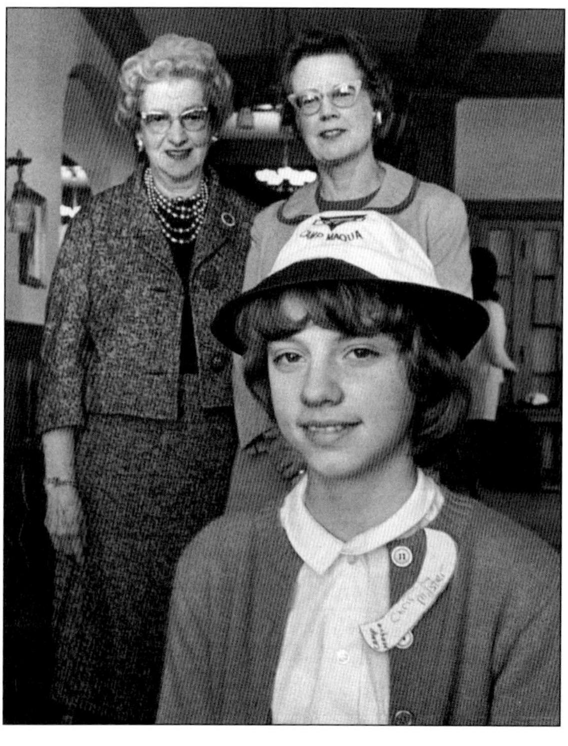

Publicity efforts to encourage registrations included the wide distribution of ads, brochures, radio ads, talks at clubs and schools, movie trailers, and rallies, which were held at the YWCA. Songs, games, introductions of the staff, and Maqua souvenirs generated excitement. Mrs. P. Herter, president of the YWCA, is seen here at left with Janet Duncan and her mother, Mrs. P. Duncan. Director Dorthe Balaskas stands in the background of this 1963 photograph. (Courtesy of YWCA Great Lakes Bay Region.)

Word of mouth was often the best publicity, especially when it was generational. Seen here at the 1965 camp rally is former camp committee chairman Mrs. Norma MacAulay (left), with Mrs. Stewart Milster and her daughter Chris—a fifth-year camper. (Courtesy of YWCA Great Lakes Bay Region.)

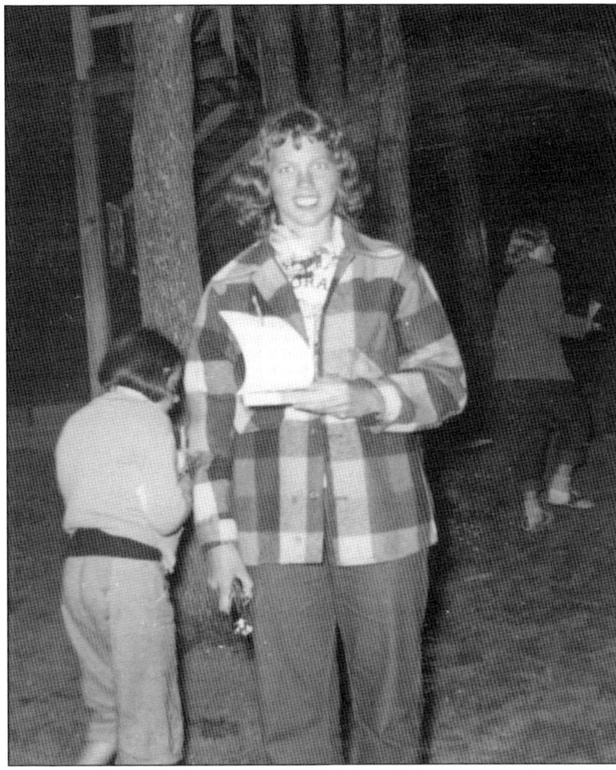

Campfires at Maqua were traditional and magical, but none were remembered as fondly as the "Wishing Boat" ceremony. Each cabin created a boat from bark, ferns, and objects from nature. Candles were affixed to the boats, and they were sent off into the night on the lake as the girls sang, "Sail, sail, my wishing boat out into the night. Bring me my golden wish, while your flame burns bright. Memories of camp, friends forever dear. This I ask my wishing boat for another year." Gay Gould is pictured at right holding her boat, while Mary Jane Keschman attends to the campfire in the image below. (Courtesy of Sascha Immerman.)

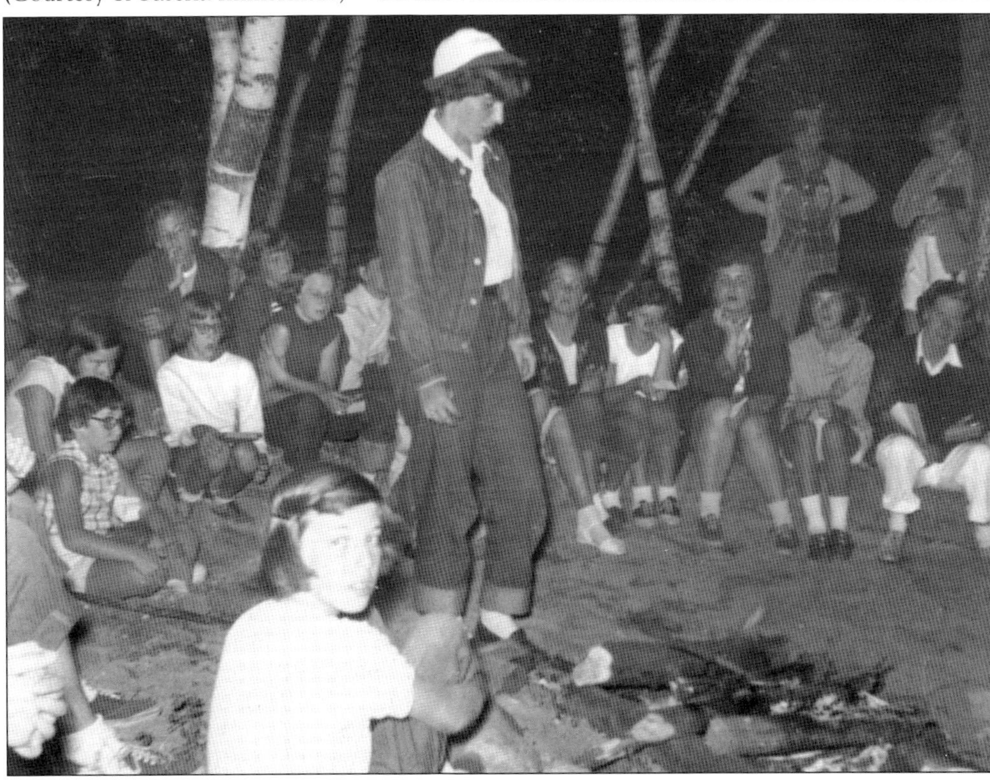

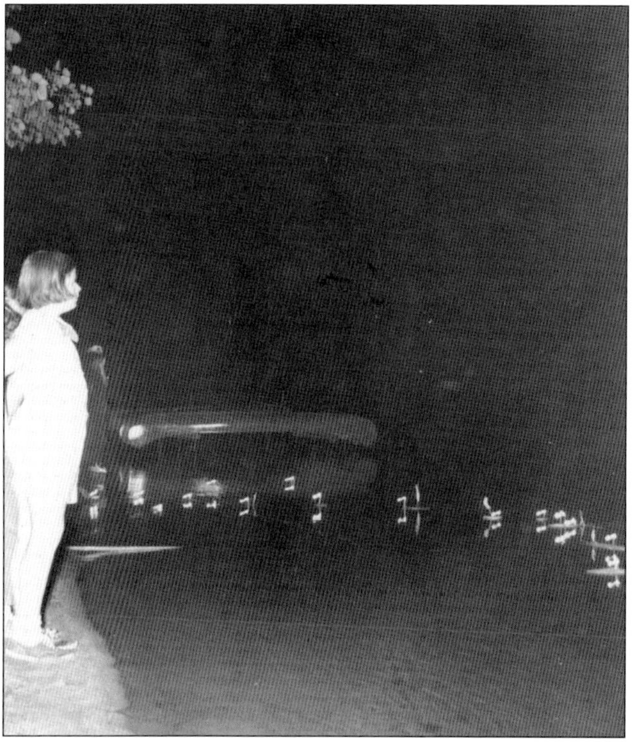

Ribbons, badges, certificates, and awards for accomplishments in sports and activities, a procession with candles to the campfire, songs and s'mores: these were the traditions that marked the emotional end of the summer session. Judy Engibous, who camped in the 1970s, observed that the girls who cried the hardest at the ceremony were usually the girls who were the most homesick in the beginning. At left, an unknown camper stands on the shore in 1959, watching the tiny candles as they twinkle on the boats floating out—accompanied by tears and hugs. Below, a photograph taken from the top of the boathouse in 1952 shows a scene that was typical of the campfires at the end of each session. (Courtesy of Pat O'Tool Smith.)

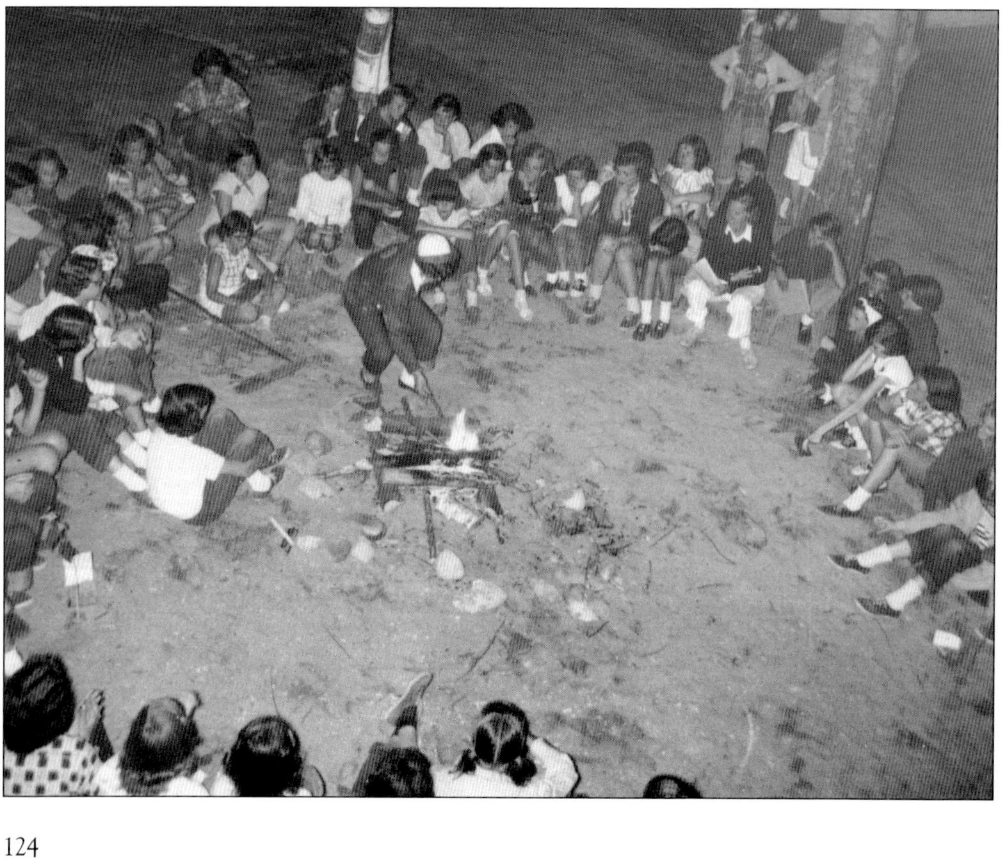

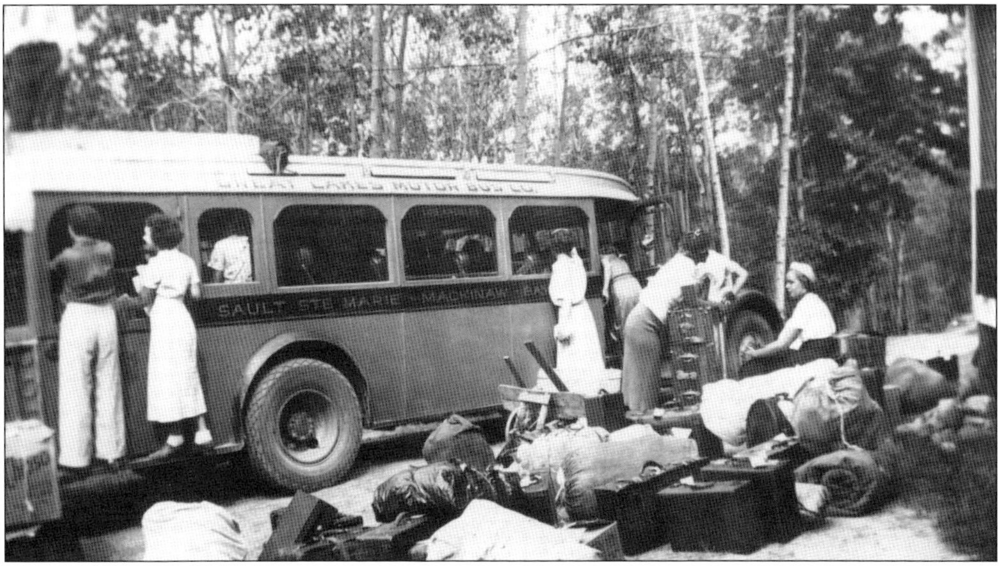

"On pick-up day when the parents arrived to get their camper, we would sing one song after another as the girls left sobbing. So many of them were emotional and it was a little contagious. We would see the girls crying and then they would run across the lodge and throw themselves into their parent's arms," wrote 1960s camper Kim Moore. In the 1920s, a round-trip bus ticket from Maqua to Bay City cost $1.25 and arrived at 12:15 p.m. An early article read, "The new girls clambered out and many greetings could be heard thrown back and forth as a girl ran into an acquaintance of the year before. Also could be heard the many goodbyes from the girls leaving and more luck to the ones who were to stay. The faces of those leaving expressed alternately grief for desire as they viewed for the last time the familiar landmarks of Maqua." (Courtesy of YWCA Great Lakes Bay Region.)

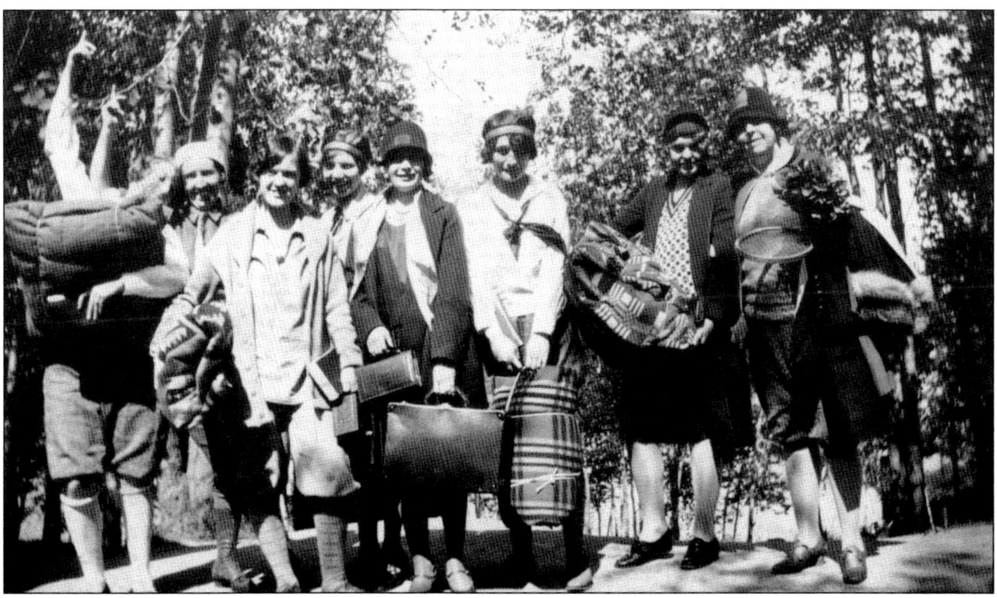

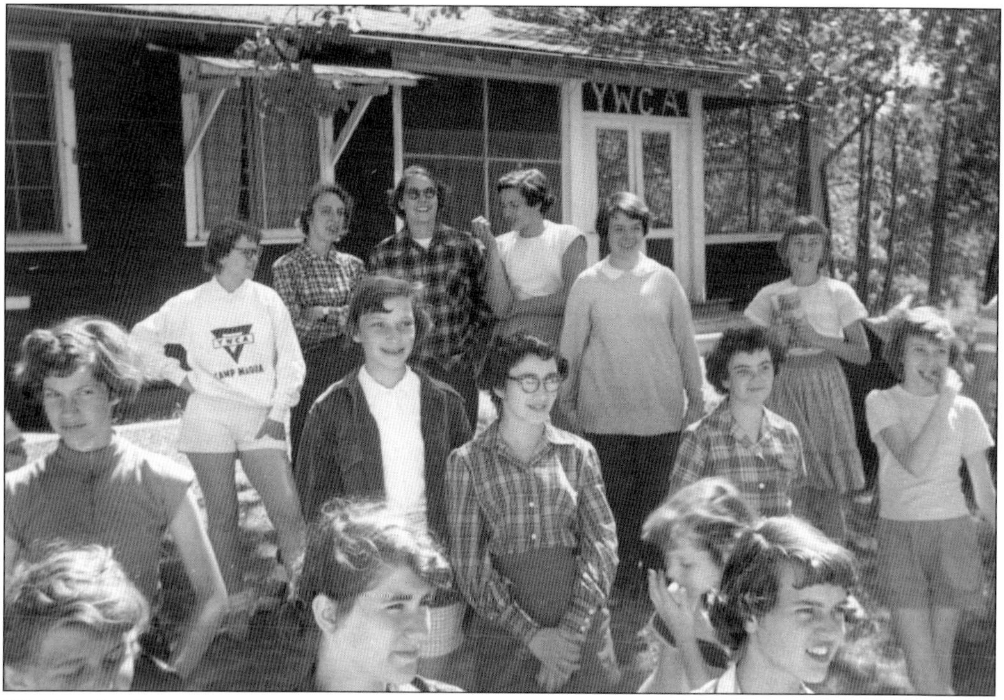

Waiting for the next group to arrive, campers and counselors gathered on the lawn outside the east side of the lodge, facing the road. The birch log YWCA sign is posted above the door frame in this scene from 1950. In the lower front, from left to right, are friends Betty Quillian, Marsha Immerman, and Molly Olson. A dark-shirted Judy Kessler stands in the middle row, to the left of sisters Marcia and Judy Sherman. (Courtesy of Sharon Wilcox Mitchell.)

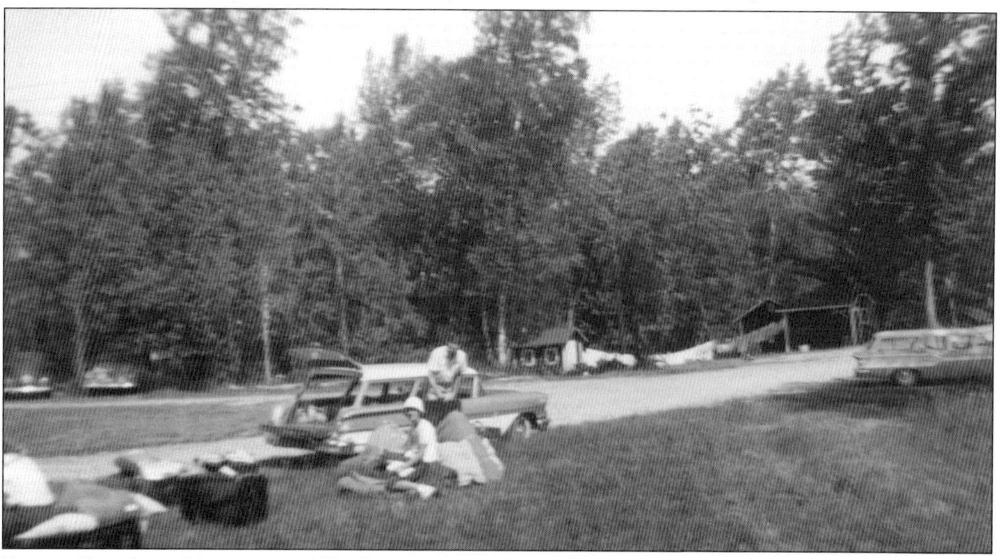

Sisters Gretchen, Minette, and Kayleen Jacques camped at Maqua in the 1950s. This photograph of "Kady" was taken by sister "Mimi" on the last day of camp in 1959, as she sits by her belongings. Their mom was late that year due to a stop at the bank for money to cover the girls' overdrawn arts and crafts bill at the camp store. Always sad to leave camp, Gretchen described the feeling as "reverse homesickness—not for home, but for camp." (Courtesy of Minette Jacques Lefkiades.)

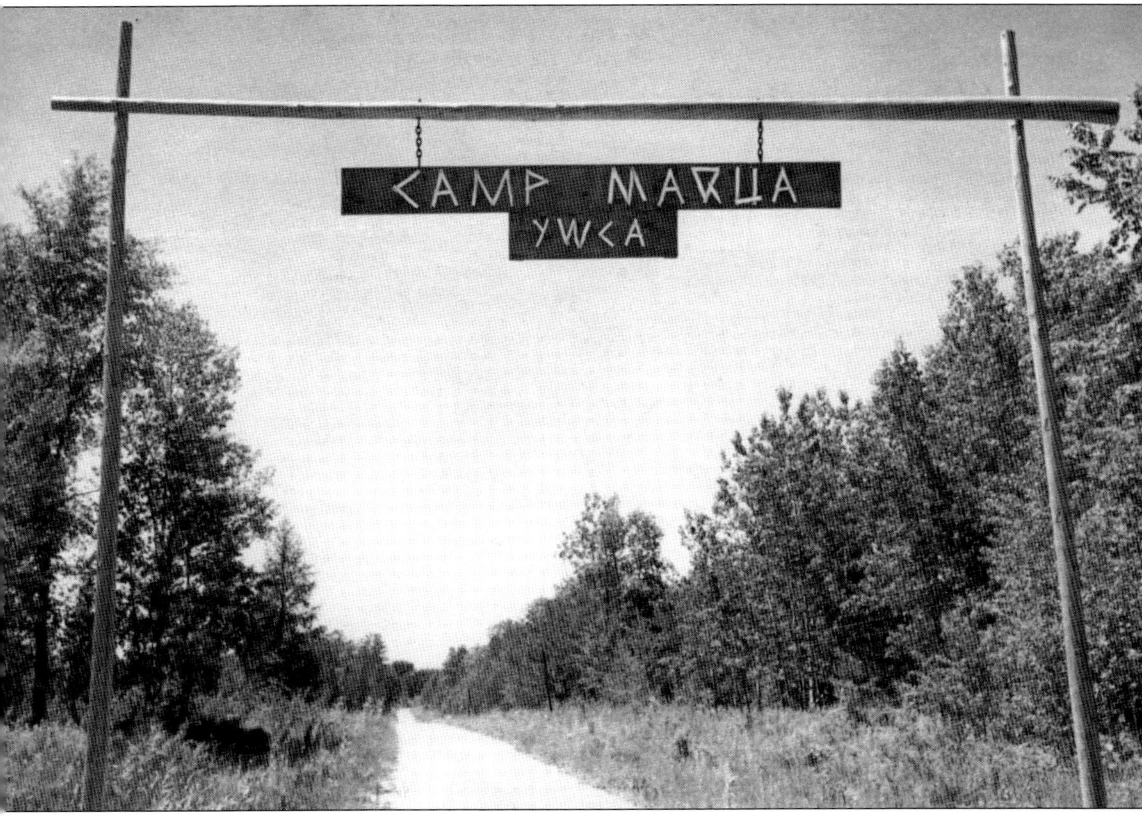

The following poem was written by Amy Falvey Carl, a Maqua camper from 1969 to 1978:

Dorthe, Beanie, Flash and Judy,
Obie, Cullen, Super Doo,
Pennington, Shelley, Pammie, C.B.
Jenifer, Magot, Doris too

Brownies, Hoppers, Buddy System
Pancakes, Cutters, Raids and Pranks
Hobo pie, s'mores, canoe trips,
Wishing boats, awards and snacks.

Counselor hunts, and capture the flag,
Poison Ivy, infirmary,
Campfire songs and smokey clothes
Remind us of what used to be.
Announcements, mail, camp store and rest hour,
Boatmen, Montague, Daddy Cool.
Girls a growing, learning, loving,
Life and friendships all anew.

Thanks to all who made the trip,
And those who made it possible.
Maqua days will never leave us
So much had changed yet not at all.

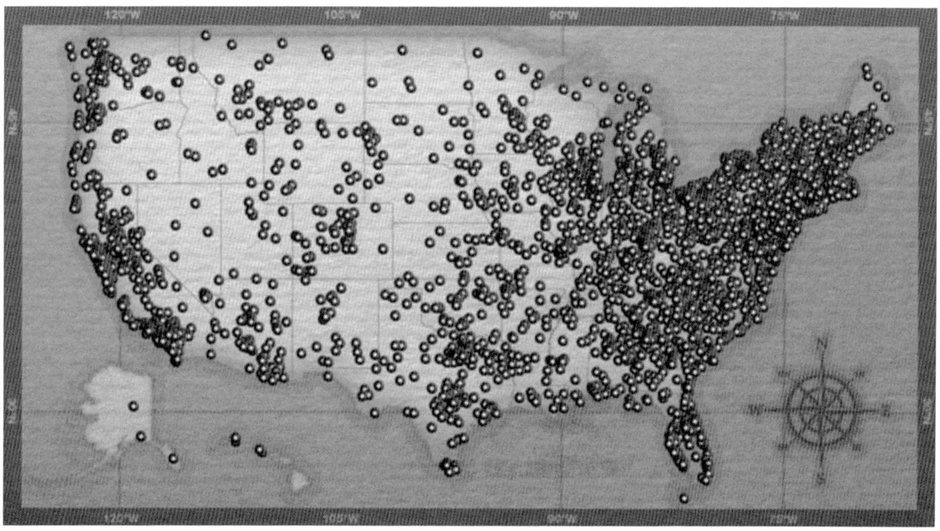